THIRD EDITION

A SHORT HISTORY
OF THE
FRENCH REVOLUTION

JEREMY D. POPKIN

University of Kentucky

Prentice
Hall

UPPER SADDLE RIVER, NEW JERSEY 07458

Library of Congress Cataloging-in-Publication Data

POPKIN, JEREMY D., [date].
  A short history of the French Revolution / JEREMY D. POPKIN—3rd. ed.
    p. cm.
  Includes bibliographical references and index.
  ISBN 0-13-060032-6
  1. France—History—Revolution, 1789-1799. 2. France—History—Consulate and First
  Empire, 1799-1815. 3. Revolutions—History—19th century. I. Title
  DC148.P67 2001
  944.04—dc21   2001021685

VP, Editorial Director: *Charlyce Jones Owen*
Acquisitions Editor: *Charles Cavaliere*
Assistant Editor: *Emsal Hasan*
Editorial/Production Supervision: *Joanne Riker*
Prepress and Manufacturing Buyer: *Tricia Kenny*
Director of Marketing: *Beth Gillett Mejia*
Cover Art Director: *Jayne Conte*

This book was set in 10/12 Palatino by East End Publishing Services, Inc.
and was printed and bound by RR Donnelley and Sons Company. The cover was
printed by Phoenix Color Corp.

© 2002, 1998, 1995 by Pearson Education, Inc.
Upper Saddle River, New Jersey 07458

Printed in the United States of America

10 9 8 7 6 5 4 3 2

ISBN 0-13-060032-6

Prentice-Hall International (UK) Limited, *London*
Prentice-Hall of Australia Pty. Limited, *Sydney*
Prentice-Hall Canada Inc., *Toronto*
Prentice-Hall Hispanoamericana, S.A., *Mexico*
Prentice-Hall of India Private Limited, *New Delhi*
Prentice-Hall of Japan, Inc., *Tokyo*
Pearson Education Asia Pte. Ltd., *Singapore*
Editora Prentice-Hall do Brasil, Ltda., *Rio de Janeiro*

CONTENTS

PREFACE   vii

CHAPTER 1

THE ORIGINS OF THE FRENCH REVOLUTION   1

The Problems of the Monarchy   1
The Failure of Reform   6
Social Structure and Social Crisis   8
The Third Estate   11
The Lower Classes   13
The Impact of the Philosophes   16
The Growth of Public Opinion   18
Notes   20

CHAPTER 2

THE COLLAPSE OF THE ABSOLUTE
MONARCHY, 1787–1789   21

The Pre-Revolution   21
The Assembly of Notables   23

From Failed Reforms to Revolutionary Crisis   25
The Meeting of the Estates-General   26
The Parliamentary Revolution   29
The Storming of the Bastille   31
Notes   35

Chapter 3

The Revolutionary Rupture, 1789–1790   36

The Concept of Revolution   36
The "Abolition of Feudalism" and the Declaration of Rights   37
The October Days   43
The Accomplishments of the National Assembly, 1789–1791   44
The Constitutional Debates   46
The Expropriation of Church Lands and the Assignats   48
The Civil Constitution of the Clergy   50
Notes   52

Chapter 4

The Defeat of the Liberal Revolution, 1790–1792   53

The New Political Culture   53
The King's Flight and the Crisis of 1791   55
The End of the National Assembly   57
The Legislative Assembly   58
The Revolt against Slavery   61
The Move toward War   62
The Impact of War   65
The Overthrow of the Monarchy   65
Emergency Measures and Massacres   69
The Failure of the Liberal Revolution   71
Notes   72

CHAPTER 5

THE CONVENTION AND THE REPUBLIC, 1792–1794   73

The Trial of the King   74
Popular Radicalism   77
The Victory of the Montagnards   78
Terror Becomes the Order of the Day   81
The Dictatorship of the Committee of Public Safety   83
Revolutionary Culture   86
The Radical Revolution and the Social Order   87
The Great Terror and Thermidor   90
The Revolution Victorious   92
Thermidor   94
Notes   94

CHAPTER 6

THE RETURN TO ORDER, 1794–1799   96

The "Bourgeois Republic" and the Search for Order   96
The Thermidorian Reaction   97
The Defeat of the Sans-Culottes   99
Counterrevolution and the Constitution of 1795   100
The Directory   103
The Directory and Europe   105
The "Politics of the Balance"   107
The "Second Directory"   108
The Fall of the Directory   110

CHAPTER 7

THE NAPOLEONIC CONSULATE, 1799–1804   111

The Consul and the Consulate   112
Napoleon's Career   114
The Constitution of the Consulate   115
Consolidation of Power   116
The Peace of Amiens and the Concordat   118
Elements of Opposition   121
Notes   123

CHAPTER 8

THE NAPOLEONIC EMPIRE, 1804–1815   124

The Resumption of War   125
From Ulm to Tilsit   126
The Continental System   127
The Empire at Home   128
Culture under the Empire   132
The Social Bases of the Empire   133
The Decline of the Empire   134
The Invasion of Russia   136
The Hundred Days   137
Note   138

CHAPTER 9

THE REVOLUTIONARY HERITAGE   139

The Postrevolutionary Settlement   140
State and Nation   141
The Broader Impact   142
The French Revolution as History   143
The Jacobin Historical Synthesis   144
The Revisionist Critique   146
Postrevisionist Studies of the Revolution   147
Notes   150

SUGGESTIONS FOR FURTHER READING   151

Bibliographies, Journals, and General Reference Works   151
Specialized Titles: Select Bibliography   152

CHRONOLOGY OF PRINCIPAL EVENTS
DURING THE FRENCH REVOLUTION   157

INDEX   163

PREFACE

From the time it occurred down to our own day, the French Revolution has always been recognized as one of those occurrences that truly changed the world. When the French people in 1789 overthrew the monarchical system under which they had lived for centuries and replaced it with a written constitution that redefined their country's political system and social structure, they were trying to implement new ideas about government and society, ideas that have become the basis of life, not only in France, but also in much of the rest of the modern world. The dramatic struggles of the French Revolution provoked debates that are still relevant today. They raised questions about the nature of liberty and equality, the extent of human rights, the legitimate powers of government, the definition of nationhood, slavery and racial prejudice, the relations between the sexes, and the ability of human beings to control their own destiny. The Revolution and the succeeding Napoleonic era saw the most extensive wars Europe had ever known and set the stage for the development of modern nation-states and ultimately for the wars and revolutions that have marked the history of the twentieth-century world.

Because of their importance, few historical events have been studied as closely as those that took place in France between 1789 and 1815. A vast literature seeks to explain the origins of the Revolution, the goals of its leaders, the role of ordinary men and women in its events, and to draw up the balance sheet of its successes and its failures. That literature continues to grow because historians continue to approach the Revolution with new questions in mind. Nineteenth-century scholars weighed the revolutionaries' contributions to the ideals of constitutional government and Napoleon's impact on the art of warfare. As modern working-class movements grew at the beginning of the twentieth century, historians focused on the importance of popular participation in the Revolution. The rise of Communist and fascist totalitarianism directed attention to the workings of the Jacobin dictatorship and the Napoleonic regime. Current interests in the role of women in the past, the cultural dimension of history, and the interaction of European and non-Western peoples have directed attention to areas often ignored in earlier studies.

This short account attempts to introduce students to the major events that make up the story of the French Revolution, and to the different ways in which historians have interpreted them. It makes no claim to be comprehensive: No single volume can hope to encompass all aspects of the revolutionary drama. It will have served its purpose if it succeeds in helping instructors share the excitement of studying this unique period of the past with their classes, and if it encourages students to undertake further exploration of the subject.

I would like to thank the following reviewers for their insight and suggestions: Laura Mason, University of Georgia; Jay Smith, University of North Carolina–Chapel Hill; Jack Censer, George Mason University; Paul Hanson, Butler University; Daniel Gordon, University of Massachusetts; Samuel Crompton, Holyoke Community College; Michael Dettelbach, Smith College, and for suggested revisions to this new edition, David Hunt, University of Massachusetts, Boston; Jill Harsin, Colgate University; Edgar Leon Newman, New Mexico State University; and Dmitri Shlapentokh, Indiana University.

CHAPTER 1

THE ORIGINS
OF THE
FRENCH REVOLUTION

Late on the night of 14 July 1789, Louis XVI, king of France, met with the duke of La Rochefoucauld-Liancourt, one of his courtiers, to discuss the dramatic news he had just received. In the capital city of Paris, fifteen miles from his royal palace of Versailles, the population had risen up and stormed the royal fortress of the Bastille. "Is it a revolt?" the bewildered king supposedly asked, thinking that the event was no more than a meaningless outbreak of violence that could quickly be brought under control. "No, Sire, it is a revolution," the duke is said to have replied.

For more than two centuries, historians all over the world have agreed with the duke's assessment. The events of 14 July 1789 marked the overthrow of a centuries-old system of government and society, and the beginning of a new era for France and the entire Western world. The storming of the Bastille caught Louis XVI by surprise. With the advantage of hindsight, however, we can see that there were many tensions in France's institutions, its social order, and its culture that made a revolution, if not inevitable, at least conceivable. Understanding the origins of the French Revolution thus requires some familiarity with the major features of eighteenth-century France.

THE PROBLEMS OF THE MONARCHY

After the French Revolution started, supporters frequently offered a very simple political explanation of their movement. They were revolting, they

Coronation of Louis XVI

Traditional symbols dominate this illustration of Louis XVI's coronation in 1775. The king takes his crown from a saint holding the cross, indicating the divine origins of his powers, while angels behind him carry banners and emblems associated with the French monarchy since the Middle Ages. This engraving gives no hint of the challenges to the church and established institutions that were to lead to the French Revolution a few years later.

Source: Bibliothèque Nationale, Paris.

said, against a system of tyranny or despotism, in which all power was monopolized by a single man, the king, and by his arbitrarily chosen ministers. As an example of this excessive power, they were likely to cite the words of Louis XV, who told some recalcitrant magistrates in 1766 that according to French law, "the sovereign power resides in my person only."[1] This was not merely rhetoric: critics of absolutism could also cite real examples of the king's arbitrary and unrestrained power, such as his ability to issue *lettres de cachet*, arrest warrants that allowed the imprisonment of any subject without a trial.

With the benefit of hindsight, historians can easily recognize that this characterization of the old regime monarchy as a despotism is greatly exaggerated. Prerevolutionary France was indeed an absolute monarchy—that is, one in which all sovereign powers, including the right to make laws and to enforce them, the right to appoint judges and officials, and the right to make war and to sign treaties, were supposedly exercised exclusively by the king. But, as French legal theorists had always taught, the king's absolute powers were neither arbitrary nor tyrannical ones. The king was obligated to rule according to laws and customs that had accumulated over the ages. He could not, for example, alter the rules of hereditary succession, which dictated that the throne passed to a king's closest living male relative. Indeed, in explaining the political difficulties that led to the Revolution of 1789, modern historians are more likely to stress the weaknesses of the absolutist system than its excessive concentration of power.

The weakness that did the most to precipitate the Revolution was the monarchy's inability to balance its income and its expenses. Laws and customs required the French government to fulfill many responsibilities that required extensive expenditures; they also limited the king's ability to raise money to pay for these obligations. Broadly speaking, the king of France was responsible for maintaining order within his kingdom and for defending it from enemies. The maintenance of internal order required keeping up police forces and guards scattered throughout territories that made up the largest kingdom in western Europe. External defense was even costlier. Like all other European monarchs, the king of France governed a state in constant rivalry with its neighbors. Kings were educated from birth not only to defend the lands they inherited but also to seek opportunities to enlarge them, thereby acquiring the glory that was an essential element of kingship.

Through a long series of conquests and acquisitions, the kingdom of France had grown from a medieval principality centered around the capital city of Paris into the largest and most populous state in Europe. The kings of the Bourbon dynasty, the line from which Louis XVI, ruler at the time of the Revolution, descended, had all engaged in warfare to enlarge their realm. They had built up a kingdom that extended from the lowlands of Flanders in the north to the Pyrenees and the Mediterranean Sea in the south, from the Atlantic Ocean in the west to the Rhine river and the Alps in the east, and that included colonies as far away as Canada, the Caribbean, and the Indian subcontinent. To do so, they had built up a costly military machine. Under Louis XIV, king from 1643 to 1715, the French army had grown to 400,000 men, the largest Europe had ever seen, and France had seemed poised to dominate the entire continent. His successors were less aggressive, but they nonetheless felt a responsibility to keep France strong and to protect its interests and its reputation abroad.

Some of the problems that led to the French Revolution stemmed from the expenses incurred in efforts to maintain France's position relative to the other European states, and especially from the increasingly costly rivalry with England that lasted all through the century. England, a naval power with a fast-growing economy, was able to concentrate on building up its colonial empire, while France also had to pay attention to its rivals on the continent, Austria and Prussia. The country's poor performance in the eighteenth century's most extensive conflict, the Seven Years' War (1756–1763), suggested that the French monarchy was unable to cope with the challenges posed by these multiple rivalries. While stubborn noblemen intrigued against each other for control of France's armies on the continent, Prussian king Frederic the Great, a brilliant commander, inflicted humiliating defeats on the French troops. The British used their control of the seas to capture French colonial possessions in India, Quebec, and the Caribbean. A decade later, France stood by helplessly as Prussia, Austria, and Russia annexed territories belonging to Poland, one of its traditional allies.

When Louis XVI came to the throne in 1774, he entrusted foreign affairs to the count of Vergennes, who was determined to restore the country's international prestige. When England's colonies in North America revolted in 1776, Vergennes took advantage of the situation. A small French army and the French fleet significantly aided the Americans, and France hosted the peace conference at which England conceded the colonies' independence in 1783. However, this success cost France a great deal of money and brought none of the tangible rewards in the form of new territories that usually went with a victory. Fear of adding even more debt was a major factor in keeping France from opposing Prussia's intervention in the Netherlands in 1787. On the eve of the crisis of 1789, the French monarchy seemed unable to maintain the country's international position.

In addition to maintaining his power and glory, the French king was expected to see to the welfare of his subjects. In earlier centuries, cities and the Catholic church had paid for many functions of local government, education, and care for the sick and the indigent, whose numbers seemed to grow relentlessly through the eighteenth century. As the monarchy had grown, however, it had taken an increasing role in many of these areas. In times of crop failure, royal intendants used royal money to provide relief supplies. The king maintained the country's main roads. His courts provided justice for his subjects. Through an ever-expanding system of royal academies, the king subsidized writers, artists, scientists, doctors, and even veterinarians. And at Versailles, outside of Paris, Louis XIV, firm in the belief that a monarch needed to dazzle both his subjects and other sovereigns, had built a palace complex of a size and magnificence that Europe had not seen since Roman days. His successors continued to add to it and to underwrite the expenses of the courtiers who encircled the royal family. Although the court at Versailles actually accounted for only a small percentage of the monarchy's annual expenses, it was a visible symbol of lavish spending. But to curtail the flow of money to the army, to the administration of the kingdom, and to the court meant changing the very definition of what the monarchy was supposed to be.

To carry out all these responsibilities, the royal government had built up an extensive administrative network. Louis XIV, the most strong-willed and efficient of the Bourbon kings, had established a system of intendants, appointed royal officials stationed in each of the country's provinces and responsible for carrying out royal orders. Subordinate officials extended the intendants' reach to smaller towns and villages. France's system of administration was considerably more centralized than that of most other European states; in theory, royal laws could be applied evenly throughout the king's vast territories.

In practice, however, this centralized administration ran into many obstacles. Each province, each region, each town had its own special laws and institutions, which the intendant could not ignore. By the eighteenth century France had become a legalistic society. From the humblest peasant to the most elegant noble, the king's subjects were imbued with the notion that they had rights and privileges they were entitled to defend. This legalistic outlook was reinforced by the conduct of the royal appeals courts, the thirteen *parlements*, whose judges claimed the right to review all royal laws and edicts to ensure that they were in conformity with the traditional laws of the realm.

Although the parlements were royal courts, the king's influence over the judges was limited because they literally owned their court seats. The sale of government posts was one of the ways in which the French monarchy made up for its inadequate sources of revenue. Jobs purchased this way became family property that could be passed down to heirs, regardless of their qualifications for the post, or sold off for a profit. These posts were desirable because offices conferred social prestige and, in many cases, granted their holders noble status. But this system of venal office-holding greatly reduced the efficiency of the royal administration. Venal office-holders, such as the judges of the parlements, could not be removed from their posts or forced to follow the instructions of the intendants.

The parlements in particular claimed that it was their duty to use this independence to resist actions that violated the traditional laws of the kingdom and the rights of the king's subjects, including most efforts to raise taxes. In the absence of institutions of representative government, the par-lements claimed to defend the interests of the "nation" against arbitrary authority. In practice, the parlements' resistance to reform often amounted to a defense of privileged groups' special interests, including those of the judges. But the parlements' denunciations of arbitrary rule and their insis-tence that the "nation" had a right to participate in political decision making spread ideas about representative government among the population. Para-doxically, the privileged noble judges of these royal courts were forerunners of a revolution that was to sweep away all special privileges.

THE FAILURE OF REFORM

Throughout the second half of the eighteenth century, royal ministers rec-ognized that the French government needed more revenue if it was going to maintain its international standing and meet its domestic obligations. But the problem of raising taxes illustrated better than anything else the institu-tional problems facing the monarchy. In theory, the king should not have had much trouble raising more money. Unlike the king of England, France's ruler had no need to negotiate with a representative body or parliament before he collected and spent money. The size of the kingdom and its rulers' need for a large army to defend it from foes who, unlike those of England, could easily threaten its borders had limited the role of the assembly of the Estates-General—France's equivalent to the English Parliament—and final-ly enabled kings to stop convening it altogether after 1614. They had estab-lished their right to collect traditional taxes without going through any legislative process. But this authority came at a price: unlike the king of Eng-land, the French ruler lacked any regular mechanism for negotiating an increase in taxes as the kingdom's needs grew. He could only collect those taxes that had become customary over the years, and many subjects were able to evade payments because of equally customary exemptions. When new taxes were imposed, they often weighed most heavily on the poorest subjects because they had the least chance of protesting effectively.

To overcome this handicap, successive French rulers and finance min-isters had adopted a wide range of expedients, including the sale of gov-ernment offices. Just as it had created the system of venal offices to raise money and ended up confronting a powerful obstacle to carrying out its own policies, so the monarchy had made arrangements about tax collection that ended up limiting its own revenues. Rather than employing tax collec-tors who worked directly for the king, the government leased out the col-lection of most taxes to wealthy entrepreneurs, called tax farmers, who paid the treasury a set fee in exchange for the right to collect taxes in a given region. This system provided the monarchy with a dependable flow of income, but it gave the tax farmers the incentive to squeeze as much as they could from the population, while forwarding as little as possible to Versailles. The hundreds of different tax-collection enterprises made rational management of the royal income impossible, and royal revenue could not be increased enough to meet the growing needs that emerged in the eighteenth century.

By the middle of the eighteenth century, royal ministers had come to realize that piecemeal measures were inadequate and had begun to propose sweeping reforms of the fiscal system. The last four decades of the monarchy witnessed repeated efforts to increase taxes and to make the French economy more productive, so that the government could extract more money from its subjects. As early as 1749, Louis XV's controller-general (the title given to prerevolutionary ministers of finance) Machault d'Arnouville had tried unsuccessfully to impose a uniform tax on all landed property in the kingdom. In the 1760s, the government adopted the program of a group of enlightened economic reformers, the Physiocrats, and tried to abolish traditional restrictions on the grain trade, hoping to encourage production and thereby expand its tax base. These plans broke down when bad harvests produced shortages and made the export of grain from the kingdom politically impossible. In 1770, the ministers Maupeou and Terray tried to write off much of the royal debt and to remove the obstructionist judges of the parlements in order to prevent the courts from hampering them.

The death of Louis XV in 1774 frustrated the Maupeou-Terray reform plans, but in 1776, one of Louis XVI's ministers, Turgot, tried to revamp the organization of France's economy along free-market lines even more extensively than his predecessors in the 1760s. In accordance with Physiocratic principles, he not only lifted restrictions on the grain trade but also tried to abolish the urban guilds, whose regulations restricted competition and governed the production of many manufactured goods. Popular protests and opposition from the parlements defeated him, but they did not stop government reform efforts. His successor, Necker, retreated from sweeping economic reforms. Necker hoped to save money, however, by eliminating unnecessary offices and collecting taxes more efficiently.

Government reform efforts were not limited to fiscal matters. In the last decades before the Revolution, the monarchy took a number of measures that foreshadowed the more sweeping changes that followed 1789. It asserted its power to regulate the Church and even to suppress some of the many convents and monasteries inherited from the past; new ideas about human rights were reflected in the abolition of torture as a way of compelling testimony in judicial cases. In the late 1770s, the minister Necker introduced representative assemblies in several provinces, trying to give public opinion some voice in lawmaking and administration. The country's Protestant minority, officially outlawed under Louis XIV, received basic civil rights in 1787, and colonial administrators tried to limit the harsh treatment of slaves in 1784 and 1785.

The fact that royal ministers had undertaken so many reform efforts shows that they were well aware of the problems undermining the French monarchy. The result demonstrated the justice of the great nineteenth-century French historian Alexis de Tocqueville's comment that "the most perilous moment for a bad government is one when it seeks to mend its ways."[2] To justify their reform proposals, the royal ministers themselves had been forced to criticize many long-established customs and institutions; they had thereby undermined the legitimacy of the existing order. At the same time, each of these prerevolutionary reform efforts implied fundamental changes in the structures of French society and threatened the privileges of important groups within it. Those who stood to lose because of proposed reforms learned to defend themselves by challenging the king's right to change laws and time-honored customs. The conflicts that provoked the French Revolution were thus not simply due to an outdated and inefficient structure of government. They were also rooted in France's complex, hierarchical social structure.

SOCIAL STRUCTURE AND SOCIAL CRISIS

French society before 1789 was structured on the principle of corporate privilege. The French king's subjects were all members of social groups—*corps* or collective bodies—that claimed certain special rights that set them apart from others. Like the institutions of the monarchy, this social order had a long history. Medieval thought had identified three main orders or estates in French society—clergy who prayed, nobles who fought, and peasants who farmed—each with its own special rights and responsibilities. Originally, for example, nobles did not pay taxes to the king, as peasants did, since they served him personally by fighting in his army. Over the centuries, privilege had become much more complicated than this simple threefold division. New groups had appeared, such as the urban populations of France's towns, who received grants of special privileges, often including certain tax exemptions. Within the towns, members of particular professions were organized into guilds, which gave them the right to monopolize certain kinds of work and to set prices and wages. As the kingdom acquired new provinces, different regions came to have differing privileges, too. New provinces might maintain their own customary laws and special institutions, such as provincial estates, and often they obtained exemptions from specified taxes. For example, Brittany, permanently joined to the kingdom only in 1532, was exempt from the unpopular salt tax, the *gabelle*.

Almost every group in eighteenth-century France could claim some sort of special privilege, but the most visible privileged groups were the Catholic clergy and the nobility, the two so-called privileged orders or estates. Because of their special status as mediators between God and humanity, members of the clergy enjoyed exemption from most taxes. They were subject to their own Church court system. The Church had the right to collect tithes, which amounted to taxes, from peasant farmers. The Church as a whole was a wealthy institution: over the centuries, the donations of the faithful had given it extensive property scattered throughout the kingdom, amounting to 10 percent or more of the country's real estate. But within the Church, some were more privileged than others. Bishops and the abbots and abbesses of wealthy monasteries and convents, normally recruited from noble families, lived in high style, but the standard of living of the parish clergy and of the nuns who staffed most of the country's hospitals and orphanages was much more modest. To critics both inside and outside of the Church, the institution's privileges seemed to have no relationship to the services it was supposed to provide to the rest of society.

Even more severe was the criticism of the privileges held by the titled nobility. Over the centuries, the nobles had changed from a military and political elite whose privileges corresponded to their special functions to an amorphous group whose members had little in common besides the special legal rights that set them apart from commoners. The nobility had long since ceased to be a closed caste descended from medieval warriors. France's kings had promoted access to this privileged group by granting titles to numerous families that had enriched themselves in trade. Noble families in financial straits married their sons to the daughters of wealthy commoners. Nonnoble families could purchase noble status by buying venal offices in the royal bureaucracy.

Noble status was worth pursuing because it brought with it many privileges. The most visible of these was exemption from many of the most onerous royal taxes, particularly the *taille*, the main tax on the peasantry. Nobles also had other special rights, however. By custom or by law, most top positions in the royal bureaucracy, the army, and the Church were reserved for men with titles. Nobles were entitled to special seating in their parish churches; they were allowed to keep doves and rabbits, despite the damage these animals often did to farm crops; and the fact that only nobles could put weathervanes on their houses emphasized their special status.

Although all nobles were privileged, not all were wealthy. Most noble families owned at least some land, but there was an enormous difference between the small elite of aristocratic courtiers, whose landholdings were often spread across several provinces and who monopolized the most lucrative posts at court and in the Church, and the hundreds of rural gentry whose income was sometimes no more than that of a wealthy peasant. Wealthier aristocrats were able to share the profits from large-scale commerce by investing in enterprises owned by commoners, thereby acquiring economic interests no different from those of their partners. Their poorer cousins, however, were often driven to fight to maintain the distinction between themselves and the rest of the population. The 1781 Ségur edict, which required army officers to prove four generations of noble descent, was a typical measure meant to reserve jobs for descendants of noble families that had no other resources to pass along to their children. Nobles recognized that any significant changes in France's political and social institutions would probably reduce their privileges. Some influential aristocrats accepted reform, assuming that they would be regarded as the natural leaders of society, but most nobles saw the government's reform proposals as a threat to their positions and openly opposed them.

Many nobles also had rights as *seigneurs* (overlords) that affected the peasants who lived near their estates and even local townspeople. These seigneurial rights were attached to landed property, not to nobility per se, and by the eighteenth century, many wealthy nonnobles had purchased estates that included such rights. Seigneurial rights included the privilege of maintaining a court to settle local disputes, the right to collect various dues from local peasants, and sometimes the right to charge tolls on roads or bridges and to compel the local population to use the seigneur's grain mill or baking oven. These seigneurial dues and monopolies, although they were often a relatively modest fraction of the seigneur's total income, caused frequent disputes between their holders and the rest of the population. Commoners resented having to make payments for which they received no visible services. In the debates of the period, objections to noble privileges and to seigneurial rights were often mixed together: both appeared to perpetuate distinctions that served no valid purpose.

The clergy and the nobility in eighteenth-century France were the most visible groups with special privileges. But many other social groups in prerevolutionary France also possessed jealously guarded rights. Townspeople were exempt from the taille, the burdensome land tax, and from many other obligations that weighed on the rural population, though they paid a much-resented tax on food and wine. Inside the towns, many trades were controlled by privileged guilds, which limited competition and maintained profitable joint monopolies for their members.

Most privilege-holding groups enjoyed benefits that made them better off than the majority of the population, but some groups lived under special restrictions. In 1685, Louis XIV had attempted to stamp out France's Protestant minority by revoking their special charter of privileges, the edict of Nantes. In 1787, Louis XVI granted some civil rights to the Protestants, who had kept up a semiclandestine existence throughout the century, but they still faced many legal restrictions. So did the small Jewish population, which included a wealthy community of Sephardim—descendants of the Jews expelled from Spain and Portugal centuries earlier—in the southwest of France and a poorer but more numerous group of Ashkenazi (German) Jews in the northeastern province of Alsace. By tradition, the Jews lived like resident aliens, governing themselves according to their own laws, but being subject to special regulations. Any systematic reform of the system of corporate privileges would inevitably raise the question of the position of these religious minorities.

THE THIRD ESTATE

The many reform plans proposed in the decades before the Revolution paid special attention to the privileges of wealthy elites such as the clergy and the nobility, because their tax exemptions made them obvious targets of any scheme for increasing government revenue. The reforming ministers of the eighteenth century recognized that it would be difficult to levy more taxes on the poorer and less-privileged sectors of the population. On the other hand, the support of this "Third Estate" might be enlisted in favor of reforms aimed at reducing the privileges of the First and Second Estates of the realm (the clergy and the nobility). Mobilizing the Third Estate would raise questions not just about France's political institutions but also about its entire social structure.

Members of the two privileged estates at least had in common their special privileges; the members of the Third Estate lacked any real unity. The Third Estate, which made up 97 percent of the population, included all the kingdom's commoners, from wealthy Parisian bankers who mixed easily with the great nobles to the beggars who trudged the highways in search of food and work. Social historians use the term *bourgeoisie* to classify the richest stratum of the Third Estate: bankers, merchants, manufacturers, lawyers, and other educated professionals. In the course of the eighteenth century, these groups profited from France's slow but steady economic expansion. The period saw an especially significant growth in overseas trade. Merchants in seaports like Bordeaux, Nantes, and Marseille enriched themselves by shipping textiles, fine wines and liqueurs, and other French products abroad and by investing in the slave trade that provided the labor force for the West Indian plantations from which France received sugar, coffee, indigo, and other tropical products. Manufacturers thrived on a growing domestic consumer market, as even the lower classes shifted from investing in durable clothing and goods that would last a lifetime to indulging in a wider variety of cheaper products meant to be replenished regularly.

Confident that they owed their success in life to their own efforts to obtain wealth and education, members of the bourgeoisie were often critical of nobles' special privileges. They also challenged the teachings of a church that condemned the pursuit of worldly goods and called routine business practices, such as lending money at interest, sinful. Members of this growing bourgeois group were to be especially prominent in the revolutionary movement that developed in 1789, so much so that historians from the time of the Revolution to our own day have often explained that movement as a bourgeois revolt. According to this "bourgeois revolution" thesis, first advanced by some of the revolutionaries themselves and most extensively elaborated by historians inspired by the nineteenth-century socialist theorist Karl Marx, the explosion of 1789 was the inevitable result of a system in which economic expansion swelled the ranks of the bourgeoisie, while the workings of the system of privilege excluded them from real social and political power.

Much recent historical research has tended to criticize this explanation of the Revolution by emphasizing the degree to which the bourgeoisie at the end of the Old Regime shared common interests with many of the nobility. Members of both groups shared characteristics that set them apart from the remaining 90 percent of the French population. They were wealthy enough to be free of daily worries about subsistence, and they were educated—in fact, literacy levels were usually higher among the bourgeoisie than among the nobility. The frontier between the two groups was not closed. Throughout the eighteenth century, successful bourgeois families migrated into the ranks of the nobility, often also investing the profits from their businesses in the purchase of landed estates and seigneurial rights. At the same time, nobles maintained their fortunes by investing in bourgeois business enterprises and marrying their children to wealthy commoners. The two groups rubbed shoulders at the theater and in the Masonic lodges that were becoming increasingly popular as the end of the century neared. In many respects, the nobility and the bourgeoisie seemed to be merging into a mixed elite, separated from the bulk of the population by its wealth and lifestyle.

The Revolution was to show, however, that the boundary between noble and bourgeois remained significant enough so that, in certain circumstances, the bourgeois members of this mixed elite could be led to turn violently against the nobles and identify themselves with the lower classes of the population. Although some prosperous bourgeois families could work their way up to noble status, the process remained a difficult and uncertain one. The practice of reserving seats for nobles in the royal academies, which were supposed to reward outstanding merit, was one example of the practices that irritated members of the bourgeoisie. While the "bourgeois revolution" thesis does overstress the tangible differences between the two groups before 1789, it is clear that the distinction between nobility and bourgeoisie remained important enough in people's minds to be exploited in a crisis situation.

Members of the bourgeoisie also had grievances against the French government. Bourgeois lawyers' interests were closely tied to the parlements. They shared the judges' conviction that France needed to be governed by regular laws, not by arbitrary royal enactments. Bourgeois families that had pinned their hopes for advancement on investment in government offices and put their savings into government bonds wanted to be sure that their positions would be protected. Merchants and manufacturers suffered in the uncertain economic climate of the 1770s and 1780s, as consumer demand stagnated and reform efforts like Turgot's abolition of the guilds were proposed and then revoked. Hopes that the newly independent American states would become a good market for French goods failed to materialize after the peace treaty of 1783. The government stirred up a wave of protest from French merchants and manufacturers in 1786 when it negotiated a free-trade treaty with Britain that exposed many French enterprises to withering competition. When the revolutionary crisis began, even many members of the better-off sectors of the bourgeoisie were receptive to the idea that they would benefit from social and political reforms.

THE LOWER CLASSES

The more prosperous and more educated members of the bourgeoisie shared the lifestyle of the nobility; their poorer bourgeois cousins were not always sharply distinguished from the lower levels of the urban population. Many a wealthy merchant or manufacturer had begun as a shopkeeper or a hard-working master artisan. Generally literate and relatively prosperous, these petty bourgeois heads of small family enterprises often exercised a strong social influence over the poorer and less settled members of the urban population, those the upper classes referred to contemptuously as the *peuple*, the common people.

The memoirs of the Parisian glassfitter Jacques-Louis Ménétra give us a rare first-hand glimpse into the life of a member of this stratum of French society. Like many skilled artisans, Ménétra learned his father's trade. He had the opportunity to spend several years making his *tour de France*, going from town to town to acquire training and experience. His adventures gave him a sense of independence, but his membership in a journeymen's organization or *compagnonnage*, which defended workers' privileges, also taught him effective methods of collective action. Ménétra's memoirs show that he was familiar with some of the enlightened ideas that circulated among the bourgeoisie, particularly those critical of the Church. In his manuscript, he wrote "Is it possible that some men lord it over others by making them believe in chimeras and that we're dumb enough to believe in all their talk?"[3] Even before the Revolution, men like Ménétra had a sense that they could think and speak for themselves.

Guild masters' sons like Ménétra were better off than the majority of the urban working population. Most journeymen had little prospect of ever becoming owners of their own shops. They floated from job to job, always at risk of sinking into the ranks of unskilled day laborers or of falling ill and ending their days begging or dying in a hospice. Women, who made up a large part of the urban working population, had even less chance to achieve a privileged position. Only a few women's occupations, such as dressmaking, had a guild structure. The wives of shopowners and guild masters worked alongside their husbands, often managing the family enterprise's money while their husbands did the physical work. Most women of the popular classes worked outside of the home, however, as street vendors, laundresses, seamstresses, and in other typically female trades. Single women often migrated to cities to work as domestic servants, a position which put them in contact with members of the wealthier classes but which exposed them to dangers such as sexual exploitation that might in the end force them onto the streets as prostitutes.

Throughout the eighteenth century, the government had regarded the urban lower classes as a potential source of danger. Even though living standards for most had slowly improved over the course of the century, the ordinary people of Paris and other large cities had simmering resentments against the wealthy and against the government that taxed them but often seemed indifferent to their needs. Conflicts between employers and their workers were a regular occurrence. Popular protest often had a political impact as well. In 1775, Parisian riots against high grain prices had defeated the minister Turgot's effort to free the grain trade, and in 1786, silk weavers and other workers in Lyon, France's second-largest city, had staged an insurrection that took three days to put down. The authorities knew that any major crisis was likely to have repercussions among the urban population.

Much of the urban population consisted of migrants from the thousands of rural villages in which some three-fourths of the French population lived. Few questions have challenged historians as much as summing up the condition of the French peasantry at the end of the eighteenth century. Even observers of the time had contradictory impressions. The English agricultural expert Arthur Young described Brittany as backward and poverty-stricken, with "husbandry not much further advanced, at least in skill, than among the Hurons," but at about the same time, another English traveler visited French Flanders and reported that "the most striking character of the country through which we passed is its astonishing fertility."[4] Most peasants were poor by the standards of city-dwellers, but conditions varied considerably from region to region, and within each village there were prosperous and impoverished families. Levels of education and literacy were usually lower in the countryside than in the towns, but some peasants could read and write. Thanks to the village priest, visitors such as traveling peddlers, and their contacts with nearby market towns, peasants had at least some sense of what was happening in the wider world.

Unlike the enserfed peasants of central and eastern Europe, the majority of French peasants had gained their legal freedom in earlier centuries. Most of them owned some land, but only a minority had enough property to make their families economically self-sufficient. To make additional income, all members of peasant families, including women and children from an early age, had to contribute. Peasants rented land or entered into sharecropping arrangements with local seigneurs or bourgeois landowners. In some regions, such as Flanders, peasants also found part-time employment in various cottage industries, such as spinning and weaving, which brought them into regular contact with bourgeois merchants. Just as the urban population ranged from prosperous skilled artisans to day-laborers, prostitutes, and criminals living on the margin of subsistence, so these rural peasants varied from well-to-do *laboureurs* who contracted to manage wealthy seigneurs' estates to impoverished migrants who lived by taking odd jobs wherever they could find them. Peasants' social conditions also varied tremendously from region to region. In France's "breadbasket," the rich grain-growing region around Paris, a market-oriented, competitive economy split the peasants into a small elite of *coqs du village*, closely linked to big landlords, and a mass of poor peasants, forced to compete for jobs as laborers to supplement what they could raise on the tiny plots of property they owned. In the western provinces, less-developed economically, the income differences between peasant families were often less extreme and the sense of tension between peasants and seigneurs less acute. These differences in rural social structure often influenced peasant reactions to the Revolution.

Although rural conditions differed considerably from region to region, most French peasants were affected by unfavorable economic trends in the last decades before the Revolution. The reign of Louis XV, from 1715 to 1774, had generally been a prosperous one for the rural population. Crop failures had been rare, and the result had been a marked rise in population. Around 1770, however, climatic conditions took a turn for the worse, and, in the two decades before 1789, economic hardship repeatedly struck the countryside. In years when bread prices rose sharply, peasants and the urban poor blamed efforts to create a free market in grain and called for government regulation. Widespread protests in the spring of 1775—the so-called Flour War (*guerre des farines*)—contributed to the failure of the minister Turgot's ambitious economic program. Even in calmer times, the growth in population meant that increased numbers of peasants competed for the available land and jobs, a situation that drove landlords' rents and food prices up but kept wages down. The growing split between rich and poor generated increased social tension. So did changing mentalities. As more secular attitudes penetrated the countryside, peasants became less tolerant of the inequitable social arrangements. As events in 1789 were to show, under the right circumstances, the peasants could become a powerful revolutionary force.

THE IMPACT OF THE PHILOSOPHES

Just as explanations of the French Revolution that emphasize social tensions were first advanced by the movement's supporters at the time, explanations stressing the influence of radical ideas go back to the movement's early critics, such as the British writer Edmund Burke. Burke and other opponents of the Revolution frequently blamed it on the baleful influence of the major French thinkers of the eighteenth century, the *philosophes*, whose criticism of established institutions had supposedly paved the way for the crisis of 1789. Over the past two centuries, historians have continued to debate the role of ideas in bringing about the Revolution. Modern scholars are less likely to attribute responsibility to specific writers and specific books. More often, they emphasize the importance of new habits of mind and behavior, many of them fostered not by radical critics of society but by the workings of Old Regime institutions themselves.

It is certainly true that eighteenth-century French intellectuals often criticized their country's leading institutions. The philosophes, the leading representatives of this movement of the Age of Enlightenment, applied to religious and social issues the rational approach to the world pioneered by philosophers and natural scientists in the seventeenth century. The baron de Montesquieu, a provincial nobleman, was among the most influential eighteenth-century political thinkers in France. His youthful satire, *The Persian Letters*, mocked Catholicism and Louis XIV's absolutist government. But Montesquieu was more than a satirist. In his masterwork, *The Spirit of the Laws*, first published in 1748, he took a systematic approach to the study of politics. He argued that each country's laws and institutions formed a system governed by a particular spirit, and he contrasted England, which he called the "one nation in the world whose constitution has political liberty for its direct purpose,"[5] with France's absolutist system, in which aristocratic honor was the only barrier to absolutism. His positive portrayal of England's constitutional monarchy, which divided power between the king and the Parliament, was an implicit criticism of the French system, which Montesquieu claimed was only kept from becoming despotic by the activity of beleaguered "intermediate bodies" such as the parlements. Throughout the rest of the century, defenders of these courts reworked and simplified Montesquieu's ideas and spread the notion that France needed independent institutions capable of limiting the power of the king and his ministers.

The poet, playwright, and pamphleteer Voltaire was another of the most influential philosophes. He aimed his sharpest barbs at religious orthodoxy. His popular plays like *Mahomet*, which was based on the life of the founder of Islam, castigated religious intolerance and fanaticism; his short novels, such as *Candide* and *Zadig*, raised troubling questions about whether God truly provided humanity with clear rules to live by. Voltaire gained particular fame near the end of his life, in the 1760s, when he devoted himself to winning justice for several victims of religious persecution in France, such as the Protestant Jean Calas, unjustly executed on charges of having murdered a son who converted to Catholicism. Although he denounced injustice and intolerance, Voltaire doubted that ordinary people could be educated enough to make good political decisions. Unlike Montesquieu, he favored an enlightened absolutist monarchy over a mixed system of government.

Jean-Jacques Rousseau, perhaps the most widely known French writer of the period, was frequently at odds with Voltaire, but the two shared a reputation for having defended the cause of the oppressed. Rousseau criticized the other philosophes' faith in reason, but he also criticized the excesses of France's sophisticated elites. In his *Discourse on the Origins of Inequality*, he contended that people had been better off when societies had been simpler and life more natural. His bestselling novels, *The New Héloise* and *Emile*, offered models of life lived according to the dictates of pure, natural feelings. More than Montesquieu and Voltaire, he urged readers to change the way they lived their private lives: his eloquent defense of "natural" motherhood and breastfeeding in *Emile* had a definite impact on many aristocratic and bourgeois women readers and is often seen as one of the sources of the subsequent movement to limit women's activities to the domestic sphere. But Rousseau was also concerned about fundamental issues of politics. His most important political work, *The Social Contract*, attempted to explain how men in complex, modern societies could retain a sense of enjoying their natural rights, provided they were able to participate effectively and on an equal basis in governing themselves. Whereas Montesquieu had argued that liberty depended on limits and divisions of power, Rousseau claimed that it depended on the citizens' uniting to follow the dictates of their common interest, which he called the general will. He insisted on the importance of equality and shared values among the citizens of a republic, even suggesting that those who didn't accept the religion of the state might be put to death. Rousseau himself feared social upheaval, but his ideas took on a new resonance in 1789 when the French people found themselves facing the challenge of making a new political system. The image of Rousseau, who had shunned luxury and always proclaimed his lower-class origins, made him a powerful icon to the leaders of the Revolution's democratic wing, who claimed his authority for their doctrines, even though they interpreted his ideas in ways he probably would have condemned.

The ideas of Montesquieu, Voltaire, and Rousseau were all reflected in a massive collaborative publication, the *Encyclopédie*, or encyclopedia, edited by the philosophes Jean d'Alembert and Denis Diderot and published in installments between 1751 and 1765. The contributers to the *Encyclopédie* applied the critical and rational approach of the Enlightenment to the full range of human knowledge and to every aspect of society. In articles carefully crafted to pass the censors, Voltaire and others cast doubt on Church dogmas and raised questions about traditional political institutions. Detailed descriptions and illustrations of farming and manufacturing processes suggested both that manual labor—and the lower classes who performed it—deserved respect, and that a scientific approach to production could improve efficiency.

The *Encyclopédie* was a bestseller. Its purchasers were part of the growing public of readers whose collective opinion loomed ever larger in national life after the middle of the century. The phrase "public opinion" entered common use in France around 1750, reflecting this new reality. It referred to what was taken to be the general outlook of the men and women who discussed cultural and political issues in the increasing number of institutions that fostered such interchange.

THE GROWTH OF PUBLIC OPINION

Whereas the opinions that mattered had once been formed at the royal court and in the royally sponsored academies, by the middle of the eighteenth century they were formulated in an informal network of institutions whose common feature was that they reflected the thinking of private individuals, independent of their social status or political position. In Paris, writers, artists, and cultured nobles and bourgeois came together regularly in *salons*, informal weekly meetings usually organized by active and intelligent women who used this means to obtain a degree of influence normally denied to them. Poems and essays first read in the salons often appeared later in one of the rapidly growing number of magazines and journals that were increasingly rivaling books as the elite's favorite form of reading material. In the provinces, regional journals served to stimulate local pride and became rallying points for local elites. Reading rooms, where for a small fee one could peruse a wide range of journals and books, also spread from Paris to most other French towns. Increasingly frequent public concerts and theater performances also served to give the public a greater sense of identity. The Masonic movement, introduced from England in the 1730s and devoted to the moral improvement of its members, became an important form of urban sociability. Masonic lodges propagated an ideology of equality. Members addressed each other as "brothers" regardless of their social rank, even though social prejudice limited recruitment primarily to the nobility and the wealthy bourgeoisie.

Participants in this increasingly lively network of cultural institutions often read the works of the great philosophes, such as Montesquieu, Voltaire, and Rousseau. But they also read a host of other texts, which often reflected very different intellectual traditions. France's politically informed public developed first in reaction to controversies spawned by quarrels inspired by the Jansenist movement for spiritual reform within the Catholic church.

Jansenists sought a purer, more rigorous faith. They blamed the papacy for corrupting the church. Louis XIV feared that the zealous advocates of this movement would undermine France's religious unity. In 1713, his lobbying led the papacy to issue an official condemnation of Jansenist doctrines, known as the bull *Unigenitus*. For the next sixty years, the French government and the Catholic hierarchy used this bull to try to root out Jansenist dissidence among French Catholics. These periodic campaigns, such as the archbishop of Paris's order in 1749 to refuse administration of last rites to suspected Jansenists unless they abjured their beliefs, inspired stubborn resistance. Persecuted Jansenists found protectors among the judges of the parlements, who used the issue to cast themselves as defenders of the rights of individuals against arbitrary authority. Pamphleteers elaborated on the parlements' case to argue that the country's traditional liberties were menaced by the growth of the central government's powers. Their works were probably more effective than the abstract treatises of Montesquieu and Rousseau in convincing the French public of the need for fixed constitutional laws and of some kind of representative institutions to defend them.

Pro-parlement pamphleteering often crossed over into exposés of the private lives of royal ministers, royal favorites, and even members of the royal family. Scurrilous *libelles* retailed unsavory details about the past of the aging Louis XV's last mistress, Madame du Barry, and titillated the public with details of the difficulties the young Louis XVI experienced in consummating his marriage with Marie-Antoinette. In 1785, scandal touched the queen herself when she was accused of having encouraged the dissolute Cardinal Rohan to purchase a fabulously expensive diamond necklace as a gift for her. This "Diamond Necklace Affair" made the king look like a cuckold, unable to perform his basic functions as both husband and member of the royal dynasty, and contributed to a broader process of undermining the sacred status the monarchy had had in the past. The authors of these pamphlets, hack writers excluded from the intellectual establishment, often emerged after 1789 as revolutionary journalists and orators.

By casting a bishop in the role of would-be seducer of the queen, the Diamond Necklace affair tarnished the Church as well as the monarchy. Writers like Voltaire and Rousseau had attacked religious orthodoxy on intellectual grounds, but the move away from strict Catholic belief had broader origins. Paradoxically, the Jansenist campaign for a more intense and spiritual faith may have contributed to the change in atmosphere. Jansenist zealotry, at its height in the first half of the eighteenth century, was too demanding for many Catholics and sometimes undermined their loyalty to the Church altogether. Although attendance at services was still legally enforced until the Revolution, the decline in the number of wills leaving money for masses for the soul of the deceased after 1750 showed that a process of secularization was already under way in many regions of the country.

This process of secularization affected not only the elites who read Enlightenment literature but also sections of the lower classes. Demographic studies show growing intervals between births in peasant families in several regions, a sign of growing willingness to ignore the Church's prohibition against contraceptive practices. Nor was this the only area in which the lower orders showed an increasing tendency to think for themselves. The frequency with which peasant communities and urban artisan groups brought lawsuits against seigneurs and employers testifies to a growing awareness that even humble subjects had legal rights and a growing expectation that the government would enforce them, even against the powerful. (In the countryside, royal officials, aware that it was in their interest to protect tax-paying peasants against tax-protected seigneurs, sometimes encouraged peasant suits.) Changes in the realm of private life, such as the growing availability of inexpensive, colorful clothing, gave the urban poor more chance to think of themselves as individuals capable of making choices. All of these developments reflected cultural changes that historians have increasingly come to recognize as contributing to the climate that made the revolution of 1789, if not inevitable, at least conceivable.

When the steadily worsening financial crisis finally forced the French monarchy to allow the population to express its views in 1788, the king's ministers soon learned that no sector of the French population was prepared simply to accept changes from above without questioning them. Nobles, peasants, and all groups in between recognized that they had interests to defend and took active measures to protect them. The resulting debate revealed the extent to which traditional cultural values had already been undermined by the impact of the philosophes' writings and other cultural changes over the course of the century. The crisis of the French Revolution had deep roots in the country's past, but in 1787, no one could have predicted how drastically France's political, social, and cultural institutions would be reshaped once the Revolution began.

NOTES

1. Cited in the University of Chicago College History Staff, eds., *History of Western Civilization* (Chicago: University of Chicago Press, 1977), 57.

2. Alexis de Tocqueville, *The Old Regime and the French Revolution* (New York: Doubleday, 1955), 177.

3. Jacques Ménétra, *Journal of My* Life, trans. Arthur Goldhammer (New York: Columbia University Press, 1986), 171.

4. Citations from Robert and Elborg Forster, eds., *European Society in the Eighteenth Century* (New York: Harper and Row, 1969), 40; and John Lough, *France on the Eve of Revolution* (Chicago: Dorsey, 1987), 34.

5. Montesquieu, *The Spirit of the Laws*, trans. Anne Cohler et al. (Cambridge: Cambridge University Press, 1989), 156.

CHAPTER 2

THE COLLAPSE OF THE ABSOLUTE MONARCHY, 1787–1789

France in the mid-1780s was a society afflicted with numerous tensions. Nevertheless, it was not obvious that the country was on the brink of a revolutionary explosion. Despite the economic difficulties of the 1770s and 1780s, most peasants were better off than their ancestors under Louis XIV. Successful members of the bourgeoisie continued to find ways to gain noble status. The questioning of traditional values had not given rise to any organized subversive movement. Repeated political crises had tested the institutions of absolutism, but each time the monarchy had emerged intact. Long-term trends had made a major crisis in France possible, but it took specific events to make it unavoidable.

THE PRE-REVOLUTION

The most important of these specific events was the fact that by late 1786 the French government was finally on the verge of complete insolvency. Charles Alexandre de Calonne, controller-general since 1783, had initially won his job because he promised that he could deal with the monarchy's financial problems without proposing controversial reforms. He now found himself having to persuade Louis XVI of the necessity for extraordinary measures to head off bankruptcy. The immediate problem was the need to repay loans floated to pay the cost of France's participation in the American War of Independence: the fiscal crisis was thus directly linked to the effort to maintain

France's role as a world power. But Calonne now advised Louis XVI that "the only way to bring real order into the finances is to revitalize the entire state by reforming all that is defective in its constitution."[1] His predecessors' failures had convinced Calonne that he could not accomplish his aims through the normal institutions of the monarchy. And so he took the first step that was to lead to a revolution: he persuaded the king to convoke an Assembly of Notables to discuss fundamental changes in the structure of French government.

The convocation of the Assembly of Notables in January 1787 was the first of a rapid series of events that historians have come to label the "pre-Revolution." During this period, which lasted from the beginning of 1787 until the meeting of the Estates-General in May 1789, the formal powers of the king and his ministers remained intact, and their bureaucratic machine continued to go through its regular routines. The authority of the absolutist state had not yet completely broken down. But that authority was rapidly eroding. In their efforts to escape from the looming shadow of bankruptcy, Calonne and his successors proposed more and more drastic reforms, thereby throwing into question more and more of France's traditional institutions. By raising so many controversial issues, these initiatives galvanized ever-wider circles of the population into organized political action, until the king's call for nationwide elections to the Estates-General extended the process of politicization to every single town and village in France.

The great French scholar Georges Lefebvre labeled this period the "aristocratic revolution" because the most vocal opposition to royal reform initiatives during this period came from members of France's titled elite rather than from the representatives of the bourgeoisie and the lower classes, who were to take such a role in events from 1789 onward. Lefebvre and other historians of the Marxist school interpreted the activity of aristocratic leaders during the pre-Revolution as the culmination of a longer process of "aristocratic" or "feudal" reaction, in which the landed aristocracy, threatened by the development of capitalism and an aggressive bourgeoisie, sought to shore up its slipping economic and social position.

More recent scholars have questioned the reality of this "feudal reaction." Nobles continued to safeguard their economic interests, as they always had, but there is little evidence that this process had become more intense just before 1789, or that most nobles thought the bases of their position were in danger. The judges of the parlements and other aristocrats who challenged royal authority during the pre-Revolution were reacting primarily to a political threat. Like the royal ministers they opposed, they also recognized the need for major reforms. But they argued that the discredited absolutist system could not be trusted to regenerate itself. They opposed measures that they feared would increase ministerial power and insisted that the French "nation" be consulted about fundamental changes in its constitution. And they saw themselves as the natural spokesmen for the rest of the population.

THE ASSEMBLY OF NOTABLES

By convening an assembly of leading noblemen, clergy, and high officials to examine his reform proposals, Calonne believed that he could enlist the force of public opinion in favor of his most important proposals. He wanted a new land tax to be levied on all property owners—nobles, clergy, and commoners—and the establishment of representative assemblies in all of France's provinces. The land tax implied the breaking down of the deep-rooted distinctions between social classes and corporate groups; the provincial assemblies suggested an abandonment of the fundamental principle of absolutism, that authority should flow from the top down. (See Document A.) But the 142 delegates who arrived in Versailles in January 1787 reacted to Calonne's projects with suspicion. They remembered that Calonne's predecessor, Jacques Necker, had tried to win public confidence in 1781 by becoming the first finance minister to make figures on royal income and expenditures public. His *Compte rendu* had purported to show that existing taxes were more than sufficient to cover normal expenditures. Since taking office in 1783, Calonne himself had borrowed and spent freely. Now he had suddenly reversed course, announcing that the treasury was empty and asking for new taxes. Few of the Notables were prepared to believe his claims without verification.

DOCUMENT A
A ROYAL REFORM PROPOSAL, 1787

On 22 February 1787, Louis XVI and his minister Calonne presented their reform proposals to the Assembly of Notables. This excerpt from the king's speech shows that they were aware of the need for major reforms.

"The projects that will be communicated to you on my behalf are large and important. On the one hand, it is my intention to increase the state's income, and make sure that it is no longer eaten up by debt payments, by a fairer system of taxes. On the other hand, the views that I have adopted after lengthy consideration are to free commerce from the different obstacles that hinder it, and to aid my poorest subjects to the fullest extent that circumstances permit. Since these [projects] all aim at promoting the public welfare, and since I know you are all eager to be of service to me, I have no fear about consulting you about the details of their execution . . . I am sure that your opinions will all tend in the same direction, and that it will therefore be easy to reconcile them. Surely no selfish interest will oppose the general interest." (*Translation by Jeremy D. Popkin.*)

Before they endorsed proposals that would overturn longstanding traditions and weaken their special privileges, they demanded a precise accounting of revenue and expenditures to demonstrate the necessity for new taxes.

Calonne responded by going over the Notables' heads and appealing to the public. He had his proposals printed, together with an introduction condemning the Notables for their defense of outmoded privileges. But the population was not ready to rally to the support of a notoriously high-handed minister against the Notables, who cast themselves as defenders of the population's traditional legal rights. By April 1787, it was clear that Calonne's gamble had failed. Louis XVI replaced him with one of his chief critics among the Notables, the archbishop of Toulouse, Loménie de Brienne. Brienne found the Assembly of Notables equally difficult to work with, however. Its members made it increasingly clear that they would not take the responsibility for approving new taxes. The most outspoken of them challenged the government to convene an elected assembly representing all elements of the population: the Estates-General of the realm, which had not met since 1614.

Brienne was naturally reluctant to make such a complete departure from the policies of absolutism. Instead, he sought to get the parlements to approve modified versions of Calonne's proposals. By a combination of concessions and pressure—he exiled the judges of the Paris parlement to Troyes for several months to weaken their resistance—he worked out a delicate compromise. The parlements would approve an extension of tax surcharges imposed during the American war, and, in return, Brienne promised to convoke the Estates-General in 1792, by which time he calculated that the worst of the government's fiscal problems would be solved. When the Paris parlement met on 19 November 1787 to ratify this plan, however, Louis XVI upset all his minister's hard work. Instead of allowing the judges of the parlement to discuss it freely, as they had been promised, the king ordered them to register it without a vote. "It is legal because I wish it," he insisted, reasserting the basic premise of absolutist government.[2] His unexpected intervention outraged the judges and much of the public.

Compromise with the parlements having failed, Brienne and his fellow ministers decided to adopt a policy of confrontation. On 8 May 1788, they promulgated a set of edicts that abolished the parlements, replacing them with a single high court for the whole country. They accompanied this radical measure with other reforms designed to make the elimination of the parlements more palatable to public opinion, such as the abolition of the fees that litigants had had to pay to judges to have their cases heard. But these did little to soften the shock of their actions, which revived the fear of an all-powerful despotism that had been raised earlier by Chancellor Maupeou's efforts to remodel the parlements in 1770–1771. The country was flooded with pamphlets that revived the traditional "parlementary" or "magisterial" themes of the need to restore a balance in the constitution by limiting royal authority.

FROM FAILED REFORMS TO REVOLUTIONARY CRISIS

Although the issues raised by the 1788 reforms were similar to those posed in 1770, the outcome of this crisis was very different. Nearly two decades of unsuccessful reform efforts from above and the unprecedented severity of the financial crisis had severely weakened the government's standing. The successful creation of a republic based on popular sovereignty in the United States provided a thought-provoking new political model. Furthermore, the political crisis was compounded by other problems. The government's attempt to stimulate trade through a treaty with England in 1786 had hurt many manufacturers. In the summer of 1788, a devastating hailstorm damaged grain crops in much of northern France, provoking a steep rise in bread prices that continued until the following summer. This crisis exacerbated the unrest among both urban and rural populations that had built up as a result of the long period of economic difficulties dating back to the early 1770s.

In this tense context, the attempt to abolish the parlements opened a debate that went beyond the issues of new taxes or court reform and raised the question of who had the sovereign power to make fundamental laws for the kingdom. Supporters of the parlements maintained that this power could only be exercised by the nation itself, not by the king and his ministers. Inspired in part by the examples of England and the United States, these protesters demanded a form of representative government for France. French historical tradition offered an example of such a body: the Estates-General, a body of representatives chosen from the three traditional Estates with the power to present grievances to the king and offer advice on taxes and laws.

As the resistance to the abolition of the parlements and the demands for a representative assembly mounted, the king and his ministers finally saw no alternative to convening the Estates-General. Royal authority was breaking down in several provinces, notably in Dauphiné, where, on 7 June 1788, pro-parlement rioters hurling stones from rooftops had driven royal troops out of the city of Grenoble in the first outbreak of the political violence that would mark the Revolution. Movements to defend local parlements and resist the government's plans also developed in several other regions, including Brittany, long a stronghold of resistance to ministerial authority. On 5 July 1788, to head off these menaces, Brienne announced that the Estates-General would be convened as soon as possible. He also suspended the censorship laws, allowing free public discussion of political matters. This announcement made government authority crumble even further. By early August, the treasury was virtually empty, and Brienne had to resign in favor of the banker Jacques Necker. Necker, who had been finance minister from 1777 to 1781, had a reputation as a reformer. His return, together with the recall of the parlements, produced a temporary calming effect, allowing the elections of deputies to the Estates-General to proceed.

THE MEETING OF THE ESTATES-GENERAL

The summoning of the Estates-General raised new and divisive questions. How were the deputies to be chosen? And how was the Assembly to be organized when it met? In previous centuries, the Estates-General had met in three separate chambers representing, respectively, the clergy, the nobility, and the Third Estate, or commoners. All three chambers had to agree before the Estates-General could pass any resolution. Under these rules, the two privileged estates—the clergy and the nobles—who collectively amounted to less than 3 percent of the population, controlled two of the assembly's three chambers and could dominate its proceedings. This perspective suited many of those who had opposed arbitrary ministerial authority under Louis XV and his successor. They saw the nobles, particularly the aristocratic judges of the parlements, as the natural leaders of the nation and its protectors against the king's arbitrary power. On 25 September 1788, the newly restored Paris parlement explicitly ordered that the Estates-General meet "according to the forms of 1614"—that is, with the three orders meeting and voting separately. The judges were probably concerned primarily with preventing the government from setting its own rules for the meeting. But the effect of their edict was to change the main focus of political debate. Arguments between supporters and opponents of royal authority gave way to equally sharp disputes between defenders of the aristocracy and the politically articulate members of the Third Estate, who now feared that their interests would be ignored at the upcoming assembly.

Movements in the provinces offered two different models of relationships between the privileged orders and the Third Estate. In Dauphiné, reformers under the leadership of a Grenoble lawyer named Joseph Mounier drafted a plan to restore its long-dormant Estates in the form of a single assembly in which half the deputies would be chosen by the two privileged orders and half by the Third Estate. They defended their plan on the grounds that, like the English constitution, it would ensure harmony among the three Estates by giving the privileged orders a stake in the new system. Events in Brittany pointed in a very different direction. In this province, dominated by impoverished petty noblemen who feared seeing themselves displaced by wealthy urban commoners such as the great merchants of the port city of Nantes, the privileged orders rejected any concessions to the Third Estate. Their opponents countered by urging the Third Estate to set itself against them and claim all authority for itself. In December and January, violence flared in the streets of Rennes, the provincial capital, as supporters and opponents of the nobility battled each other. The royal intendant was unable to control the situation.

The Breton Third Estate's argument against the privileged orders was transferred to the national level in one of the most influential pamphlets written in the late fall of 1788, the abbé Sieyès's *What Is the Third Estate?*[3] Sieyès began with a ringing declaration: "The plan of this work is very simple. We have three questions to ask: 1st. What is the Third Estate? Everything. 2nd. What has it been in the political order up to now? Nothing. 3rd. What does it demand? To become something." The Third Estate, Sieyès asserted, "has . . . within itself all that is necessary to constitute a complete nation," since its members did all the useful work in the country. "If the privileged order were abolished," he concluded, "the nation would be not something less but something more." He called for a single assembly representing those who made real contributions to the public welfare, from the humble peasant to the wealthy merchant and the learned lawyer. This group, Sieyès maintained, had a single common interest: "it is the nation." Its representatives had every right to proceed on their own, disregarding any objections of deputies from the privileged orders. Other "patriotic" pamphleteers, such as the Protestant minister Rabaut Saint-Etienne, seconded Sieyès's arguments and added their own. Rabaut, for example, urged his readers not to "follow the conduct of your ancestors," but to be guided by "good sense" and "the law of nature." (See Document B.)

As the elections to the Estates-General proceeded in the first four months of 1789, compromise between the privileged orders and the Third Estate still seemed possible. The harsh logic of Sieyès's radical arguments was not yet translated into reality. Necker had managed to get Louis XVI to defuse some opposition by announcing the "doubling of the Third" on 27 December 1788: as in the Dauphiné assembly, the commoners would elect twice as many deputies as each of the other two orders. But this decree said nothing about whether the 600 deputies from the Third Estate and the 300 from each of the other two orders would meet together in a single assembly or in separate chambers, in which case the Third Estate's predominance would be meaningless.

The elections to the Estates-General transformed the notion of government according to public opinion from an abstract slogan into a living reality. In every parish and district of the country, all adult men—and, in exceptional cases, a few women—were called together not only to choose representatives but also to voice their views on what issues the Estates-General should consider by drawing up *cahiers de doléance*, or lists of grievances. The cahiers provided a complex and ambiguous picture of the population's concerns on the eve of the Revolution. All three orders' cahiers indicated a consensus in favor of major constitutional reforms, above all the creation of a system of representative government that would modify the king's absolute powers. The nobility and clergy were ready to accept some major modifications of their privileges, such as equality of taxation. There was strong sentiment for reform of the legal system, and most nobles favored abolition of censorship. The nobility's cahiers hardly foresaw the complete abolition of their order, however, and the clergy were far from favoring the creation of an essentially secular society.

DOCUMENT B
THE REVOLUTIONARY SPIRIT IN 1788

Together with the abbé Sieyès's What Is the Third Estate? *the future deputy Rabaut Saint-Etienne's* Considerations on the Interests of the Third Estate *provided the clearest statement of the revolutionary challenge to France's existing institutions that developed in the months before the meeting of the Estates-General. In this excerpt, Rabaut Saint-Etienne expresses the revolutionaries' general attitude toward the past and calls on the Third Estate to adopt a new mentality.*

"It is obvious that there is only one real interest, and that is the interest of all. Where the interest of all is not properly understood . . . , one should at least follow the interest of the largest number. The largest number is the Third Estate composed of twenty-five million subjects, as against five or six hundred thousand with privileges. The distinction of ranks does not justify any distinction of political rights. If there were such a distinction, it would be unjust that power should belong to the smallest group, and this sub-aristocracy would be unconstitutional. Since national assemblies are assemblies of taxpayers, only taxpayers should be included, and those who do not pay taxes should not be included. Since those who are included have this right only as taxpayers, and therefore form only one category, the Estates-General are only a single body, a body of taxpayers.

"These are the true principles, this is your code, these are your true instructions, Third Estate, and I invite you to meditate on them. Don't bother to open your books, you will find them full of contradictions. Don't try to follow the conduct of your ancestors, they had no principles to follow and they were degraded. Don't ask what was done before, because you know what it was: you were sacrificed. Consult only good sense, which is the same in all countries and all epochs, and the law of nature, the basis of all rights, whose principles can never be overridden.

"Reclaim your proper place and your ascendancy, because you are the nation. The time has come when, evils being at their peak, order will arise from disorder itself. The taxes on the people have reached their highest level, they cannot be increased. It is the time that the two orders that lord it over you should share the burden with you." (From Rabaut Saint-Etienne, *Considerations sur les intérêts du Tiers-Etat* [1788] pp. 35–37. *Translation by Jeremy D. Popkin.*)

Cahiers representing peasant villages mixed appeals for broad reform with local concerns, calling for repair of bridges, abolition of specific tolls and dues, and measures against specific privilege-holders, such as the postmaster of the village of Ecommoy whose neighbors complained that he was evading taxes. Taken as a whole, they represented a serious protest against the workings of the seigneurial system and the privileges of the nobility. As deputies from the villages came together to elect regional representatives, members of the urban Third Estate, usually bourgeois lawyers, office-holders, and other professionals, reworked these demands, giving them a more general form. Even so, the Third Estate cahiers were still something less than a revolutionary program. They revealed strong dissatisfaction with existing conditions and a widespread demand for the end of most special privileges, but they did not call for the elimination of social distinctions or the abolition of the monarchy. The summoning of the Estates-General raised special controversies in France's colonies, where white colonists feared that the campaign for liberty in France itself would lead to attacks on slavery; many leading Paris radicals were members of the *Société des amis des noirs*, a group founded in February 1788 to promote the eventual abolition of that system. Some colonists demanded the right to elect deputies to the Estates-General to protect their interests; others suggested that the colonies imitate their North American neighbors and declare independence from France.

THE PARLIAMENTARY REVOLUTION

On 3 May 1789, the approximately 1,200 deputies to the Estates-General assembled in Versailles. They included well-known participants in the public debate that had occupied the country ever since Calonne had convoked his Assembly of Notables more than two years earlier, as well as obscure parish priests, provincial noblemen, and small-town lawyers. Contrary to the allegations of critics then and since, many of the members of the Estates-General had practical experience in public affairs as royal officials, in local government, or as administrators in the Church. Among the assembled deputies, there was an articulate minority of self-proclaimed Patriots, bent on a sweeping transformation of French public life. Their program included a fixed, written constitution for France that would severely limit the king's powers, the abolition of legal privileges, a representative assembly, religious toleration, and press freedom. Initially, however, most of the deputies rejected the Patriots' radicalism and looked for leadership to Louis XVI, whose popularity had soared since he had agreed to the convocation of the Estates-General, and to the chief minister, Necker. Necker's budgetary wizardry, the deputies assumed, would produce a solution to the fiscal crisis.

Unfortunately for the monarchy, the king and Necker proved unprepared for the extraordinary situation they now found themselves in. Louis, an honest and well-meaning man, lacked the vision and determination to take the lead in a radical reform movement; Necker had little sense of how to handle a crisis. Charged with presenting the government's program to the Estates-General in its opening session, he stupefied the deputies with a long-winded account of the monarchy's fiscal problems but offered them no specific proposals to debate. The king and Necker left the Estates-General itself to decide the burning question of whether to vote by head or by order.

With no commitment to significant reform from the king, the deputies of the Third Estate had every reason to fear that subsequent proceedings would be dominated by the two privileged orders. This fear drove even the moderate members of the Third Estate to support a radical decision: the Third Estate paralyzed the assembly by refusing to organize itself and begin work unless the other two orders immediately agreed to meet and vote in common. The underlying issue was fundamental: was France to become a country of citizens enjoying equal rights, or was it to remain divided into different status groups with differing privileges?

On 10 June, after five weeks of futile negotiations, the Third Estate deputies had become sufficiently impatient to endorse Sieyès's motion to send a final invitation to the nobles and the clergy to form a single assembly and then to proceed without them if they declined. Joined by a handful of deputies from the clergy, they then voted on 17 June 1789 to assume the new name of National Assembly, thus proclaiming that they were speaking for the national community as a whole. News of their actions reached a wider public through the regular letters that many of the deputies sent home and via hastily created newspapers that summarized the Estates-General's debates. In coffeehouses and public places throughout the nation, ordinary citizens, living embodiments of the public opinion that had taken on a new level of importance with the monarchy's virtual abdication of power, eagerly followed the debates.

The Third Estate's decision to transform itself into a National Assembly was a challenge not only to the other two orders but also to the authority of Louis XVI. Three days later, on 20 June, he announced a special royal session of all three orders on 23 June. In the meantime, royal officials locked the deputies of the National Assembly out of their regular meeting hall. Fearing that the king would try to quash their decisions, the members of the Assembly held an emergency session in the only building they could find that was large enough to accommodate them, the king's indoor tennis court. There, they swore the dramatic "Oath of the Tennis Court," pledging not to allow themselves to be sent home until they had given France a new constitution.

The king's speech on 23 June 1789, offering limited reforms but insisting on the maintenance of the privileged orders, failed to halt this defiance of royal authority. When royal officials ordered the deputies to disperse after the king's speech, Count Mirabeau, a renegade nobleman who had been elected to represent the Third Estate of his native Provence and who had already established himself as one of the National Assembly's dominant figures, defiantly replied, "We are here by the will of the French people, and we will only be dispersed by the force of bayonets." Faced with the intransigence of the Third Estate deputies, the king was forced to back down. On 27 June 1789, he himself ordered the deputies of the clergy and the nobility to join the National Assembly. The former deputies of the Third Estate seemed to have won, and the National Assembly began drafting a constitution. But the bayonets to which Mirabeau had referred were not out of the picture. The government had begun to assemble troops near the capital; the incipient revolution still risked being put down by force.

THE STORMING OF THE BASTILLE

While the troops assembled and the deputies debated, the rest of the French population had begun to take a hand in determining the country's fate. The agitation accompanying the elections to the Estates-General and the unrest stemming from difficult economic conditions had already led to popular insurrections in several parts of the country. In April 1789, artisans and workers in Paris's populous Faubourg Saint-Antoine had sacked the mansion of the wallpaper manufacturer Reveillon, who had been accused of trying to lower wages. Although not directly connected to the summoning of the Estates-General, this incident of violence was a warning of the strength of social tensions. But political excitement was more visible in Paris than social unrest. Crowds gathered every day in open spaces like the gardens of the Palais-Royal to listen to reports from Versailles and speeches by self-appointed orators. Popular sympathies were overwhelmingly with the leaders of the Third Estate and hostile to the "aristocrats" of the other two orders. Political agitation affected even the soldiers stationed in and around Paris, some of whom openly expressed their sympathies for the National Assembly.

In Versailles, the king's most conservative advisers had now gained the upper hand. On 11 July 1789, Louis dismissed Necker, who, in spite of his ineffectual performance at the opening of the Estates-General, had still been regarded as an advocate of reform. Even before the deputies in Versailles could respond to this move, the people of Paris took to the streets in protest. On July 12 and 13, as fears grew that the troops ringing the capital would be sent in to put down the patriotic movement, crowds besieged several royal arsenals in the city, demanding arms. Meanwhile, army commanders warned Versailles that they could not count on their men to fight against the Parisians.

REVEIL DU TIERS ETAT.

Ma foute, il étoit tems que je me réveillasse, car l'oppression de mes fers me donnoient le cochemar un peu trop fort.

The Awakening of the Third Estate

This caricature was one of many that communicated the significance of the dramatic events of July 1789 even to those who could not read. In this striking image, representatives of the nobility and the clergy recoil in alarm as a figure representing the commoners of the Third Estate frees himself from his chains and prepares to take up arms. In the background, supporters of the Revolution are demolishing the fortress of the Bastille and carrying the severed heads of victims killed in the uprising.

Source: Library of Congress.

On 14 July 1789, a large crowd composed primarily of skilled artisans and shopkeepers, aided by soldiers from one of the regiments stationed in the city, surrounded the Bastille, an imposing medieval fortress-prison that had become a symbol of despotic authority. Defended by only a few hundred troops and housing at that moment only seven prisoners, the Bastille had little real significance, but when the Parisians, infuriated by the commander's refusal to give up the weapons it contained, stormed and captured it, their victory became an immediate symbol of the newly born popular revolutionary movement. The "victors of the Bastille" had defeated the forces of the old government and of the privileged groups that had depended on it. Their support enabled the reform-minded deputies to stand up to the king. But the National Assembly also recognized that it would have to reckon with these popular allies' demands. (See Document C.)

DOCUMENT C
AN ACCOUNT OF THE STORMING OF THE BASTILLE

The Révolutions de Paris *was one of the first newspapers founded after 14 July 1789. Its breathless account of the capture of the Bastille reflects the electric atmosphere of the Revolution's first days.*

"At first, we approached from the Rue Saint-Antoine to reach the fortress, where no one entered unless admitted by the will of the terrible despotism, for it was there that the monster still lived . . .

"The action became ever more intense. The citizens no longer feared the gunfire. They scrambled all over the rooftops, into the rooms, and as soon as one of the garrison appeared on the tower, he attracted the fire of a hundred sharpshooters, who immediately knocked him down . . . The fury was at its height, no one cared about death or danger. Numerous women helped us with all their strength. Even children, after each salvo from the fort, ran here and there to pick up the cannonballs . . . We pressed ahead, we reached the staircase, we seized the prisoners, we penetrated everywhere. Some seized the guards, others scrambled to the top of the towers. They waved the country's sacred flag, to the cheers and the delight of an immense crowd . . .

"This glorious day should astonish our enemies, and promise us the triumph of justice and liberty." (From *Révolutions de Paris*, no. 1 [12–19 July 1789]. *Translation by Jeremy D. Popkin.*)

The storming of the Bastille was accompanied by several outbreaks of violence against officials of the old regime that showed how quickly popular action could go beyond the bounds of peaceful reform. The crowd lynched de Launay, the fortress's military commander, and the *prévôt de marchands* Flesselles, the head of the royal municipal administration, who was accused of having tried to delay the insurrectionary movement long enough for additional troops to arrive. Their severed heads were carried through the streets in a gory celebration of the popular victory. The reform-minded Patriot leaders who had helped set off the insurrection moved quickly to restore order, however. The committee of electors who had chosen Paris's deputies to the Estates-General turned themselves into an improvised city government, choosing one of their members, the astronomer Sylvain Bailly, as mayor. They created a civic militia, the National Guard, to maintain order in the streets; it was put under the command of the Marquis de Lafayette, the reform-minded nobleman famous for his participation in the American Revolution. From the outset, it was clear that there was a potential cleavage between leaders like Bailly and

Lafayette, willing to profit from the success of the popular movement but determined to keep it under control, and the mass of the population, whose direct action had ensured the revolutionary movement's success but who were now expected to return quietly to their homes.

A similar combination of elite and popular action characterized the wave of revolutionary uprisings that swept over other French cities in July 1789, some before and some after the Parisian events. Crowds assaulted local buildings that symbolized royal authority and forced the royal intendants and the appointed municipal officials to yield power to improvised councils of men loyal to the National Assembly. This "municipal revolution" paralyzed the royal administration and transferred responsibility for enforcing the laws to officials who owed their authority to the support of the local population, thereby reversing several centuries of administrative centralization.

Even more threatening to the traditional social order was the wave of peasant violence that followed the storming of the Bastille. In many rural regions, peasants terrified by rumors that "brigands" in the pay of aristocratic opponents of the Revolution were about to devastate their crops turned on the manor houses of the local nobles in a mass movement that came to be known as the "Great Fear." Relatively few nobles were actually killed, but a number of chateaux were burned. More often, the rioting peasants forced local seigneurs to turn over the charters and deeds that consecrated their special privileges. "After having broken the locks on my cabinets that held my documents . . . , they burned them in the woods near my chateau," one noble victim complained.[4] The peasants' actions made it clear that they demanded an end to the exactions of the seigneurial system. This rural insurrection, the largest outbreak of peasant revolt in France in many centuries, completed the breakdown of royal authority. As a result, the National Assembly had the chance to make important reforms. But the deputies of the National Assembly, many of whom were themselves owners of rural property, faced the daunting challenge of restoring order not just in Paris and other towns but throughout the vast French countryside.

All over the country, royal authority dissolved and power rested in the hands of those who declared their loyalty to the Assembly and adopted the new symbols of patriotism, such as the red, white, and blue tricolor cockade that the Paris Patriots had created. This largely spontaneous movement from below ensured the success of the National Assembly and of what was now openly proclaimed to be a revolution. In the face of the crowd's actions in Paris, Louis XVI on 15 July 1789 announced the recall of his troops and the reappointment of Necker. Two days later, he traveled to his capital city. Large crowds lined his route and applauded when he accepted a tricolor cockade from Bailly, the new mayor. Louis's action symbolized the reconciliation of the king and his people, once again joined together like a father and his children. But the atmosphere of euphoria and the applause for the monarch could not conceal the fact that the former absolute ruler had had to recognize the authority of an official installed by a popular insurrection.

NOTES

1. Cited in Jean Egret, *The French Pre-Revolution, 1787–1788,* Wesley D. Camp, trans. (Chicago: University of Chicago Press, 1977), 2.

2. Cited in William Doyle, *Origins of the French Revolution* (New York: Oxford University Press, 1980), 109.

3. Sieyès, cited in John Hall Stewart, *A Documentary Survey of the French Revolution* (New York: Macmillan, 1951), 42–44.

4. Cited in J. M. Roberts, ed., *French Revolution Documents* (Oxford: Basil Blackwell, 1966), 141.

CHAPTER 3

THE REVOLUTIONARY RUPTURE, 1789–1790

THE CONCEPT OF REVOLUTION

The dramatic events of July 1789 generated many slogans. One of the most expressive was the motto of the *Révolutions de Paris*, a weekly newspaper founded just after the storming of the Bastille: "*Les grands ne nous paraîssent pas grands que parce que nous sommes à genoux. Levons-nous!*" ("Those above us look powerful only because we are on our knees. Let's stand up!") In two short sentences, the anonymous creator of this slogan captured the essence of the experience that the French people had suddenly found themselves caught up in. By taking action—by getting off their knees and adopting a new posture—the participants in the Revolution changed their sense of who they were: instead of royal subjects, they became free citizens. They also imposed a new identity on their former overlords: *les grands* would no longer be *les grands* if they no longer towered over their supposed inferiors, and the hierarchies of power and privilege that had structured French society would cease to exist. The *Révolutions de Paris*'s motto provided a powerful definition of what carrying out a revolution meant.

Historians ever since have used the term "revolution" to describe the drama that began in 1789. In the era of the Renaissance, when history was seen as running in cyclical patterns, the concept of revolution implied a return to a prior state of things. By the eighteenth century, it had come to mean any sudden and unexpected political event. In this sense, revolutions

were frequent and occurred, like natural disasters, without human intervention. In 1789, however, as historian Keith Baker has shown, the word
quickly took on a new meaning. Rather than speaking of "revolutions" in
the plural, the French and the foreign observers who followed the events in
France with keen interest now spoke of "the Revolution," a unique and sin-
gular event. The French Revolution, furthermore, was an open-ended event
that human beings shaped, not one they simply endured. The very rapid
adoption of this new terminology showed that even contemporaries recognized how profoundly the events of June and July 1789 had altered the situation. Among the first results of these events had been the creation of the
modern notion of revolution.

As they recognized the special character of their situation, the deputies
of the National Assembly, along with much of the French population, were
both exhilarated and alarmed. Making a revolution offered the opportunity
to create a new world, but it also risked plunging French society into a violent breakdown. Conscious of what was at stake, the deputies moved rapidly to enunciate the basic principles of a new society, strikingly different from
the hierarchical world of the past. Within a few months they had abolished
the seigneurial system, the absolute monarchy, and the system of privileges
that had pervaded French society. In their place, they had proclaimed the
primacy of the rights of individual citizens and created a system of representative government to protect them. Completing the details of the new
constitution would occupy the Assembly until September 1791, but the radical direction of its work was clear before the end of the summer of 1789.

THE "ABOLITION OF FEUDALISM" AND THE DECLARATION OF RIGHTS

In the wake of the Paris crowd's storming of the Bastille on 14 July 1789, the
1,200 deputies to the National Assembly in Versailles found themselves in an
extraordinary position. The danger from the king was gone. His army and
his bureaucracy had ceased to function, and the most ardent opponents of
the Revolution, such as the king's younger brother, the Count of Artois, had
fled abroad. The deputies could count on a national groundswell of popular
support. But the violence that had resulted in the lynching of the Bastille's
commander and of the head of the royally appointed municipal government
in Paris on 14 July and the wave of reports of peasant revolts in the countryside showed that the revolutionary process could easily get out of the assembly's control. The deputies needed to establish a new social and political
order before the disintegration of the old one plunged France into chaos.

In the six weeks after the fall of the Bastille, the Assembly took two
decisive steps that defined the ways in which the new society and the new
government would differ from the old. The first was to eliminate the dense

thicket of special privileges that had blocked all previous efforts at change. On the night of 4 August 1789, the Assembly, spurred by the reports of rural insurrection arriving from around the country, held a special session to consider abolishing some of the nobility's special privileges. They hoped that this would satisfy the peasantry and end the burning of chateaux and legal documents. This limited reform was unexpectedly upstaged by a sweeping proposal to do away with the whole complex of "feudal" privileges that had distinguished nobles from commoners. The success of this motion launched a chain reaction of further renunciations. Representatives of the clergy moved to abolish tithes; deputies from the provinces and privileged cities gave up their immunities from taxes, customs fees, and other regulations. The sale of government offices was done away with, and recruitment to church, government, and military positions formerly reserved for nobles was thrown open to all citizens, regardless of status. By the time the exhausted deputies staggered out into the dawn on 5 August, they had gone far to "abolish the feudal regime entirely," as the preamble to their edicts promised.

The deputies later qualified much of the language they had initially voted for. Peasants, for instance, soon discovered that the National Assembly had made complex distinctions between "feudal" obligations supposedly derived from medieval serfdom and "real" obligations considered analogous to rent. Peasants were required to pay their landlords compensation for the abolition of "real" obligations. Nevertheless, the basic thrust of this radical package of reforms remained intact. The Assembly had decided that France would henceforth be a community of legally equal citizens. The legal distinctions between clergy and laity, between social classes, and between the inhabitants of different geographic regions of the kingdom had been leveled. No subsequent French regime has been able to reverse this fundamental accomplishment.

Having dismantled the old order, the National Assembly began establishing the new on 26 August 1789 when it endorsed the seventeen articles of the "Declaration of the Rights of Man and Citizen." (See Document D.) This document, the most important creation of the French Revolution, clearly defined the fundamental principles of a new society based on equality and individual rights and a new system of government based on the consent of the governed.

The decision to enact a Declaration of Rights before any other part of the new constitution had been agreed on caused controversy. Many deputies feared that such a sweeping statement of principles would give ordinary citizens exaggerated notions of their rights and undermine respect for the law. The Assembly's majority, however, decided that it would be more dangerous to start creating new institutions without having agreed on the basic principles they were supposed to reflect. The procedure the Assembly adopted was the reverse of what the drafters of the American

The Declaration of the Rights of Man and Citizen, voted by the National Assembly on 26 August 1789, laid down the basic principles of the new constitutional order. At the same time, its provisions expressed the liberal revolution's ambivalence about the prospect of political participation by the lower classes.

"The representatives of the French people, organized as a national assembly, considering that ignorance, neglect, and scorn of the rights of man are the sole causes of public misfortunes and of corruption of governments, have resolved to display in a solemn declaration the natural, inalienable, and sacred rights of man, so that this declaration, constantly in the presence of all members of society, will continually remind them of their rights and their duties, so that the acts of the legislative power and those of the executive power, being subject at any time to comparison with the purpose of any political institution, will be better respected; so that the demands of the citizens, based henceforth on simple and incontestable principles, will always contribute to the maintenance of the constitution and the happiness of all.

"Consequently, the National Assembly recognizes and declares, in the presence and under the auspices of the Supreme Being, the following rights of man and citizen.

Article 1. Men are born and remain free and equal in rights; social distinctions can be established only for the common benefit.

2. The aim of every political association is the conservation of the natural and imprescriptible rights of man; these rights are liberty, property, security, and resistance to oppression.

3. The source of all sovereignty is located in essence in the nation; no body, no individual can exercise authority which does not emanate from it expressly.

4. Liberty consists in being able to do anything that does not harm another person. Thus the exercise of the natural rights of each man has no limits except those which assure to the other members of society the enjoyment of these same rights; these limits can be determined only by law.

5. The law has the right to forbid only those actions harmful to society. All that is not forbidden by the law cannot be hindered, and no one can be forced to do what it does not order.

6. The law is the expression of the general will; all citizens have the right to concur personally or through their representatives in its forma-

Continued

DOCUMENT D, *continued*

tion; it must be the same for all, whether it protects or punishes. All citizens being equal in its eyes are equally admissible to all honors, positions, and public employments, according to their capabilities and without other distinctions than those of their virtues and talents.

7. No man can be accused, arrested, or detained except in cases determined by the law, and according to the forms which it has prescribed. Those who solicit, draw up, execute, or have executed arbitrary orders must be punished; but any citizen summoned or seized by virtue of the law must obey instantly; he renders himself culpable by resisting.

8. The law must establish only penalties that are strictly and clearly necessary, and no one can be punished except in virtue of a law established and published prior to the offense and legally applied.

9. Every man being presumed innocent until he has been declared guilty, if it is judged indispensable to arrest him, all severity that is not necessary for making sure of his person must be severely repressed by the law.

10. No one may be disturbed because of his opinions, even religious, provided that their public demonstration does not disturb the public order established by law.

11. The free communication of thoughts and opinions is one of the most precious rights of man: every citizen can therefore freely speak, write, and print: he is answerable for abuses of this liberty in cases determined by the law.

12. The guaranteeing of the rights of man and citizen necessitates a public force; this force is therefore instituted for the advantage of all, and not for the private use of those to whom it is entrusted.

13. For the maintenance of the public force, and for the expenses of administration, a tax supported in common is indispensable; it must be assessed on all citizens in proportion to their capacities to pay.

14. Citizens have the right to determine for themselves or through their representatives the need for taxation of the public, to consent to it freely, to investigate its use, and to determine its rate, basis, collection, and duration.

15. Society has the right to demand an accounting of his administration from every public agent.

16. Any society in which guarantees of rights are not assured nor the separation of powers determined has no constitution.

17. Property being an inviolable and sacred right, no one may be deprived of it unless public necessity, legally determined, clearly requires such action, and then only on condition of a just and prior indemnity." (From Paul Beik, ed., *The French Revolution* [New York: Harper and Row, 1970], pp. 95–97. Reprinted by permission.)

constitution, who worked in a calmer situation, were doing at almost the same time: only after finishing the constitution in 1787 did they propose a Bill of Rights, which was enacted in 1791 to define the limits of governmental power.

The French declaration's eloquent preamble asserted that "ignorance, neglect, and scorn of the rights of man are the sole causes of public misfortunes," implying that the new order being inaugurated with the Declaration would be completely different from the past. Its first article echoed the opening sentence of Jean-Jacques Rousseau's *Social Contract* in proclaiming that "men are born and remain free and equal in rights." Article 2 stated that the purpose of government was to protect the rights of "liberty, property, security, and resistance to oppression." Article 4 defined liberty in broad but vague terms as "anything that does not harm another person." Many future debates would be required to determine what this phrase meant, but it clearly suggested that each individual should have the right to make important decisions without interference either from the government or from corporate groups such as guilds, which would be formally abolished in 1791. Other articles of the Declaration fleshed out the notions of liberty and security by giving citizens explicit protection against arbitrary arrest and promising them freedom of religious belief and freedom of expression. The Declaration's final article gave special emphasis to the "inviolable and sacred right" of property. In a society where there was a huge gap between rich and poor, the legislators felt compelled to emphasize that the equality proclaimed in the Declaration's first article did not entitle the latter to a share of the former's goods.

Citizens' rights were to be protected not only by prohibitions against government intrusion but by provisions giving them the right to participate in making laws and overseeing their administration. Article 3 asserted that "the source of all sovereignty is located in essence in the nation," thereby abolishing the king's claim to supreme authority and transferring it to the community of citizens. Article 6, again borrowing language from Rousseau, proclaimed that "law is the expression of the general will" and promised all citizens a right to participate in the making of it. The statement that they had "the right to concur personally or through their representatives in its formation" straddled a crucial question, however. Rousseau had insisted that the only free people were those who participated personally in lawmaking, like the citizens of the ancient Greek city-states, all of whom voted in public meetings. The Declaration foresaw the possibility that most citizens would delegate this power to others, but its wording allowed radical critics to insist that it could only really be fulfilled by a system of direct democracy. In addition to sharing in the making of the laws, the Declaration promised citizens that their representatives would have the right to approve taxes and expenditures and to review the conduct of public officials (Articles 14 and 15).

The Declaration's drafters saw a direct connection between liberty and equality: if all human beings possessed rights simply by virtue of being born, these rights necessarily had to be "the same for all," as Article 6 stated. This implied the end of all special privileges, except those granted to public officials so that they could carry out their duties. Every citizen had the right to compete for "all honors, positions, and public employments," all of which were to be awarded solely on the basis of "virtues and talents," without regard to considerations such as noble birth. Although it would take almost a year before the Assembly explicitly abolished hereditary titles, the Declaration effectively ended the centuries-old distinction between nobles and commoners.

Although most of their wording emphasized citizens' rights, the drafters of the Declaration believed in the necessity of government. They stressed that citizens were obliged to obey laws, pay taxes, and submit to arrest warrants "instantly." Article 12 called for the maintenance of a "public force" to uphold the law "for the advantage of all." The articles guaranteeing freedom of religion and the press contained clauses stating that even those fundamental rights could be limited by law. Article 16 tried to ensure that no future government would abuse these powers by setting conditions for recognizing a legitimate political system: it had to protect individual rights, and there had to be a division of powers to prevent any sort of tyranny. The later course of the Revolution would show that the drafters of the Declaration had been too optimistic in assuming that this statement and the provisions on popular participation would prevent any oppression of the citizens.

It is hard to exaggerate the importance of the Declaration of Rights of Man and Citizen. In less than two pages, it explicitly condemned the basic ideas underlying absolute monarchy and social systems based on hierarchy and privilege. In their place, the Declaration called into being an "imagined community"[1] of equal citizens endowed with extensive rights and a participatory political system meant to protect them. The French Declaration was broader in scope than the American Bill of Rights. It was formulated in abstract and universal terms, suggesting that its principles were valid not only for France but also for all nations. For more than two centuries, the Declaration has served as a model for other countries seeking freedom. It was the inspiration for the the United Nations' "Declaration of Human Rights" of 1948.

At the same time, however, the Declaration of the Rights of Man and Citizen, like the decrees of 4–5 August 1789, incorporated significant ambiguities. Did the term "man" include all human beings, or only members of the male sex? Who was entitled to the status of citizen? How was its promise of equality to be reconciled with its explicit defense of private property, the unequal distribution of which left some citizens better off than others? Did property include the black slaves in France's colonies? Did the repeated clauses stating that individual rights could be limited by law indicate an excessive concern to maintain government power? Did the promise of liberty include the liberty to oppose the Revolution itself? And who was entitled to speak for the nation, the new repository of political legitimacy? Much more than the American Revolution, the French movement raised fundamental political questions. The men of the National Assembly have often been blamed for this, and for not trying harder to salvage what they could from the French past. Their optimistic faith that France was uniquely suited to give the world an example of enlightened political reform did prove excessive. In the face of the old regime's inability to reform itself before 1789 and the pressure from the popular movements in the cities and the countryside, however, their actions are understandable.

THE OCTOBER DAYS

Although he had appeared ready to bow to the power of the Revolution after the fall of the Bastille, Louis XVI was not prepared to endorse the drastic restructuring of government and society implied by the 4 August decrees and the Declaration of Rights. Throughout the month of September, the king refused to make a public statement accepting them. According to the principle of national sovereignty proclaimed by the Assembly, these decrees did not need the king's approval, but the deputies, having kept him on his throne, wanted his cooperation. Louis' footdragging raised public suspicions, not only among the deputies, but also in the general population. In Paris, the high bread prices that had provoked public unrest earlier in 1789 exacerbated discontent.

When reports reached Paris that an army regiment recently summoned to Versailles had held a raucous banquet in which the patriotic tricolor cockade was supposedly trampled on the floor, popular anger exploded. The first to react were women, upset about the still-elevated price of bread in the markets as well as the king's apparent counterrevolutionary maneuvers. On 5 October, a large crowd of women assembled at the Hôtel de Ville to demand that the city government take action to protect the Revolution. Dragging cannon, and accompanied by male members of the National Guard, the women set out to march on the royal palace. The Guard commander, Lafayette, though he opposed direct popular action, joined the expedition to avoid losing control over his own troops.

The marchers reached the royal palace late at night. After bloody clashes that led to the killing of several palace guards, the king agreed to demands that he and his family should come to Paris; the National Assembly, relegated to the sidelines during the confrontation, had no choice but to agree to follow. On 6 October 1789, the royal family set off, accompanied by the marchers who were carrying the severed heads of the royal guards on pikes and noisily celebrating their success in bringing "the baker, the baker's wife, and the baker's boy" (the king, queen, and their son) back to the city. Like the storming of the Bastille on 14 July, the "October Days" showed that popular violence could have major political effects: the king and the Assembly, brought to Paris by force, were now much more exposed to organized pressure from the populace. The uprising demonstrated that women, normally excluded from politics, could influence the course of events.

THE ACCOMPLISHMENTS OF THE NATIONAL ASSEMBLY, 1789–1791

After the October Days, the political tension in Paris declined. For the next year and a half, although violent episodes affected some of the provinces, the capital was relatively calm, and the National Assembly's deputies were able to concentrate on their task of constitution-making. Many historians have called this period the "liberal revolution" because it was characterized by the enactment of fundamental legislation incorporating the principles of individual liberty announced in the Declaration of Rights, but this phase of the movement has also been labeled the "bourgeois revolution" because the Assembly's interpretation of liberty favored educated property owners. Only they could fully exercise the rights of citizens, as the new constitution outlined them. The new order did open many new possibilities for members of the bourgeoisie, but to define the liberal phase of the Revolution as the capture of the movement by a self-interested minority overlooks the extent to which the revolutionary legislators were actually striving to transform all French citizens into something new. The National Assembly did not hesitate to abolish the privileges of major bourgeois interest groups as well as those of the nobility and the clergy. In August 1790, it did away with the requirement that defendants in court cases be represented by certified members of the bar, and the March 1791 law allowing all citizens to practice any profession led to the end of licensing for doctors. Anyone who wanted to could now practice law or medicine.

By the fall of 1789, the 1,200 men who had arrived in Versailles at the beginning of May, uncertain about their role and for the most part unacquainted with one another, had found leaders and organized into informal parties. Those who considered themselves the most determined supporters of the Revolution stationed themselves in seats on the left side of the speaker's desk; the most vehement opponents of the Revolution claimed the right side of the room, and the terms "left" and "right" have served ever since to characterize radicals and conservatives, not only in France but also throughout the world. Although the Assembly had abolished the privileges of the nobles and the Church, the fact that half its members had originally been elected to represent those groups meant that there was strong support for conservative and moderate views. It took a combination of popular pressure,

Louis XVI's intransigent refusal to accept the new system, and unforeseen circumstances to push the Revolution steadily in a more radical direction.

The size and diversity of the Assembly made it difficult for any one figure to dominate it. The strongest potential leader was the Count Mirabeau. He was a master of the spoken word and also one of the first to sense the importance of the newspaper press. Mirabeau believed that the Revolution offered an opportunity, not to destroy the monarchy, but to strengthen it. By working with the Assembly to abolish outmoded institutions and draft a constitution that would give him genuine powers, the king could win the country's trust. Mirabeau embarked on a delicate strategy of trying to control the National Assembly while simultaneously making secret efforts to persuade the king and queen to commit themselves to accept the basic results of the Revolution. "There is no hope for the State and for the king except in the closest possible alliance between the ruler and the people," he wrote to the king.[2] But Mirabeau's transparent personal ambition and his dissolute private life made many other deputies distrustful of him. The Assembly's decision in November 1789 to prohibit any of its members from serving as royal ministers, as members of Parliament did in England, was aimed at keeping Mirabeau out of power.

No other deputy came close to obtaining sway over the Assembly and the revolutionary movement. The abbé Sieyès, whose ideas had had such influence during the critical days of June 1789, lacked the oratorical skills to dominate the Assembly, and he soon dissipated much of his prestige by defending the Church's privileges. The Marquis de Lafayette, well known because of his participation in the American War of Independence, lost much of his popularity because his position as commander of the Paris National Guard required him to repress public demonstrations in the capital. Some deputies, such as Maximilien Robespierre, a small-town lawyer from northern France who became the leading advocate of the common people's interests in the debates, and the abbé Maury, a clergyman from humble origins who proved to be the most eloquent defender of royal authority and Church interests, established themselves as representatives of minority viewpoints. But the National Assembly, setting a precedent that has had lasting influence in France, made its decisions collectively, through debate and bargaining, and blocked the emergence of strong leaders.

Certainly the king was no longer in a position to fill the leadership vacuum. Louis XVI stubbornly resisted Assembly measures he regarded as undermining royal authority or religion, but he put forward no positive program. The queen, Marie-Antoinette, had a firmer character but a limited comprehension of the revolutionary situation. Her widely rumored efforts to get foreign powers to intervene against the Revolution made her and the monarchy increasingly unpopular. With real power concentrated in the National Assembly, the king's ministers, so influential under the Old Regime, no longer had much authority.

THE CONSTITUTIONAL DEBATES

Even before the October Days, the Assembly had started to debate the question of what powers the king should have in the new constitution. At first, a moderate group, the *monarchiens*, dominated the Assembly's constitutional committee. Their leaders included several reform-minded nobles and Joseph Mounier, the lawyer who had led the revolutionary movement in Dauphiné in 1788. The monarchiens epitomized the fusion of property-owning elites that had seemed poised to govern the country at the end of the Old Regime; their proposed constitution, similar in many ways to that of England, represented a compromise between the old order and the principles of the Revolution.

The monarchiens' proposal gave the king extensive powers: he would have a large budget to spend as he pleased and the right to veto laws he disapproved of. The legislature would have consisted of two houses, as in England, one of peers and one representing the common people. More radical deputies, including Mirabeau, rejected this scheme: they feared that the king would use his veto to paralyze the Assembly and that the division of the legislature would leave the aristocracy too much power. The Assembly settled instead on a plan that gave the king greatly reduced authority and put real power in the hands of an elected one-house legislature, free to act almost without restrictions because it directly represented the will of the people. The king was given only a suspensive veto—the right to delay legislation for three two-year sessions of the Assembly.

Another contentious issue concerned the right to vote. Most deputies accepted the argument that only citizens who owned a certain amount of property, and thus had tangible individual interests to defend, could be expected to make intelligent political choices. In December 1789, they voted to restrict the franchise to adult males who paid taxes equivalent to three days of an ordinary laborer's wage, with an even higher wealth qualification for deputies. In March 1790, the Assembly voted to let the colonies determine voting qualifications for themselves, allowing the whites who controlled politics there to exclude the mulattoes (mixed-race) and free blacks whose representatives had hoped the deputies would take up their cause. By the standards of the time, the property qualification for voting was quite modest—it would have allowed well over half the adult male population to vote in national elections. The restriction on eligibility to the legislature was much tighter: only about 72,000 men, many of them nobles rather than bourgeois, met the qualifications. Having declared that all French citizens were equal, defenders of these provisions were hard put to answer Robespierre's challenge, "Can the law be termed an expression of the general will when the greater number of those for whom it is made can have no hand in its making?"[3]

Although the majority of the Assembly voted to bar the poorest citizens from any direct participation in politics, the deputies did not consciously neglect the needs of the lower classes. The Assembly's Committee on the Needy made a full-scale inquiry into France's social problems and proposed that the government assume responsibility for assuring a decent standard of living for orphans, the poor, the ill, and the elderly. The new constitution included provisions for a permanent Committee of Public Instruction, with a mandate to make elementary education available to all citizens. Unfortunately, neither the National Assembly nor any subsequent revolutionary government ever had the resources to implement these sweeping proposals. And, in some areas, the laws it drafted did adversely affect the poor. The Le Chapelier law of June 1791, for example, which barred all "coalitions" aimed at affecting wages and prices, made workers' organizations and strikes illegal and is frequently cited as evidence of the Assembly's dedication to bourgeois interests.

Unable to make significant improvements in the lot of the poor, the National Assembly was more successful in extending the definition of individual liberty. French Protestants had already been granted limited civil rights in 1787. The Assembly, which included several Protestant deputies, quickly declared that they were now full citizens. The status of other minorities proved more controversial. Despite the efforts of deputies such as the abbé Grégoire, a Catholic priest who defended civil rights on religious grounds, longstanding prejudices kept the Assembly from granting rights to the majority of French Jews until one of its final sessions in September 1791. For the first time in Europe, religious belief was thus separated from citizenship. The legal system was reformed to abolish arbitrary detention without trial and to give defendants a better chance of proving their innocence. The censorship system had collapsed in the summer of 1789; the Assembly debated several proposals to limit the "excesses" of the press, but in practice left it completely uncontrolled. In March 1791, the Assembly voted to abolish the guilds and to give all citizens equal access to all trades, thus consecrating economic individualism.

An unsuccessful mulatto revolt in France's most important colony, Saint-Domingue, in the fall of 1790 forced the Assembly to reconsider its stand on racial issues. In May 1791 it passed a decree granting full citizenship to nonwhite children born to free parents in the colonies. Even this limited concession was too much for the white population of the Caribbean colonies, but by the time their lobbyists had persuaded the Assembly to reverse its decision in September 1791, the great slave rebellion in Saint-Domingue that was to lead eventually to that colony's independence had already broken out.

One of the Assembly's most enduring accomplishments was its division of France into new administrative districts, called departments. These units, of approximately equal size and named after prominent geographic features such as rivers or mountains, were intended to rationalize France's administrative system and also to break down provincial loyalties that might conflict with loyalty to the nation as a whole. The maps of the many overlapping court districts, religious dioceses, and other administrative divisions of the Old Regime were redrawn to correspond to departmental boundaries, which made citizens' relations with the government much simpler. With minor modifications, the departments created in 1789 have survived to the present day. Along with its redrawing of the administrative map, the Assembly abolished all the various tolls and customs boundaries that had divided France economically. The entire country thus became a unified market, and the deputies assumed that this would encourage manufacturing and commerce.

The decentralized system of local government initially set up in 1790 proved far less enduring than the creation of the departments and the elimination of trade barriers. Local officials were to collect taxes, administer justice, and enforce laws. The central government became almost totally dependent on the cooperation of these local authorities, whom the government could not control, to carry out its directives. In the first flush of revolutionary enthusiasm, the system seemed attractive, but before long, conflicts between local and national officials proved that it contained dangerous weaknesses. The redrawing of administrative boundaries also pitted towns against their neighbors, as rival communities fought to capture as many government agencies for themselves as possible. Participation in this scramble was one of the ways in which local elites throughout the country learned the ropes of the new political culture.

THE EXPROPRIATION OF CHURCH LANDS AND THE ASSIGNATS

The liberal legislation enacted by the National Assembly had the potential to create a conflict between the wealthy bourgeoisie, who stood to benefit most from the new system, and the mass of the population: the Third Estate was no longer a united block. But the issue that most visibly threatened the liberal revolution grew out of the Assembly's attempt to reform the French Catholic church.

The Assembly had first faced this issue in November 1789, when it voted to expropriate the Church's accumulated property. Decades of denunciation of the clergy's mismanaged wealth had paved the way for this idea. Furthermore, since the Assembly intended to have the civil government take over many of the functions traditionally performed by the Church, such as schooling and aid to the poor, it seemed logical that the government should inherit the resources that the Church had used to pay for these ser-

Provinces and Departments

The boundaries of France's prerevolutionary provinces kept alive memories of the long process by which the kingdom had been built up. The new departments, created in 1790, fostered a sense of national unity and also allowed for a more efficient system of administration.

vices. Most important in the deputies' minds, however, was the idea that by selling off the Church lands, the government would be able to repay the massive debts left over from the Old Regime. In addition, as proponents of the measure pointed out, the purchasers of this property would acquire a vested interest in defending the Revolution. Opponents warned that if the government could confiscate the Church's property, it could eventually take over other citizens' goods as well. "We are attacked today . . . your turn will come," the abbé Maury told the nonreligious members of the Assembly.[4] But even many of the clergy, particularly the underpaid parish priests who were now to receive salaries from the state, supported the move.

Since the Church's landholdings were too extensive to be sold off at one time without flooding the market, the National Assembly issued certificates backed by the presumed value of the church lands, known as *assignats*, that could be redeemed for property when it came on the market. Government creditors were paid in assignats, which soon became a form of paper currency, used for ordinary business transactions and the payment of taxes. Initially, the quantity of this paper money in circulation was limited and the bills were accepted at close to their face value. But when tax revenues fell short, successive revolutionary governments were constantly tempted to issue more of them. Eventually, the depreciation of the assignats became one of the Revolution's most pressing problems.

The expropriation of Church property obligated the National Assembly to undertake a thorough restructuring of the Church. Church reform had been a widespread demand throughout the eighteenth century, and numerous cahiers had encouraged the Estates-General to carry it out. "Establishments without any purpose, useless men highly salaried, useful men without recompense . . ."—so the deputy Jean-Baptiste Treilhard summed up the revolutionaries' view of the Old Regime church.[5] Even most of the clergy recognized that reform was long overdue. It was the nature of the reforms imposed and the lack of consultation with the Church that caused conflict. For many Catholics, the granting of full civil and political rights to religious minorities was a jarring change. In regions where Catholics and Protestants had long been in conflict with each other, such as the southern city of Nîmes, this change in the religious status quo led to bloody violence, and some Catholics came to regard the Revolution as a Protestant plot against their faith. In February 1790, the Assembly abolished monastic religious orders, except for those devoted to teaching and charitable activities. Monks and nuns were now free to renounce their vows and become ordinary citizens.

THE CIVIL CONSTITUTION OF THE CLERGY

Additional conflicts resulted from the deputies' internal restructuring of the Church. The Assembly redrew the boundaries of dioceses to correspond to the boundaries of the departments it had established, abolishing more than one-third of the prerevolutionary bishoprics. More controversial was the decision to have local voters elect their priests and to have the priests choose their bishops. The French kings had long had the right to nominate bishops. Now that authority was vested in the people rather than the king, it seemed logical to the legislators that this power should pass to the voters. But the reform overturned the hierarchical structure of the Church, under which authority descended from God through the Pope to the bishops, who in turn consecrated priests. Devout Catholics also objected that the electoral assemblies charged with selecting priests would be open to Protestants, Jews, and atheists.

Most of the Assembly's members had little patience with these Catholic loyalists. Deputies who shared the Enlightenment's critical attitude toward the church were eager to remodel the institution. Others, though religious, were imbued with traditional Jansenist distrust of the Pope and favored thoroughgoing reforms. In July 1790, the deputies enacted a set of laws known as the Civil Constitution of the Clergy. When many priests objected to its provisions, the Assembly decided to require those who wanted to keep their posts to take an oath of fidelity. Every French priest soon had to make a public choice. To take the oath was to endorse the Revolution and the nation; to refuse it was to challenge both. The issue split France almost in half. Slightly more than 50 percent of the parish clergy took the

The Civil Constitution of the Clergy

The National Assembly's radical reform of the Church forced priests and Catholic congregations throughout the country to take a position for or against the Revolution. In this cartoon, "A New Method to Make Curés Take the Oath," patriotic members of the bourgeoisie and the National Guard force a priest to swear an oath accepting the new arrangements. Several women and clergymen are shown in postures suggesting their opposition to the Church reforms, which sharply divided the population.

Source: Bibliothèque Nationale, Paris.

oath, but the remainder, including all but seven French bishops, refused. Where parish priests refused the oath, the government sought to install newly promoted priests who had accepted it, often in the face of violent local resistance to the "intruder" from laypeople who blamed the Revolution for destroying the "true" faith. The imposition of the Civil Constitution thus raised in acute form the issue of how far the revolutionary government could go in imposing its decisions on citizens who opposed them in the name of their individual freedom. The controversy caused by the Civil Constitution left the country deeply divided. Some modern historians, particularly the American scholar Timothy Tackett, have claimed that this dispute, more than anything else, served to determine which regions would identify themselves with the revolutionary reforms and which would remain opposed to the new ideas for decades to come.

The growing controversy over the clergy's oath foreshadowed a major change in the course of the Revolution. For most of the twelve months following the storming of the Bastille, the movement had appeared to have overwhelming support. Opposition to it had come primarily from circles close to the Court and from some of the nobility, small groups associated with the most discredited aspects of the old society. The argument over Church reform proved different. For the first time, a significant part of the population, including large numbers of commoners, resisted a major piece of revolutionary legislation. Supporters of the Revolution now faced the question of how far they were prepared to go to impose their program on those members of the population who refused to accept it.

NOTES

1. The phrase comes from the influential essay of anthropologist Benedict Anderson: *Imagined Communities* (London: Verso, 1991).

2. Cited in Guy Chaussinand-Nogaret, *Mirabeau* (Paris: Seuil, 1982), 224.

3. Cited in George Rudé, ed., *Robespierre* (Upper Saddle River, N.J.: Prentice Hall, 1967), 14.

4. Cited in Florin Aftalion, *L'économie de la Révolution française* (Paris: Hachette, 1987), 91.

5. Cited in Paul H. Beik, ed., *The French Revolution* (New York: Harper & Row, 1970), 138.

CHAPTER 4

THE DEFEAT OF THE
LIBERAL REVOLUTION,
1790–1792

A crowd of 300,000 attended the Festival of the Federation held in Paris on 14 July 1790 to commemorate the first anniversary of the storming of the Bastille. The celebration began in pouring rain. As the ceremonies proceeded, however, the sun broke through the clouds. Participants saw it as a good omen: perhaps the difficulties besetting the first stages of the Revolution would also blow over. Instead, however, the conflicts inspired by the radical effort to remake French society became more severe. The deputies to the National Assembly hoped that the completion of the new constitution would put an end to these disputes. By the time they finished their elaborate plan for a constitutional monarchy in September 1791, however, it was already clear that there would be continuing resistance to many parts of it, both from conservatives opposed to the Revolution and from groups who claimed that the new laws failed to carry through the promises of the Declaration of Rights. Less than a year later, a new revolutionary insurrection, the *journée* of 10 August 1792, would demolish both the French monarchy and the work of the National Assembly.

THE NEW POLITICAL CULTURE

One reason for France's continuing instability was the growth of a new political culture that made it possible for a growing part of the population to express its views. The political institutions worked out by the National

Assembly were meant to limit participation to the wealthier male members of the national community, but the informal institutions of revolutionary political culture were more open. Three fundamental features of this new political culture were newspapers, political clubs, and public festivals. Anyone could read a newspaper or hear it read aloud; club meetings were frequently open to the poor and to women, and even children participated in festivals. There was thus from the start a potential conflict between the constitution makers' efforts to limit and channel political activity and the expansive tendencies embodied in these informal institutions.

The periodical press was the most important medium by which the public at large could follow the proceedings of the National Assembly and the other events of the Revolution. Prior to 1789, France's domestic newspapers had been tightly controlled by censorship. As soon as the Estates-General convened, this system broke down. Over 130 new journals were launched before the end of 1789. Circulating throughout the country, these periodicals helped create a political arena on a national scale, in which readers all over the country followed the same debates at the same time.

The press was one of the first professions in which the revolutionary promise of "careers open to talent" was fully realized. Previously unknown writers quickly established themselves as national political figures when readers responded to their productions. Camille Desmoulins, a young lawyer who had participated in the public demonstrations that led to the storming of the Bastille, used his weekly *Révolutions de France et de Brabant* to denounce the lingering influence of the aristocracy and to criticize the moderation of the deputies. Jean-Paul Marat, an eccentric doctor and scientist, gave himself a new identity as *L'Ami du peuple* ("The Friend of the People") in his daily paper of the same name. He addressed himself especially to the common people of Paris, and his encouragement of popular violence soon made him a power to be reckoned with. The new medium was no monopoly of the Revolution's supporters: counterrevolutionary polemicists used it just as skillfully as did advocates of change. Throughout the Revolution, the press was a cacaphonous chorus of conflicting voices, commenting on events and frequently undermining the legislators' efforts to bring them under control.

Clubs channeled and organized the public's participation in the new politics. The first ones grew out of the informal gatherings in coffeehouses and other public places that had accompanied the elections to the Estates-General. By October 1789, a group of Patriot deputies had founded a club that met regularly to plan common strategy in the Assembly. The club soon expanded to include private citizens as well as legislators and named itself the *Society of Friends of the Constitution*, but it was more commonly referred to as the Jacobin Club, because it met in a church formerly owned by the Jacobin order. The Paris Jacobins and the numerous provincial clubs that affiliated with it became a vast political machine to support the Revolution.

By mid-1791, there were 434 Jacobin clubs, and the number grew into the thousands during the Revolution's radical phase during the period 1793–1794. These clubs brought supporters of the Revolution together to hear the latest news from the Assembly, discuss the issues of the day, and plan local political initiatives. Until 1791, membership in the Jacobins was restricted by a relatively high admission fee, and the early Jacobins tended to be substantial members of the middle classes who distrusted radicalism. In later years, however, as membership in the Jacobins was opened up to poorer citizens, the club network supported increasingly radical policies.

The Jacobins' national network gave them a unique importance, but there were numerous other political clubs, particularly in Paris. Radical revolutionaries including the journalists Desmoulins and Marat and the future popular leader Georges Danton led the Cordeliers Club, which welcomed disenfranchised "passive" citizens and campaigned against what it saw as the National Assembly's bias in favor of the rich. Cordeliers members helped start a network of "popular societies" to organize support among the capital's working classes. Women, excluded from the electoral politics of the Revolution, participated in many of the clubs, such as the *Cercle social*, founded by Parisian supporters of political and religious democracy. Women also formed their own clubs in at least sixty provincial towns. Counterrevolutionaries had their own groupings, such as the Club Massiac, formed by representatives of the plantation owners in France's Caribbean colonies to oppose any move to abolish slavery. Patriot hostility obstructed the spread of counterrevolutionary groups, however; in some instances, violent demonstrations broke up their meetings.

Public festivals provided a symbolic representation of the movement's achievements that all groups could participate in. The first of these revolutionary celebrations were largely spontaneous, like the planting of "liberty trees"—poles festooned with revolutionary symbols—in many towns in 1789. Toward the end of that year, local patriotic groups and units of the National Guard began organizing "federations," bringing together groups from several towns or regions for ceremonies honoring the new constitution. This movement culminated on 14 July 1790 in the national Festival of Federation celebrated on Paris's Champ de Mars, now the site of the Eiffel Tower. Before an enormous crowd, the King and the leaders of the Assembly and the National Guard swore loyalty to the new constitution. Press reports and the accounts of those who had come from the provinces gave the entire country a sense of having taken part.

THE KING'S FLIGHT AND THE CRISIS OF 1791

The growing number of people who followed political events and wanted to influence them made it difficult to confine conflicts to the Assembly in

Paris. As the National Assembly tried to impose the Civil Constitution of the Clergy on a growing number of reluctant "refractory" priests and their congregations in the fall of 1790, local incidents of opposition multiplied. This religious conflict led directly to the undermining of the National Assembly's constitutional system because it helped drive Louis XVI to make an open break with the Assembly in June 1791. A devout Catholic, the king was deeply troubled when the Pope condemned the Civil Constitution of the Clergy in March 1791, after Louis XVI had signed it into law. The king was also under pressure in early 1791 because he had refused Assembly demands for strong measures against the nobles and members of the royal family who fled abroad after July 1789. From their refuges in the small German principalities along the Rhine, these emigrés sought to organize an army to invade France. They also lobbied foreign powers to invade France and free the king. Louis issued token appeals to his relatives but failed to convince the supporters of the Revolution that he meant them. In any event, the emigrés retorted that the king was acting under duress and ignored his injunctions.

On 20 June 1791, the king finally tried to get out of his increasingly awkward situation by fleeing abroad himself. By the time the king's disappearance was discovered, he and his family had already escaped from the capital. A nervous National Assembly immediately sent couriers in pursuit while announcing to the public that the monarch had been "abducted." The discovery that Louis had left behind a manifesto denouncing the Revolution that had replaced "the monarchical government under which the nation has prospered for fourteen hundred years"[1] discredited this story, but the Assembly hesitated to condemn the king and commit itself to replacing him: the entire constitutional edifice so painfully erected since July 1789 would be called into question. For the royal family, the attempted flight turned into a tragedy of errors. Their large and conspicuous coach attracted attention along the road, and delays caused them to miss their rendezvous with the loyal troops who had been recruited to escort them. In the small town of Varennes, near the northern frontier, the fugitives were recognized and arrested by the local authorities. Heavily guarded, the royal party traveled back to Paris.

The flight to Varennes was a clear indication that the Revolution had reached a crisis. Counterrevolutionaries hailed the king for finally showing "that the pure blood of the Bourbons runs in your veins."[2] The king's actions forced supporters of the Revolution to consider the possibility that France might be better off without a monarch at all. The Cordeliers Club urged the National Assembly "in the name of the fatherland, to declare immediately that France is no longer a monarchy. . . ."[3] The idea of a republican government, in which all political leaders were chosen by the people, had been considered impossible in a large country. The Varennes crisis for the first time made republicanism appear as a viable political option in France.

The leaders of the National Assembly quickly decided, however, that they needed to preserve the monarchy in spite of the king. Barnave, one of the most eloquent spokesmen for the Third Estate in June 1789, now became the leading defender of this policy. He spoke for many who had supported the Revolution's assault on noble privileges but who had become increasingly alarmed by the success of radicals who tried to convince the common people that the unequal distribution of wealth and property violated the natural rights proclaimed in 1789. If France was to become a stable country in which the rights of property owners were secure, Barnave argued, there had to be a strong executive authority, independent of public opinion, to maintain the laws. To remove the king from office would be to "begin the Revolution anew," and it would invite demands for complete democracy and the redistribution of property.

Barnave and his followers prevailed in the National Assembly, which voted to absolve the king for his flight, but they also split the revolutionary movement. On 16 July 1791, Barnave and most of the other deputies quit the Jacobin club, leaving a small rump organization in the hands of Robespierre, and founded a rival club, the Feuillants. On the following day, Paris radicals called for a mass demonstration to protest the Assembly's decision. When disorders broke out, the National Guard commander, Lafayette, and the mayor of Paris, Bailly, both sympathetic to the Feuillants, sent in the National Guard. About sixty demonstrators were shot down in this "massacre of the Champ-de-Mars" (near the present day site of the Eiffel Tower). This repression appeared to confirm the radical claim that the Assembly despised the common people. A constitution put into effect under these conditions rested on shaky foundations.

THE END OF THE NATIONAL ASSEMBLY

With the king's fate resolved and the radicals temporarily silent, the National Assembly hastened to conclude its work. In August and September 1791, the deputies "revised" the entire constitution, altering a number of clauses to strengthen safeguards for property owners. The conflict over the Civil Constitution of the Clergy, the king's flight, and the massacre of 17 July 1791 showed that grave difficulties threatened the new liberal order, but the deputies could be forgiven for taking pride in what they had accomplished. They had broken the political deadlock that had prevented necessary political reforms for decades. They had given France a complete, new constitutional system, based on the principles of legal equality for all male citizens and individual liberty. If they failed to solve some of the most pressing problems they had come up against, such as poverty and education, they had at least measured the size of the tasks and proclaimed principles that, a century or more later, would become the basis for effective legislation.

Critics at the time and since have blamed the National Assembly for trying to do too much at once and for failing to provide sufficient checks and balances in their constitutional system. As early as February 1790, an English observer, Edmund Burke, had published a scathing indictment of the entire revolutionary enterprise. "You began ill, because you began by despising every thing that belonged to you. You set up your trade without a capital," Burke warned the French, arguing that historic tradition was a better guide for political reform than the abstract reason to which the National Assembly had appealed. He predicted that the expropriation of Church lands would become a prelude to a general attack on property, and that the weakening of the king's power would ultimately lead to the complete demise of the monarchy. Burke's eloquent denunciation of the Revolution and his defense of tradition made him the first great spokesman for conservatism, the principled opposition to sudden and thoroughgoing social and political change.

To the revolutionaries of 1789, however, well aware of the decades of unsuccessful reform efforts that had preceded the summoning of the Estates-General, criticisms like Burke's seemed exaggerated and unreasonable. In their eyes, the opportunity that appeared in July 1789 was too valuable to be passed up and the danger of political deadlock too serious to permit a real division of powers. The first two years of the Revolution had been accompanied by a certain amount of violence, but, in view of the scope and complexity of the issues the movement had raised, the amount of overt conflict had been relatively modest. The National Assembly had tried to balance the need for reform with some respect for established interests—it had, for example, offered nobles compensation for most of the seigneurial rights they had lost. Unlike Burke, who thought that the Revolution's fundamental principles were unsound, the majority of the deputies in 1791 still thought that the difficulties they had encountered were merely teething pains that would soon be overcome.

THE LEGISLATIVE ASSEMBLY

Fewer than 25 percent of the "active" citizens entitled to vote under the new constitution actually took part in the 1791 elections. Those who did vote were usually supporters of the Revolution, and the deputies they elected were probably more enthusiastic about the movement than the population as a whole. Most of the 745 deputies who assembled for the first time on 1 October 1791 were from the bourgeois groups that had gained the most from the National Assembly's reforms. Because of the National Assembly's "self-denying ordinance" forbidding its members to seek re-election, all were newcomers to national politics. Unlike the deputies of the National Assembly, few of them came from the old privileged classes, and they were

Patriot Journalists

This engraving of leading Patriot journalists from 1791, shown holding their publications, demonstrates the development of a self-conscious prorevolutionary movement. The journalists surround an allegorical figure representing the new constitution, which put "the nation" and "the law" above "the king." The hand rising from underground represents the radical writer Jean-Paul Marat, who had gone into hiding to avoid arrest for criticizing policies he claimed favored the rich.

Source: Newberry Library, Chicago.

much less willing to seek compromises with opponents of the Revolution. Many had served as local officials and had had to deal with refractory priests and other opponents of the new order. Determined to ensure the triumph of the revolutionary movement, they were also concerned about protecting social order and the rights of property.

At the outset, the moderate Feuillant group formed after the flight to Varennes and dedicated to making the new constitutional system work had more supporters in the new assembly than the radical Jacobins, who had lost all trust in the king. Outside the Legislative Assembly, however, the more radical revolutionaries, such as Robespierre, had managed to hold the loyalty of most of the provincial club network, giving them a powerful propaganda tool, and the Jacobins soon gained the initiative over their rivals. The debates of the Paris Jacobin Club, whose members included prominent former National Assembly deputies who were now out of office as well as the more radical members of the Legislative Assembly, often attracted more attention than the Assembly's own proceedings. Pro-Jacobin newspapers publicized the most important speeches delivered at the club and had a strong influence on public opinion. The radicals also had strong support in the Paris population, particularly from groups like the Cordeliers Club, a stronghold of advocates of political participation for the common people.

While the radicals pressured the Legislative Assembly from the left, the deputies also had to contend with counterrevolutionary agitation from the right. There were no openly declared counterrevolutionary deputies in the Legislative Assembly, but outspoken royalist journalists and caricaturists kept up a vociferous campaign for the overthrow of the new constitution. They criticized the king for his apparent willingness to accept the role of a constitutional monarch, openly urged army officers to join the emigrés, and looked forward to a foreign invasion to quash the Revolution. "Refractory" priests who had refused to accept the Civil Constitution of the Clergy often became rallying points for local resistance to the revolution in the provinces.

In this tense atmosphere, the Legislative Assembly continued to work on the details of legislation to fit the new constitution. In general, its members shared their predecessors' determination to create a society of independent individuals with equal rights. For example, the Legislative Assembly completed the secularization of citizenship by making the registration of births, marriages, and deaths—known in France as the *état civil*—a function of the government rather than the Church. The new legislation authorized divorce and allowed husbands and wives equal rights to initiate proceedings. Divorces could be granted not just for adultery and other violations of the marriage contract, but also on the basis of mutual consent or "incompatibility of temperament." This reform made marriage a voluntary agreement between consenting adults, just as the revolutionary legislators claimed that society was the result of a voluntary agreement among all citizens.

THE REVOLT AGAINST SLAVERY

The increasingly agitated political atmosphere diverted most of the Legislative Assembly's attention to immediate threats to the Revolution, however. These threats included troubles in the colonies, domestic social unrest, and the threat of war. News of a massive slave revolt in France's most important colony, the Caribbean sugar island of Saint-Domingue, reached Paris in October 1791 two months after the insurrection had begun. Through contacts with sailors and domestic servants whose masters discussed the news from France, some slaves had heard rumors about the movement for liberty that had begun in 1789. They were also inspired by the example of earlier slave resistance movements, such as the Makandal conspiracy of 1757, which had spread fear throughout the colony's white population. Black slaves in Guadeloupe and Martinique had revolted unsuccessfully in late 1789, inspired by rumors that "the white slaves in France had risen, and killed their masters, and were now enjoying the fruits of the earth."[4] The Saint-Domingue slave rebellion proved much more difficult to control. The rebels burned plantation buildings and massacred slaveowners, and the movement brought to the fore a leader of genius, Toussaint L'Ouverture, who skillfully took advantage of the divisions between the wealthy white slaveowners, the *petits blancs*, the less prosperous whites who lived in the colony's cities, and the mulatto population which had already staged an unsuccessful movement of its own in October 1790.

The National Assembly in France had been pressed by antislavery activists such as the abbé Grégoire to take up the issue of rights for people of color and the abolition of the slave trade. But representatives of the colonial plantation owners had successfully responded that abolition would ruin not only the economy of the colonies but also that of the port cities, like Bordeaux, that depended on overseas trade. In May 1791, the Assembly did pass a law granting political rights to the small minority of free blacks in Saint-Domingue, but it had been unable to enforce this law before the August 1791 uprising. In the wake of the revolt, the Legislative Assembly dispatched commissioners to try to restore order. While the deputies continued to grapple with France's domestic problems, the fate of its most lucrative overseas possession remained completely unsettled.

The Legislative Assembly had to cope with spreading social unrest closer to home as well. The 1791 grain harvest was a poor one, and by the fall there were outbreaks of social violence in a number of rural areas. In February 1792, crowds in Paris, angered by the high price of sugar, attacked merchants' shops. The deputies, who saw the Revolution as a movement on behalf of the people, could not understand why ordinary men and women would blame the revolution for economic problems. They found it easier to claim that members of the former privileged orders had incited these disturbances. Although the deputies supported a political system based on individual rights, many of them were now ready to back laws curtailing the rights of groups blamed for obstructing the new order. In November 1791, the Legislative Assembly voted stringent laws against refractory priests, who had to take a new oath to defend the constitution. Another law ordered emigré nobles to return to France by the end of 1791 or face the loss of their property and execution if they returned to France later. Louis XVI vetoed both these laws. His actions made prorevolutionary deputies and the public even more dubious about his willingness to make the new constitution work.

THE MOVE TOWARD WAR

The issue of the emigrés was one of the main factors that drove the Legislative Assembly to its most important decision: its vote on 20 April 1792 to declare war against Austria. The revolutionaries of 1789 had been persuaded that war, the result of kings' greed for conquests and glory, was one of those evils of the Old Regime that they could abolish. In May 1790, when Spain appealed for French support against England under a treaty between the two Bourbon monarchies, the National Assembly stripped the king of his traditional right to declare war. The Constitution of 1791 announced that "the French nation will never undertake any war of conquest, and will never employ its forces against the liberty of another people."

From the start, however, the Revolution affected France's neighbors. The principles contained in the Declaration of the Rights of Man and Citizen challenged the bases of absolute monarchy and social privilege, not just in France, but everywhere in Europe. Spain banned the circulation of news from France in December 1789, to protect its king's subjects from the bad example of their neighbor's revolt. Furthermore, the National Assembly's insistence that all Frenchmen had the right to be part of the nation affected several foreign rulers who owned lands surrounded by French territory. In Alsace, the Assembly annexed territorial enclaves that longstanding treaties had assigned to various German princes, offering them financial compensation but refusing to negotiate on the principle of its sovereignty. Events in Avignon, an island of territory belonging to the Pope, raised an even more explosive issue. In June 1790, local revolutionaries overthrew the Papal government and demanded to be annexed to France. Cautious at first about endorsing the idea that any population could throw off its old ruler and vote to join France, the National Assembly finally took the plunge in September 1791. Although the territory involved was small, the arguments used to justify this annexation had the potential to upset the entire traditional European order.

For their part, Europe's other governments had initially shown little hostility to the Revolution. Some assumed that the Revolution would weaken France's power and give them a free hand to pursue their own interests. Prussia, Russia, and Austria, for example, turned their attention to blocking efforts at national reform in Poland, where a liberal constitution similar to the new French one had been proclaimed in May 1791. Louis XVI's flight to Varennes finally stirred Europe's rulers to make verbal gestures on behalf of their fellow monarch. Leopold II of Austria, brother of Marie-Antoinette, and Frederic William II of Prussia met in Pillnitz in August 1791 and issued a declaration asserting that events in France were "a matter of common concern to all the sovereigns of Europe" and suggesting possible intervention.[5] This fueled the French Patriots' contention that the Revolution was in danger from abroad. The continued presence of the French emigrés in territories in Austria's sphere of influence that were close to France's borders gave the revolutionaries another pretext for complaining about foreign hostility. (See Document E on page 64.)

In France, support for war came from the extremes of right and left. The Feuillant moderates opposed the idea, fearful that the fragile constitutional monarchy would not survive such an ordeal, but a majority of the radical Jacobin supporters of the Revolution openly favored hostilities. The leaders of the pro-war faction in the Jacobin Club came to be known as the Girondins, because many of their most prominent members were deputies from the Gironde, the department of Bordeaux. Their most prominent spokesman was the journalist-deputy Jacques-Pierre Brissot; their true leader was Madame Roland, the spirited wife of another leading member, in whose salon the Girondin deputies regularly met. The Girondins tended to be talented and ambitious individualists who had made their way in the world by virtue of their own abilities. No friends of the Old Regime, they were nevertheless susceptible to the concerns of France's bourgeois elites; many of them represented the country's big trading cities, such as Bordeaux and Marseille. These deputies, representatives of the middle-class urban revolutionary movement, joined with intellectuals and journalists from Paris to spur the Revolution forward over the opposition of the moderates, who thought the movement had achieved all that could be hoped for with the passage of the 1791 Constitution.

In the war debates, the Girondins' leading spokesman Brissot argued that war would exalt patriotic fervor and expose traitors who hoped for the defeat of the Revolution. Furthermore, the radicals were confident that, as soon as French troops crossed their borders, the populations of neighboring countries would embrace the revolutionary cause and rise up against their own rulers. "Volcanoes are everywhere in readiness; . . . only a spark is needed to bring about a universal explosion," Brissot proclaimed.[6] His enthusiasm overrode Robespierre's farsighted warning that "no one loves armed missionaries."

The Jacobin war party found unlikely allies among the king's closest supporters. Once war was declared, they thought, the king, as commander-in-chief of the army, would have expanded powers. If France was successful,

DOCUMENT E
AN EMIGRÉ MANIFESTO

After the Holy Roman Emperor and the King of Prussia had been persuaded in August 1791 to issue the Pillnitz Declaration, warning the revolutionaries not to take further measures against Louis XVI, the king's brother, the Comte de Provence, who had successfully fled from the kingdom at the time of Varennes, issued his own proclamation. Its aggressive tone, characteristic of the French emigrés, helps explain why the revolutionaries reacted so strongly to their actions:

"If the rebels stubbornly and blindly oppose this wish [the foreign monarchs' desire to see the king's powers restored] and foreign armies are forced to enter the kingdom, it will be entirely their own fault. They alone will have made it necessary; they alone will bear the guilt for the blood that will have to be shed; the war will be their work. The only goal of the allied Powers is to support the healthy part of the nation against the delirious part, and to put out the volcano of fanaticism in the heart of the kingdom whose eruptions menace all countries.

"Furthermore . . ., one cannot believe that the French, no matter how many efforts are made to inflame their natural pride by exalting and electrifying all minds with misleading ideas of patriotism and liberty, really want to go on much longer sacrificing their tranquility, their goods and their blood to support an extravagant experiment that has only made people unhappy. Intoxication doesn't last; the successes of crime have their limits, and one quickly gets tired of such excesses, when one is oneself their victim." (From L. G. W. Legg, *Select Documents Illustrative of the History of the French Revolution* [Oxford: Clarendon Press, 1905], pp. 129–30. *Translation by Jeremy D. Popkin.*)

his position would be strengthened; if the French army was defeated, the foreign powers would do away with the revolutionaries. The king himself had private doubts about the wisdom of these arguments, but in the end, he went along with them. On 10 March 1792, he appointed a new team of ministers close to the pro-war Girondin group: Madame Roland's husband became Interior Minister and a fiercely anti-Austrian general, Dumouriez, took over management of foreign affairs. When the Austrian government rejected a French ultimatum to expel the emigrés from German territory, the king asked the Assembly to declare war, and so, on 20 April 1792, France entered into a conflict that would last, with brief interruptions, for more than two decades.

THE IMPACT OF WAR

The declaration of war had an immediate and long-lasting impact on the course of the Revolution. It raised the stakes of political debate enormously. For patriots, opposition to any aspect of the Revolution now looked like treason and deserved the harshest possible punishment. Political disputes now took on a life-and-death character that made compromise harder to accept than ever. The war also marked a further step in the political mobilization of the common people. As members of the lower classes were drawn into the war effort, the National Assembly's decision to exclude these "passive citizens" from full political rights became harder to justify.

The outbreak of war focused attention on the condition of the French army. Until July 1789, the army had been the king's, not the nation's. It consisted primarily of long-term professional soldiers, some of them recruited from abroad. The officer corps was entirely aristocratic; regardless of merit, rank-and-file soldiers could not hope to rise above the rank of noncommissioned officers. The National Assembly had undertaken to reform the army, like every other French institution. Soldiers and officers were given the same rights as other citizens, and the officer corps was opened to commoners. New units, composed of prorevolutionary volunteers drawn from the National Guard, were created alongside the old "line" regiments, whose political attitudes were often suspect.

By 1792, these reforms had been only partially successful in creating an army in accordance with the Revolution's new conception of the nation. Many aristocratic officers' loyalty to the new revolutionary order was less than certain, and relations between the officers and their men were strained, as a bloody soldiers' mutiny at Nancy in August 1790 had shown. At the start of the war, army morale was low. The troops were quick to blame their commanders for any reverses they suffered; at Lille, panicked French soldiers massacred their own commander. In Paris, news of these defeats plunged the institutions of the constitutional monarchy into a fatal crisis.

THE OVERTHROW OF THE MONARCHY

By the start of the war, the constitutional system put into effect in 1791 was already coming apart. Particularly in Paris, the large population of artisans and shopkeepers who had made up most of the crowd that stormed the Bastille had never accepted their exclusion from politics. In the spring of 1792, prorevolutionary political activists had mobilized strong support among these *sans-culottes*, so called to distinguish them from the educated classes, who wore elegant knee-breeches or *culottes*, not the worker's long trousers. Sans-culotte activists began to mobilize against both the king and

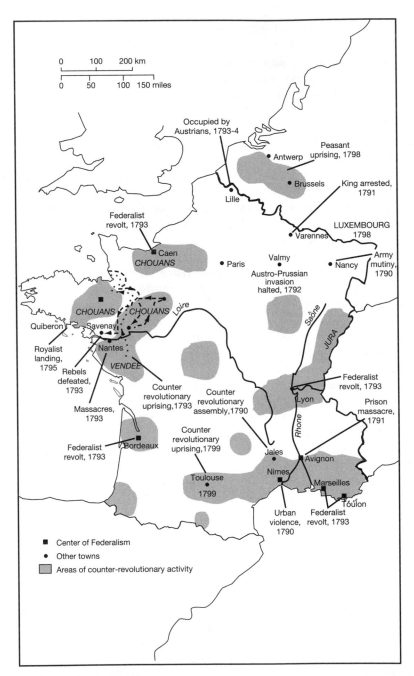

The Revolution in the Provinces

Events in the provinces had a major impact on the direction of the Revolution. The "Great Fear," the Nancy army mutiny, the king's flight to Varennes, the Vendée revolt, and the federalist uprisings all posed major crises for the revolutionary government in the capital.

an Assembly that seemed indifferent to the Austro-Prussian army's advance into France. Along with these male activists, a small but determined group of women made their presence felt as well, participating in street demonstrations and even demanding the right to bear arms, as male citizens did.

By the summer of 1792, activists from the popular movement had gained control of many of the 48 sections into which Paris had been divided in 1790. Each section had a political assembly in which all citizens could participate, as well as a National Guard battalion that could be mobilized in a crisis. Even though voting in the sections and participation in the National Guard were theoretically limited to "active" citizens, by the summer of 1792, many poorer members of the population refused to accept this exclusion. The growing strength of this popular movement became visible on 20 June 1792, when a sans-culotte crowd invaded the royal palace to protest the king's veto of several measures aimed at strengthening the war effort. The demonstrators surrounded the king and forced him to drink a toast to the nation, but he defied their demands to withdraw his vetoes. The Jacobin deputies kept their distance from this protest, whose organizers came primarily from the radical Cordeliers Club, but they shared the crowd's fear that the king was deliberately dragging his feet to give the Austro-Prussian invaders time to reach Paris.

At the beginning of July 1792, a small group of revolutionary militants, including both radical journalists and sans-culotte leaders, evolved a plan for an uprising leading to the summoning of a National Convention, which would remove the king, take emergency measures to defend the country, and give France a new constitution. In addition to the armed battalions of the more radical Paris sections, the plotters relied on the armed *fédérés*, volunteer units from all over the country that had come to Paris for the celebration of 14 July. The unit from Marseille was especially noted for its revolutionary ardor. Its members had arrived in Paris singing a new marching song composed a few months earlier whose verses called on all "children of the Fatherland" to take arms and let "the blood of our enemies water our fields." This "song of the Marseillais" became a rallying cry for the assault on the monarchy. (See Document F.)

On 28 July 1792, the commander of the allied forces, the Duke of Brunswick, issued a proclamation holding the inhabitants of Paris responsible for any attack on the king. When the news of this "Brunswick manifesto" reached Paris, the insurrectionary leaders decided to act. By 9:00 A.M. on 10 August, thousands of their supporters were converging on the Tuileries. The king and his family took refuge with the Legislative Assembly, leaving their loyal Swiss guards behind to defend the palace. In the course of the day, fighting broke out; the outnumbered guards killed at least 100 of the insurgents. This infuriated the sans-culottes, who retaliated by massacring the guards who fell into their hands. The tenth of August thus became by far the bloodiest of the revolutionary insurrections, or *journées*. It was also among

DOCUMENT F
THE JOURNÉE OF 10 AUGUST 1792

When French armies suffered defeats during the first months of the war against Austria and Prussia in 1792, Jacobin radicals and sans-culotte activists, who controlled the Paris city government, put pressure on the Legislative Assembly to remove Louis XVI from office. The city's mayor, Jérôme Pétion, expressed their sentiments in a speech to the Assembly a few days before the journée of 10 August 1792.

"The head of the executive branch is the first link in the chain of counterrevolution . . . So long as we have such a king, liberty cannot put down solid roots, and we want to remain free. Out of a spirit of indulgence, we would have liked to ask you simply to suspend Louis XVI from office, as long as the country is in danger, but the Constitution prevents this. Louis XVI constantly invokes his constitutional rights; we now invoke ours, and call for his removal from office.

"This important act being taken, it would be very doubtful that the nation could have confidence in the present ruling dynasty. We ask that a team of ministers be chosen, mutually responsible for their actions, named by the Legislative Assembly, but not picked from its members, as the Constitution requires, elected by the public vote of free men, to run the government on a provisional basis until the will of the people— our sovereign and yours—has been legally expressed in a national convention to be summoned as soon as the safety of the state permits. Meanwhile, let our enemies, whoever they are, range themselves along our frontiers. Let the cowards and the traitors flee the soil of liberty. Let three hundred thousand slaves advance on us. They will find themselves faced with ten million free men, ready for death or victory, fighting for equality, for their family's homes, for their wives, their children, and their parents. Let every one of us take our turn as soldiers, and, if we have to have the honor of dying for the country, let each one of us leave a heroic memory behind by accounting for the death of a slave or a tyrant." (From Buchez and Roux, *Histoire parlementaire de la Révolution française* [Paris: Paulin, 1835], vol. 16, pp. 318–19. *Translation by Jeremy D. Popkin.*)

the most decisive politically. The Legislative Assembly suspended Louis XVI from his functions and voted to call nationwide elections for a Convention that would determine the fate of the monarchy; it thus scrapped the Constitution of 1791. By declaring that all adult males were eligible to vote for the Convention, the Assembly abandoned the effort to keep power in the

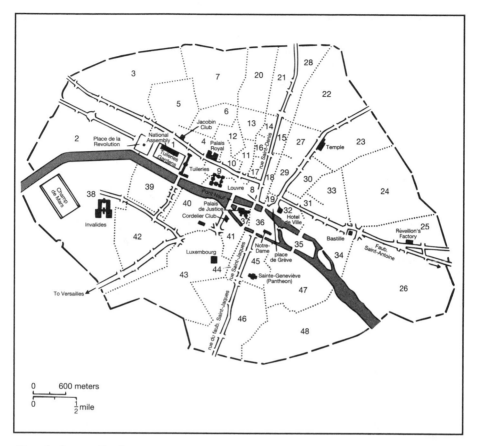

Revolutionary Paris

The revolutionary legislatures occupied buildings near the old royal palaces, the Louvre and the Tuileries, in the center of the city. The Hôtel-de-Ville, seat of Paris's municipal government, was closer to the eastern faubourgs, home of the sans-culotte militants whose organized marches put pressure on the government at many critical moments during the Revolution. Dotted lines show the boundaries of the 48 sections into which the city was divided after 1790.

hands of the propertied classes. The liberal or bourgeois Revolution had ended; the democratic and radical Revolution had begun.

EMERGENCY MEASURES AND EMERGENCIES

The six weeks between the uprising of 10 August and the first session of the National Convention gave France its first taste of what came to be called revolutionary government, in which ordinary legal processes were suspended in the name of defending the Revolution. During this period, control of Paris was shared uneasily by the Legislative Assembly—half of whose members had ceased to attend meetings after the uprising—and a municipal assembly, the Commune, whose members included leaders of the sans-culotte movement and Jacobin radicals such as Robespierre. For the moment, the most visible leader was a veteran member of the radical Corde-liers Club, Georges Danton. A fiery speaker with a gift for communicating with ordinary people, Danton had played a key role in the sans-culotte cap-ture of the Paris sections (neighborhood assemblies) before the uprising. Named minister of justice after 10 August, he pushed his colleagues to sat-isfy radical demands for fast action. "We must dare, and dare again, and dare forever, and so France will be saved," he proclaimed.

To satisfy this popular pressure for action, the Legislative Assembly set up a Revolutionary Tribunal on 17 August 1792. Its procedures superseded many of the guarantees in the Declaration of the Rights of Man. There was no appeal from its sentences, and those condemned to death were executed with a new mechanical beheading device that experts had created for the National Assembly, which was supposed to be painless and efficient—the guillotine, named for Dr. Guillotin, a legislator who had wanted to abolish cruel punishments. Other emergency measures included the deportation of all "refractory" priests and the dispatch of commissioners to the provinces to bring local governments in line with the new atmosphere in Paris.

These actions were not enough to satisfy the sans-culottes' demand for immediate measures to defeat the counterrevolution, however. On 2 Sep-tember 1792, reacting to news that the key fortress of Verdun was about to surrender, political activists surrounded the principal Paris prisons. They set up improvised tribunals and forced the jailers to bring out the prisoners. In all, some 1,300, most of them guilty of nothing more tangible than having held privileged status before 1789, were killed. The massacres continued for several days, and neither the Legislative Assembly nor the Commune made any effort to stop them. These killings stained the Revolution's reputation throughout Europe; they also made the incoming Convention acutely aware of the need to convince the sans-culottes that it was doing everything nec-essary to defend the Revolution.

In the aftermath of the September massacres, the Revolution's destiny depended on the outcome of the Austro-Prussian invasion. On 20 Septem-ber 1792, the day the Convention first assembled in Paris, the issue was set-tled by the battle of Valmy. The French, now somewhat better organized than in the first battles of the war, profited from their superiority in numbers and their artillery to halt the Austro-Prussian advance. The great German author Goethe, who accompanied the Prussian troops, recognized the sig-nificance of the French citizen army's success. "A new era of world history begins here," he told his companions.[7] The commanders of the invading force were less foresighted: they decided it would make no difference if they retreated and resumed operations in the spring. Their decision gave the radical revolutionary government precious time to consolidate its position.

THE FAILURE OF THE LIBERAL REVOLUTION

Was the collapse of the constitutional monarchy inevitable? If so, why? Critics have pointed to some shortcomings in the design of the 1791 constitution that helped hasten its demise. The logic of national sovereignty may have favored the idea of a one-house legislature, but practical experience in France and elsewhere has suggested that a bicameral system provides for more thorough airing of controversies and more careful legislation. Giving the king the power to delay legislation with the suspensive veto but not to reject it altogether made him the target of protests if he opposed popular proposals, but it didn't give him real authority to defend his point of view. Even so, the internal flaws of the constitution were not so obvious as to make it unworkable. Experience in a number of European countries during the nineteenth century demonstrated that constitutional monarchy could be a successful form of government, capable of evolving in the direction of fuller democracy.

In 1791, however, the French attempted to install a constitutional monarchy with a king who had proven his ill-will toward such a system and with a legislature bent on enforcing controversial policies such as the Civil Constitution of the Clergy. At the same time, the king and the new assembly had to face a growing challenge from below to the principle of limiting political rights to the propertied classes. There was also a vocal counterrevolutionary opposition that openly sought to destroy the new institutions. In addition to all these internal difficulties, the new government had to contend with a dangerous international environment. The absence of consensus about how to deal with these problems certainly undermined the new political system.

Historians in the Marxist tradition, such as Georges Lefebvre, see the disintegration of the constitutional monarchy and the "second revolution" of 1792 as a logical continuation of the original Revolution of 1789. By proclaiming the principle of popular sovereignty, the original revolutionaries had fatally undermined hereditary authority. The principle of equality discredited their own effort to limit political rights to property owners. For these historians, it was inevitable that the common people would demand a system of government that truly represented their will. All historians recognize, however, that the decision to go to war in April 1792 changed the character of the Revolution. The war created unanticipated problems and greatly accelerated the move toward radicalism. Some non-Marxist scholars see this as evidence that the Revolution had "deviated" from its original path. Many of them also stress that the "second revolution" was never a true mass movement. The Jacobins and the sans-culotte movement represented highly organized minorities, and in the countryside, many areas were clearly hostile or indifferent to the new revolutionary radicalism. While historians generally agree that the constitutional monarchy set up in 1791 had little chance of success, there is thus substantial debate about the nature of the forces that destroyed it.

NOTES

1. Cited in Beik, ed., *French Revolution*, 167.

2. *Journal général de la cour et de la ville*, 27 June 1791.

3. Cordeliers petition, 21 June 1791, in A. Mathiez, *Le Club des Cordeliers* (Paris, 1910), 47.

4. C. L. R. James, *The Black Jacobins* (New York: Vintage, 1963), 81.

5. Cited in John Hall Stewart, ed., *Documentary Survey of the French Revolution* (New York: Macmillan, 1951), 223.

6. Cited in Beik, ed., *French Revolution*, 201.

7. Cited in Claus Träger, ed., *Die Französische Revolution im Spiegel der deutschen Literatur* (Leipzig: Reclam, 1975), 250.

CHAPTER 5

THE CONVENTION AND THE REPUBLIC, 1792–1794

Like the National Assembly, the National Convention that convened in September 1792 made fundamental changes in French life that broke radically with the past. Even more than the National Assembly, its work has been controversial. To some, this first attempt at the creation of a democratic republic laid the groundwork for the basic institutions that make France a democratic society today. Others see the Convention as a violent and destructive regime comparable to the totalitarian dictatorships of the twentieth century. However it is viewed, no historian can deny that the three years of the Convention's session were among the most momentous in all of French history.

The National Convention was born in crisis, and its entire three-year existence was shaped by a series of urgent problems. The deputies elected in September 1792 had to deal with both the Austro-Prussian invasion and the issue of constitution making. The 749 new deputies were on the whole similar to the members of the outgoing Legislative Assembly. In fact, many had sat in that body or in the National Assembly, since there was no repetition of the "self-denying ordinance" of 1791 that had kept deputies from running for reelection. Lawyers and former government officials still predominated, and the deputies were still overwhelmingly members of the bourgeoisie. They were young—two-thirds were under forty-five—and strongly committed to the Revolution.

These deputies had little in common with the Parisian sans-culottes. The deputies still wanted to govern through orderly legal processes, whereas the sans-culottes were men—and women—of direct action, who considered the crisis facing the Revolution too grave to be dealt with through slow-moving legislative debates. The tension between the Paris population and the Convention continued throughout the new assembly's three-year tenure in office and explains much about the policies it adopted.

THE TRIAL OF THE KING

Even before the arrival of news from the battlefield at Valmy, the Convention had set its political course. At its opening session on 20 September 1792, it immediately voted to proclaim France a republic and thus cut the last institutional link between the Revolution and the Old Regime. But what was to be done with Louis XVI? The debate on his fate revealed that the Jacobin deputies who dominated the Convention were deeply divided. The two main groups in this debate, the Girondins and the Montagnards, had already taken shape during the period of the Legislative Assembly. Both had participated in the campaign against the king that had begun with the military defeats of June 1792. Even as the pressure to remove Louis XVI mounted, however, the Girondins had begun to reconsider the idea of using popular pressure to force him out of office. Some Girondin leaders now thought their group could more easily control a weak king than a turbulent assembly. Their hesitation did much to discredit the Girondin group in the eyes of the popular revolutionary movement.

The more radical Montagnards now controlled the Jacobin Club. Their most prominent leader was Maximilien Robespierre, the small-town lawyer whose numerous speeches on behalf of the less privileged during the National Assembly had given him a national reputation. In the Convention, his main allies were the popular agitator Danton, who had dominated the government in the critical days between the 10 August insurrection and the convening of the new legislature, and the radical journalist Marat. Compared to the Girondins, the Montagnards voiced greater concern for the lower classes. Their rhetoric tended to be more moralistic than the Girondins', their political positions more uncompromising. They had favored the abolition of the monarchy and had accepted the results of the 10 August uprising without any hesitation.

The two rival groups clashed regularly from the first weeks of the Convention's sessions, with the Girondins accusing the Montagnards of plotting to establish a dictatorship and the Montagnards responding that their opponents were in collusion with the imprisoned king. Even though the 1791 constitution had declared the king legally immune to punishment, pressure for action against him was too strong for the Girondins to resist. The Montagnards and the sans-culotte leaders contended that no trial was necessary: the king's guilt was obvious, and he should be executed forthwith. A majority of the Convention decided, however, to follow legal procedures and give the king a trial, with the deputies voting on his fate. The legislators thus set the stage for a great public drama that would do much to define the nature of the radical revolution.

Louis was aided by a legal team headed by one of his prerevolutionary ministers, Lamoignon de Malesherbes, who later paid with his life for volunteering for this role. His lawyers argued that the Convention had no legal authority to judge the king, and they reminded the deputies that the king had convoked the Estates-General in 1789 and approved its initial reforms. Determined to maintain his dignity, even in defeat, Louis XVI told

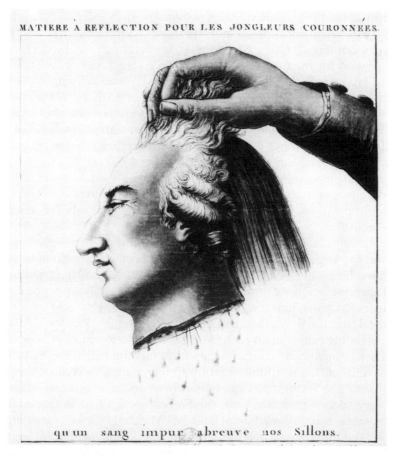

MATIERE À REFLECTION POUR LES JONGLEURS COURONNÉES.

qu un sang impur abreuve nos Sillons.

The Execution of Louis XVI

The execution of Louis XVI in January 1793 was a declaration of war against all vestiges of the Old Regime, and against the other European monarchies. Before 1789, depictions of the king served to maintain royal authority. This striking engraving of his severed head was meant to publicize the French people's total rejection of the institution of kingship.
Source: Bibliothèque Nationale, Paris.

the deputies, "In speaking to you, perhaps for the last time, I declare to you that my conscience reproaches me for nothing. . . ."[1] The evidence of his contacts with the emigrés and with the Austrian government, much of it furnished by documents discovered in the *armoire de fer*, a secret safe found in the Tuileries palace after the 10 August uprising, convinced an overwhelming majority of deputies to judge the king guilty of "attempts against liberty and of conspiracy against the general security of the state."[2]

The deputies then had to decide on the king's punishment. The Girondins, still looking for some way to avoid the irreparable step of execution, suggested several alternatives. Thomas Paine, elected to the Convention out of respect for his contribution to the American Revolution, wanted to banish Louis to the United States, where "he may learn . . . that the true system of government consists, not in kings, but in fair, equal, and honorable representation."[3] Other Girondin leaders argued that the decision was too important for the Convention to take on its own authority. They called for a national referendum in which the citizens themselves would determine the king's fate. The Montagnards responded that delaying his punishment would plunge the country into confusion and undermine the war effort. Their most effective orator, the twenty-five-year-old Louis-Antoine Saint-Just, declared that "those who worry about whether it is fair to punish a king will never establish a republic."[4] The crucial roll call vote on execution took 36 hours; most deputies felt obliged to explain their decisions. The final vote was close, with a number of legislators still trying to find a compromise that would postpone the king's death, but a narrow majority favored immediate execution.

Four days later, on 21 January 1793, the king was conveyed from his prison to the large public square now known as the Place de la Concorde. The crowd lining the streets was mostly silent. When the king tried to make a final speech from the scaffold, the National Guard commander ordered his drummers to drown him out. The fall of the guillotine's blade underscored the radical turn the Revolution had taken on 10 August 1792: the Convention had irreversibly ruled out any compromise with the Revolution's opponents.

There was also no compromise in the factional struggle that divided the Convention. The resulting instability became more and more dangerous as the problems facing the Convention became more critical. After some temporary successes in late 1792, the French armies had to face new foes, most notably Britain and Spain, and by March 1793 the Austrians had regained the initiative in Belgium and the Rhineland, while the Spaniards launched an invasion in the south. Dumouriez, the defeated French commander in Belgium, tried to lead his troops against the Convention and then went over to the enemy, leaving the main French army in disarray. The fact that he had been friendly with members of the Girondin group offered the Montagnards a new opening to attack their rivals.

Danger to the Revolution was also mounting at home. In March, an attempt to draft new troops for the army set off an uprising in rural western France, centered in the department of the Vendée. The peasants who started the insurrection soon recruited local nobles with military experience to lead them; by June, their "Catholic and Royal Army" had grown to 40,000. The rebellion became a veritable civil war, waged with unrelenting cruelty on both sides. The Vendeans captured several small towns and threatened the port city of Nantes, the capture of which would have allowed them to receive support from England. Although resistance to the draft set off the uprising, the Vendeans had broader grievances against the Revolution. The deeply Catholic rural population in western France resented the Civil Constitution of the Clergy, and many peasants had had to watch as the prorevolutionary town-dwellers in their region bought up many of the former Church lands. The drastic methods used to put down the Vendée rebellion, which included mass drownings of prisoners in the Loire river and the burning down of entire villages, together with the massacre of their inhabitants, have been one of the main justifications for claims that the Revolution resembles twentieth-century totalitarian regimes. It is impossible to justify the excesses committed by the revolutionary forces, but civil wars, especially when they coincide with foreign invasions, as the Vendée rebellion did, do frequently generate deadly cycles of extreme violence. Revolutionary leaders in Paris realized that the brutalities committed in the Vendée threatened to discredit them, and such methods were rarely used elsewhere; the deputy on mission Carrier, responsible for many of the mass killings, was recalled after three months.

POPULAR RADICALISM

In addition to the war and the Vendée rebellion, the Convention had to deal with a worsening economic crisis. A poor grain harvest in 1792 sent food prices soaring again, and this inflation undermined the assignats, the paper currency that the National Assembly had begun to issue in 1789. Wages failed to keep up with the rise in prices, leading to popular protests. The issue of the government's relationship with the common people of Paris, the sans-culottes, became ever more critical.

The sans-culottes were a very mixed group. Although their spokesmen claimed that the movement represented the poor, the most active members were usually skilled artisans and shopkeepers. They tended to be better educated and more prosperous than the common run of day laborers and journeymen. Membership in the sans-culotterie was as much a matter of cultural attitudes as it was a question of economic status. A popular journalist defined a sans-culotte as "a being who always goes on foot, who has no millions, . . . no castle, no valets to serve him, and who lives simply with his wife and children. . . . He is useful, because he knows how to plow a field, to forge, to saw, to file, to roof a building, to make shoes, and to spill out his last drop of blood for the salvation of the Republic."[5]

To ensure that the Revolution benefited the common people, the sans-culotte movement advocated a program of direct participatory democracy. They insisted on the primacy of the Paris sections, the forty-eight neighborhood assemblies where any citizen could come and help decide political questions. To prevent elected legislators from defying the will of the people, the sans-culottes insisted that deputies should be subject to recall at any time. The sans-culottes' grievances were articulated most forcefully by several agitators and journalists who came to be known as the *enragés*. The best known was the "red priest" Jacques Roux, a former clergyman. He and the other enragé leaders accused the Convention of favoring the wealthy. They demanded price controls, measures against hoarding and speculation in foodstuffs, and severe punishment of the "conspirators" they blamed for the suffering of the poor. (See Document G.)

The enragés' program appealed strongly to the lower classes in Paris, and especially to women. Traditionally responsible for buying their families' food, they were especially aware of the increase in bread prices. In May 1793, the most militant women activists formed the Society of Revolutionary Republican Women under the leadership of the actress Claire Lacombe. Although the number of articulate women activists was small, they were often able to draw larger groups into street demonstrations. Women's participation in revolutionary politics reached its peak in the spring and summer of 1793. To calm the unrest, the Convention passed a law setting maximum prices for wheat and flour and giving the government the right to requisition supplies from reluctant growers. The maximum was a major deviation from the Revolution's original support for free-market principles. Its enactment showed the Convention's growing fear of the popular movement. It also showed the legislators' willingness to meet crises by restricting the individual freedoms guaranteed in the Declaration of the Rights of Man and strengthening the powers of the national government.

THE VICTORY OF THE MONTAGNARDS

In the face of the mounting pressure from the sans-culottes, the split between the Girondins and the Montagnards became more and more bitter. The Girondins publicly blamed the Montagnards for encouraging the prison massacres in September 1792. They supported a new constitutional plan, introduced in February 1793 by Condorcet, one of their leaders, that would have allowed for popular referenda to overturn legislation. The Montagnards condemned the plan as unworkable and as a plot to turn the country

---

DOCUMENT G
THE ENRAGÉS' CHALLENGE TO THE NATIONAL CONVENTION

In the summer of 1793, the former priest Jacques Roux, the leader of the radical group known as the enragés, expressed the dissatisfaction of the poorer members of the Paris population, who demanded quick action to relieve their economic distress. The vehement terms of Roux's speech to the National Convention on 25 July 1793 reflect the tension between the popular movement and the Jacobin deputies.

"Delegates of the people, for a long time you have promised to end the calamities the people are suffering from, but what have you done about it? You have just finished writing a constitution that you are going to submit to a vote of the people. But did you include a ban against speculation in it? No! Did you announce punishments for hoarders and monopolists? No! All right: we tell you that you haven't finished the job . . . Take care, the friends of equality won't be fooled by charlatans who want to contain them through famine, by these vile hoarders whose warehouses are the gathering-places of cheats.... What could possibly be the goal of those speculators who take over factories, commerce, and the products of the earth, except to drive the people to despair and force them to throw themselves into the arms of despotism? How long will you allow rich egoists to drink the people's pure blood from gilded cups?

"If you show that you don't care about wiping out speculation and hoarding, it will be an act of cowardice that will make you guilty of a crime against the nation. Don't be afraid of having the rich—that is, the evil ones—hate you: everything must be sacrificed for the people's welfare . . . No doubt suffering is unavoidable in a great revolution, and we intend to make all the sacrifices necessary to maintain liberty. But the people remembers that it has been betrayed twice by two different assemblies. It is time for the sans-culottes, who have broken the scepter of tyrants, to overthrow every kind of tyranny. Find a quick remedy for our urgent problems." (From Buchez and Roux, *Histoire parlementaire*, vol. 28, pp. 216–17. *Translation by Jeremy D. Popkin*.)

---

against Paris. When there was renewed rioting against high food prices in February and March 1793, the Girondins set a precedent that was later used against them by stripping the Montagnard journalist-deputy Marat of his parliamentary immunity and having him tried for inciting violence. His acquittal sparked popular demonstrations that reminded the Girondins how unpopular they had become among the Paris population.

The political crisis in the Convention had echoes throughout the country, as moderates and radicals struggled for control of local governments. In several big provincial cities, violent local disputes pitted moderate and radical republicans against each other. By the end of May, enemies of the Montagnards controlled such strategic centers as Lyon, Marseille, Bordeaux, and Caen. In concert with the Girondin deputies in Paris, who controlled a number of the most influential newspapers, these anti-Montagnard groups denounced the excessive influence of Paris on the Convention. It was undemocratic, they asserted, for the Paris sans-culotte activists to be able to impose their political demands, while the mass of the population in the provinces was ignored.

To the Montagnard leaders and to the radical sans-culottes in Paris, this challenge cried out for action before it was too late. On 31 May 1793, the radical Paris sections staged a repetition of the 10 August 1792 insurrection: National Guard units, by this time made up mostly of sans-culottes, surrounded the Convention, and two days later the intimidated assembly suspended twenty-two Girondin deputies. The defeated Girondin leaders fled to the provinces. The Montagnards were left in control of the Convention, which itself was clearly at the mercy of whoever could rouse the armed sans-culotte battalions.

The journée of 31 May–2 June 1793 gave the Montagnards control of the Convention, and they were now able to push through whatever laws they wanted. On 24 June, the deputies hurriedly endorsed a new constitution to replace the now-defunct document of 1791. The provisions of this Constitution of 1793 were much more democratic than those of its predecessor. It called for a unicameral legislative assembly chosen by universal manhood suffrage, eliminating the distinction between active and passive citizens. Furthermore, the constitutional plan made the government responsible for giving all citizens the possibility of exercising their rights. Although it continued to safeguard property rights, the 1793 constitution also defined a "right of subsistence," entitling all citizens either to a job or to adequate welfare benefits, and promised a system of universal free public education. These provisions anticipated modern-day social-welfare legislation in most Western countries. If the government violated the people's rights, the 1793 constitution explicitly recognized their right to rise up against it. The provisions of the Constitution of 1793 were never put into effect, however. The Convention voted to postpone its inauguration until the crisis facing the country had been overcome.

Although the Montagnards now dominated the Convention, they seemed likely to lose much of the rest of the country. France's foreign enemies continued their advances, the Vendée rebels remained a threat, and there was a new danger: a series of revolts against the Jacobin-dominated Convention in some of the major provincial cities. These uprisings, known as the federalist movement, took place in towns whose deputies had been among the purged Girondins and where local governments had been taken over by their supporters, places such as Caen, Bordeaux, Lyon, and Marseille. Unlike the Vendée rebels, the federalists proclaimed their loyalty to the Revolution and the Republic. But they condemned the influence of the radical sans-culotte movement and the centralization of authority in Paris.

Luckily for the Convention, the revolts in different parts of the country remained uncoordinated, and the federalists' essentially negative program failed to rally widespread support, whereas the Convention had the advantage of being the focus of patriotic resistance to the foreign threat. As the Convention's forces advanced on the federalist strongholds, the originally republican rebels had to accept support from avowed royalists. In the Mediterranean port city of Toulon, they even welcomed the British fleet. These alliances further discredited the insurrections, however. The federalist movement, together with Charlotte Corday's assassination of the journalist-deputy Marat on 13 July 1793, added to the Montagnards' sense of being under siege and made them even more reluctant to compromise with opponents. They put down the provincial rebellions with the utmost severity. At Lyon, cannon loaded with chain-shot were used to mow down hundreds of captured rebels, in a mass execution that was intended to dramatize the Revolution's determination to stamp out its enemies. The Convention even tried to remove the rebel city's name from the map: Lyon was to be renamed "Liberated City."

TERROR BECOMES THE ORDER OF THE DAY

Although the Montagnard-dominated Convention was able to overcome the federalist revolts during the summer of 1793, its control of the streets of the capital was still not secure. Under his pen name, *Père Duchesne*, the popular journalist Jacques Hébert joined the enragé group and the Society of Revolutionary Republican Women in denouncing the Convention for its moderation toward traitors. The assembly responded to the crisis atmosphere with a series of new measures, such as imposing the death penalty for hoarding grain. On 23 August 1793, the Convention voted the *levée en masse*. For the first time in modern history, the entire population of a country was called upon to rally to its defense, and the entire national economy was, in theory, put under government control. According to the terms of the law, "young men shall go to battle; married men shall forge arms and transport provisions; women shall make tents and clothes, and shall serve in the hospitals . . . " Even children and the aged were to contribute whatever help they could. State-owned workshops were set up to produce weapons for the army. With this decree, the revolutionaries asserted a democratic nation-state's right to conscript all citizens and all resources to meet a national emergency. The limitations the men of 1789 had attempted to impose on governmental power were swept away, and the revolutionary regime established a precedent that would be copied extensively in the wars and revolutions of the twentieth century.

Increasingly, the Convention delegated day-to-day responsibility for running the government to its Committee of Public Safety. This body, first set up in April 1793, had been reconstituted after the defeat of the Girondins. Robespierre, Saint-Just, and several other Montagnard leaders replaced more moderate deputies, including Danton, whose influence was rapidly diminishing, and gave the Committee's policies a radical direction. Within the Committee, some members handled particular problems: Lazare Carnot directed the armies, Robert Lindet dealt with finances. Others, like Robespierre himself, had a more general role. All committee members participated in the spirited, often angry debates over major policies. To ensure that its policies were carried out, the Committee sent its own members or other Montagnard Convention deputies "on mission," with authority to override local officials and army commanders.

The levée en masse and the establishment of the "great" Committee were major steps toward the consolidation of a revolutionary dictatorship. The sans-culotte leaders remained unsatisfied, however. On 5 September 1793, an armed crowd once again surrounded the Convention. Bowing to this pressure, the deputies announced that "terror is the order of the day" and added two prominent radicals, Collot d'Herbois and Billaud-Varennes, to the Committee of Public Safety. In the weeks that followed, the Convention passed a further series of laws to strengthen government powers and show its revolutionary zeal. These new laws ensured that the government of France would remain "revolutionary until the peace," as a decree passed on 10 October 1793 put it. For the next ten months, France lived under a full-fledged revolutionary dictatorship, in which almost all individual rights were officially suspended.

The revolutionary regime moved quickly to control much of the national economy. On 29 September, the Convention voted a general maximum, extending the price controls earlier imposed on grain to a long list of products classified as "necessities" and setting workers' wages at a level meant to raise living standards above what they had been in 1790. A "revolutionary army" of militant sans-culottes was sent to the countryside to force reluctant farmers to turn over requisitioned grain. The government also silenced all political opposition. A system of censorship muzzled the newspapers. The "law of suspects," passed on 17 September, set up surveillance committees throughout the country and ordered them to list all people "who, by their conduct, associations, talk, or writings have shown themselves . . . enemies of liberty." "Suspects" could be jailed indefinitely. In the wake of the law, the Revolutionary Tribunal tried a whole series of prominent political figures: the Queen, the Girondin leaders, and such prominent symbols of the liberal revolution of 1789 as Barnave and Bailly, the mayor of Paris who had put down the Champ de Mars demonstration in July 1791. Their executions dramatized the revolutionary government's determination to eliminate all potential opposition.

THE DICTATORSHIP OF THE COMMITTEE OF PUBLIC SAFETY

The revolutionary dictatorship set up in the fall of 1793 fulfilled many of the sans-culotte movement's demands. But it did so by creating a powerful centralized government that increasingly made itself independent of the Paris popular movement. By giving the Committee of Public Safety the authority to nominate members of all its other committees, the Convention made it the real center of the government. The Convention had to vote to renew the Committee's membership and its powers every thirty days. In the crisis atmosphere that prevailed until the summer of 1794, however, there was little chance of the deputies deciding to undermine the Committee's authority. The Committee gave orders to the ministers and the commanding generals of the French armies. It worked closely with a second group, the Committee of General Security, which oversaw the police. Its *mouchards*, or spies, listened to conversations in the streets and cabarets and kept the government abreast of public opinion.

A law passed on 4 December 1793 specified that the Convention's decrees took precedence over all local measures and gave the central government authority to remove and replace local administrators, reversing the movement toward decentralization that had characterized the liberal stage of the Revolution. This centralized power was enhanced by the tremendous growth in the government's bureaucracy: hundreds of new clerks were hired to see that the new laws were carried out. In the provinces, local Jacobin militants threw themselves into implementing national policies. Urged on by deputies sent from Paris, they denounced violators of the maximum, identified suspects, helped recruit soldiers, and organized care for the wounded. This largely improvised system, dependent on enthusiastic amateurs, nevertheless permitted the Montagnards to govern the country more effectively than any of the earlier revolutionary regimes.

Both contemporaries and historians have recognized Maximilien Robespierre as the leading figure among the Committee of Public Safety's members. It would be hard to imagine a politician more different from Mirabeau, the strongest personality in the National Assembly. Mirabeau had been passionate, profligate, a whirlwind of energy who loved crowds and intrigue; Robespierre was cold, restrained, an intellectual especially influenced by Rousseau's writings. In his own way, however, Robespierre was as skillful a politician as Mirabeau. His carefully thought-out speeches helped maintain support for the government in the Convention and the Jacobin Club. His reputation for disinterested devotion to the public good gave him the nickname "the Incorruptible." In the end, Robespierre would be brought down by his obsession with the vision of an ideal republic and his indifference to the human cost of installing it, but historians who see him as nothing more than a ruthless fanatic overlook his equally real commitment to the principles of democracy, the basis of his popular support.

Robespierre was better known than his colleagues on the Committee of Public Safety because he was called on most often to justify its actions and the system of revolutionary government. His speech of 25 December 1793 argued that a temporary dictatorship was the only way to achieve the constitutional freedoms that had been the original object of the Revolution. "Revolution is the war waged by liberty against its enemies; a constitution is that which crowns the edifice of freedom once victory has been won and the nation is at peace." Until the "enemies of the people" who opposed the movement had been definitively defeated, Robespierre argued, the government had to have virtually unlimited powers. "Those who call them arbitrary or tyrannical," he thundered, "are foolish or perverse sophists who seek to reconcile white with black and black with white: They prescribe the same system for peace and war, for health and sickness . . . "[6] (See Document H.)

This doctrine clearly reflected the circumstances of 1793, in which the men of the Convention had had to combat armed enemies on all sides and take extraordinary measures to keep the population fed. But the idea of using the power of an unfettered government to remake the French people tempted the Montagnard leaders. In a manuscript he left unpublished, Robespierre's young colleague Saint-Just planned an austere modern-day Sparta, in which children would be taken from their parents at the age of seven and raised in state schools, so that their only loyalty would be to the nation. Robespierre talked of a Republic of Virtue, from which private selfishness would be banished. "All has changed in the physical order; all must change in the moral and political order. One half of the world revolution is already achieved, the other half has yet to be accomplished . . . ," he wrote, suggesting an almost limitless program.[7]

DOCUMENT H
MADAME ROLAND AND ROBESPIERRE ON THE TERROR, 1793

The following two passages demonstrate the passions generated by the Reign of Terror. In the memoirs she wrote shortly before her execution, Madame Roland, imprisoned along with her Girondin friends after the journée of 31 May 1793, denounced the Terror as a betrayal of the Revolution's ideals.

"Will history ever be able to paint the horror of these terrible times and the abominable men who filled them with their crimes? . . . What can one compare to the rule of these hypocrites who, always dressed in the mask of justice, always speaking the language of the law, have set up a tribunal to carry out their vengeance, and send to the scaffold, after parodies of judicial procedure, all those whose virtue offends

Continued

DOCUMENT H, *continued*

them, whose talents put them in the shade, or whose wealth makes them envious?

"What Babylon ever matched the spectacle of this Paris, fouled by blood and debauchery, governed by officials who make it their business to spread lies, to sell reputations, to encourage murder? What people has ever corrupted its morals and its instincts to the point of becoming addicted to seeing public executions, and of boiling over with rage when they are delayed . . . ?"

(From *Mémoires de Madame Roland* [Paris: Mercure de France, 1966], pp. 235-36, translation by Jeremy D. Popkin)

In his speech on revolutionary government, Robespierre defended extraordinary measures as necessary to create conditions in which true liberty could flourish.

"The theory of revolutionary government is as new as the Revolution that created it. It is as pointless to seek its origins in the books of the political theorists, who failed to foresee this revolution, as in the laws of the tyrants, who are happy enough to abuse their exercise of authority without seeking out its legal justification.... It behooves us to explain it to all in order that we may rally good citizens, at least, in support of the principles governing the public interest.

"It is the function of government to guide the moral and physical energies of the nation toward the purposes for which it was established.

"The object of constitutional government is to preserve the Republic; the object of revolutionary government is to establish it.

"Revolution is the war waged by liberty against its enemies; a constitution is that which crowns the edifice of freedom once victory has been won and the nation is at peace.

"The revolutionary government has to summon extraordinary activity to its aid precisely because it is at war. It is subjected to less binding and less uniform regulations, because the circumstances in which it finds itself are tempestuous and shifting, above all because it is compelled to deploy, swiftly and incessantly, new resources to meet new and pressing dangers.

"The principal concern of constitutional government is civil liberty; that of revolutionary government, public liberty. Under a constitutional government little more is required than to protect the individual against abuses by the state, whereas revolutionary government is obliged to defend the state itself against the factions that assail it from every quarter.

"To good citizens revolutionary government owes the full protection of the state; to the enemies of the people it owes only death." (From George Rudé, ed., *Robespierre* [Upper Saddle River, N.J.: Prentice Hall, 1967], pp. 58–59. Reprinted by permission of the publisher.)

REVOLUTIONARY CULTURE

The dream of creating a moralized revolutionary utopia was embodied in efforts to create a new revolutionary culture. On 5 October 1793, the Convention replaced the Christian calendar with a new revolutionary one, meant to show that the Revolution had begun a new era in human history. Years were to be counted from the establishment of the French Republic on 22 September 1792, so that 1793–1794 became the Year II. The year was divided into twelve months, each given a poetic name based on its weather—*nivôse* was the month of snow, *floréal* the month when flowers bloomed—and each month was divided into three ten-day weeks, or *décades*.

The new calendar was part of a program of rationalization that included the introduction of the metric system on 1 August 1793, a reform that lasted, and the division of the day into ten hundred-minute hours, which did not. But it was also related to the de-Christianization campaign that reached its height in late 1793. Whereas the National Assembly had intended to reform the Church, the de-Christianizers aimed to abolish it altogether. The movement was initiated by revolutionary militants in provincial areas where anticlerical attitudes were already strong at the end of the Old Regime. They accused Catholic priests of "having kept us stupid, kept our souls enchained by absurd mysteries, play-acting and useless ceremonies."[8] Activists intimidated priests and nuns into renouncing their vows and marrying. They destroyed religious statuary and confiscated church buildings for granaries and other secular purposes.

In November 1793, the de-Christianizers turned Paris's Notre Dame Cathedral into a Temple of Reason and staged a ceremony in honor of a Goddess of Liberty, impersonated by an actress from the Opera. Robespierre and the leaders of the Convention stood aloof from the de-Christianization campaign and eventually reined it in: they feared its potential for further inflaming religious conflict. But to much of the French population, de-Christianization became synonymous with the Revolution. The split between devout Catholics and ardent republicans was to remain one of the main divisions in French life for well over a century.

The revolutionaries also undertook to root out dialect languages and regional cultures, which they saw as threats to national unity. If the Breton peasants resisted the Revolution, one deputy asserted, it was because "they speak a language as different from ours as German or English."[9] Revolutionary militants sought to use language to propagate the new values of the revolutionary regime. They encouraged their fellow citizens to address each other with the familiar "tu" rather than the more formal "vous" that had traditionally been used to show respect for social superiors. Instead of calling each other *Monsieur*, a traditional form of address that literally meant "my lord," men addressed each other as *citoyen* ("citizen"). By promoting a national language and doing away with words that recalled the difference between classes, supporters of the Revolution hoped to create a national community of equal citizens.

In place of France's traditional culture, the revolutionaries of the Year II propagated new symbols and new values. Plays like Sylvain Maréchal's *Last Judgment of Kings*, in which a volcano swallowed up the major European sovereigns, used melodramatic techniques to portray the war as a crusade for the welfare of humanity. On public buildings and government agencies' letterheads, slogans like "Liberty, Equality, Fraternity, or Death" and icons like an all-seeing eye, a reminder of the vigilance every patriot was expected to maintain, replaced the symbols of Catholicism and the monarchy. Revolutionary playing cards featured effigies of Liberty or portraits of the philosophes in place of kings and queens. Jacques-Louis David, the country's most prominent artist, put his talents to use for the revolutionary cause. His posthumous portrait of the assassinated Montagnard journalist Marat, the one real masterpiece of painting from the revolutionary decade, used the techniques normally employed to depict the crucified Christ to glorify the memory of an actual historical figure. David also designed the decorations and costumes for the elaborate public festivals, such as the Festival of the Supreme Being, that were a major part of the Montagnards' cultural campaign. This revolutionary cultural propaganda reinforced the consciousness of a break with the past at the level of everyday life, but its enforced nature created much resentment against the new regime.

THE RADICAL REVOLUTION AND THE SOCIAL ORDER

Along with their program of cultural transformation, the Montagnards also enacted a number of measures meant to favor the lower classes. In the countryside, peasants had often acted to defend their interests without waiting for approval from the Convention. They had refused to make the compensation payments to their landlords that the decrees of 4 August 1789 had called for, and they defended communal rights that the legislators had tried to abolish. Shaken by the peasant revolt in the Vendée and rural uprisings in parts of southern France, the deputies passed several laws aimed at satisfying peasant sentiment. The Convention settled disputes about the interpretation of the National Assembly's decrees of 4 August 1789 in favor of the peasants, rather than the landlords. The redemption payments for feudal dues that peasants had refused to pay were abolished. The Convention also ordered that Church and emigré lands put up for auction be divided into smaller lots so that peasant bidders would have a better chance of purchasing them. In February 1794, the Convention, at Saint-Just's urging, passed its most radical social legislation, the so-called ventôse decrees, which called for the confiscated estates of counterrevolutionaries to be divided up and

distributed free to indigent patriots. Twentieth-century Marxist historians
have interpreted the ventôse decrees as a sign that the revolutionary government was ready to question the sanctity of private property. In practice,
however, this radical proposal was never really implemented.

It was during the period of the Committee of Public Safety's domi-
nance that the nature of the Revolution's impact on women became clearest.
In the Declaration of the Rights of Man and Citizen, the ambiguous word
"man" was used, in its general sense, with no indication whether it was
meant to include both sexes, but the revolutionary constitutions reserved
political rights exclusively for males. The abolition of noble privileges eliminated the wealthy female patronesses who had often played a major role in
French culture; the break-up of convents abolished a sphere in which religious women had been able to live largely outside of male control. Some
revolutionary legislation went against this trend: the 1792 divorce law gave
both sexes the right to initiate proceedings. In general, however, revolutionary reforms changed a situation in which some privileged women had
enjoyed more rights than most unprivileged men into a society in which all
men enjoyed more rights than all women.

A few feminist militants, such as Olympe de Gouges, a self-educated
playwright, saw liberating possibilities in the Revolution's principles. In
1791, she published a "Declaration of the Rights of Woman," proclaiming
that "woman is born free and lives equal to man in her rights,"[10] thereby
employing the revolutionary idea of natural rights to make an argument for
citizenship rights for women. (See Document I.) Woman militants were
active in the revolutionary street demonstrations of 1792, alongside men
from the lower classes, who were also excluded from full citizenship during
that phase of the Revolution. Women were also active in the enragé movement in 1793. Once the Montagnard Convention had established the principle of universal manhood suffrage, however, the revolutionary movement
turned against its female allies. In November 1793, the Convention banned
all public political activity by women and closed down the most important
of the women's political clubs, the Society of Revolutionary Republican
Women, for promoting street agitation. At the Paris Commune, the sans-
culotte leader Chaumette claimed that "it is contrary to all the laws of nature
for a woman to want to make herself a man" by taking on public responsibilities. Women were to confine themselves to the home, where they could
serve the nation by raising their children as patriots.[11] Accused of creating
disorder that favored the enemies of the Revolution, several women
activists, including Olympe de Gouges, were guillotined.

Excluded from the revolutionary movement, some women turned
against it. Female participation in bread riots had served to radicalize the
Revolution in 1789, but by 1794 such protests often expressed counterrevolutionary sentiments. Women were prominent in many protests against the
Civil Constitution of the Clergy. Many historians have concluded that it was

DOCUMENT I
FRENCH WOMEN ADDRESS THE NATIONAL ASSEMBLY, 1791

*Etta Palm d'Aelders, one of the leaders of the movement for political rights for
women, published this address to the National Assembly in the summer of 1791.*

"Gentlemen,
The chains of Frenchmen have fallen with a crash; the sound of their fall
caused despots to grow pale and shook their thrones; an astonished
Europe fixed an attentive eye on the star that illuminates France and on
the august senate which represents a people who join the love of being
just to the will to be free.

"Yes, Gentlemen, you have broken the iron sceptre in order to replace
it with the olive branch; you have sworn to protect the weak. It is a question of your duty, your honor, your interest, to destroy down to their
roots these gothic laws which abandon the weakest but [also] the most
worthy half of humanity to a humiliating existence, to an eternal slavery.

"You have restored to man the dignity of his being in recognizing his
rights; you will no longer allow woman to groan beneath an arbitrary
authority; that would be to overturn the fundamental principles on
which rests the stately edifice you are raising by your untiring labors for
the happiness of Frenchmen. It is too late to equivocate. Philosophy has
drawn truth from the darkness; the time has come; justice, sister of liberty, calls all individuals to the equality of rights, without discrimination of
sex; the laws of a free people must be equal for all beings, like the air and
the sun. For too long, alas, the imprescriptible rights of nature have been
misprized; for too long, bizarre laws, the worthy product of centuries of
ignorance, have afflicted humanity; finally, for too long, the most odious
tyranny was consecrated by absurd laws." (From Darline Gay Levy, Harriet Branson Applewhite, and Mary Durham Johnson, eds., *Women in
Revolutionary Paris* [Urbana: University of Illinois Press, 1979], pp. 75–76.
Reprinted with permission of the University of Illinois Press.)

during the revolutionary period that the division between a male population attracted to liberal and rationalist ideas and a female population loyal
to traditional religious beliefs, which was to characterize France throughout
the nineteenth century, first emerged.

Although the Montagnard Convention firmly excluded women from
the public sphere, it took an important symbolic step by becoming the first
European government to abolish slavery and grant full political rights to
blacks. The fighting that had continued in the key French colony of Saint-
Domingue since the slave revolt of August 1791 prompted this step. The

Convention had dispatched commissioners and troops to the island in September 1792. They threw their support to the slaves, against the white planters who were prepared to accept British intervention to restore their positions. The Jacobin delegate Sonthonax proclaimed a partial emancipation of the slaves in August 1793, and the Convention confirmed this policy in February 1794. It also seated a black deputy, the former slave J.-B. Belley. The Convention's actions failed to save France's control over its Caribbean colony, but they set an important precedent in the struggle against slavery.

THE GREAT TERROR AND THERMIDOR

Obsessed with maintaining national unity, the Montagnard leaders engaged in a constantly intensifying hunt for hidden conspirators whose activities they blamed for the Revolution's continuing difficulties. In the provinces, some of the deputies on mission interpreted their mandate to "make terror the order of the day" in extreme terms. At Nantes, Jean-Baptiste Carrier, sent to crush the peasant guerrilla war that had continued even after the defeat of the Vendean army in the summer of 1793, rid himself of the several thousand suspected rebels crowding the prisons by mass executions in which victims were thrown into the Loire River. To end rural resistance, "infernal columns" of republican troops scoured the countryside, burning villages and fields, and killing civilians indiscriminately. The guerrillas retaliated by massacring local republican loyalists and government troops. The total loss of life in the region, where fighting continued for several years after the fall of Robespierre, may have exceeded 100,000.

Another spectacular feature of the Terror was its use against an increasing number of the Revolution's most dedicated supporters. Already in 1793, the arrested Girondin deputy Vergniaud had commented prophetically that "the Revolution, like Saturn, is devouring its children." Those executed in October and November 1793 had included prominent leaders of the revolutionary movement of 1789 as well as dedicated republicans from 1792. In the winter of 1794, the Terror swept up the major enragé spokesmen and a number of Convention deputies accused of corruption or involvement in a murky "foreign plot" against the Revolution. Tension and fear reached a peak with two spectacular show trials in March and April 1794. First, the Committee of Public Safety arrested the most prominent spokesmen of the Paris sans-culotte movement. The journalist Jacques Hébert, author of the *Père Duchêne*, the pamphlet-journal that had become the symbol of radical patriotism, and several of his supporters were tried and executed on trumped-up charges. Hébert's real crime was his personal popularity. He represented a possible alternative to the Committee, whose harsh measures were undermining its support. His execution was also intended to forestall any further sans-culotte agitation against the Committee of Public Safety's policies. Already in the previous fall, the Convention had limited the Paris sections to two public meetings a week, and by voting to pay those who attended section meetings, it had deprived those assemblies of their spontaneous character. An extensive police network made sure that there would be no repetitions of the bread riots and protests that had been so frequent in 1792 and 1793.

Having brought the sans-culottes under control with the execution of Hébert, the Committee then turned against a group of Convention deputies who had raised their voices against the extension of the Terror and who seemed to have support among the middle classes. Whereas Hébert and his followers had been "ultras" who wanted to push the Revolution too far, Robespierre charged, these men—particularly the famed orator Danton and the journalist Camille Desmoulins, who had criticized the Committee in his paper, the *Vieux Cordelier*—were "citras" who wanted to stop the Revolution before it had gone far enough. In powerful speeches before the Revolutionary Tribunal, Danton threatened to turn the tables on the Committee and show the baselessness of the charges against him. The Convention hurriedly passed a decree changing the trial procedures to silence him. The Danton group's execution on 5 April 1794 seemed to show that there were no remaining limits to the process of the Terror.

Rather than reassuring the Committee, the executions of the Hébertists and Dantonists merely accelerated the pace of the Terror. The atmosphere of enforced conformism and the evident lack of genuine enthusiasm that the Terror itself had engendered made the movement's leaders even more fearful. Saint-Just complained that "the Revolution has become frozen" and called for ever more drastic measures against hidden counterrevolutionaries. On 8 June 1794, Robespierre presided over an elaborately staged Festival of the Supreme Being, designed by the artist Jacques-Louis David and meant to demonstrate the nation's spiritual unity and adherence to revolutionary principles. But just two days later, Robespierre rammed through the Convention a law that stripped suspects sent before the Revolutionary Tribunal of all rights to defend themselves. Convention deputies no longer enjoyed any special immunity from arrest. This "law of 22 prairial" unleashed the so-called Great Terror of the summer of 1794. In six weeks, the guillotine decapitated over 1,300 victims in Paris alone.

How a revolutionary movement begun in the name of individual liberty could have culminated in so much bloodshed, and how Robespierre, an eloquent advocate of human rights, could have become the Terror's main proponent, are questions that continue to be debated after more than two hundred years. Critics of the Revolution, from Edmund Burke to modern historians such as François Furet, have seen the Terror as an outgrowth of the movement's utopian and unrealistic aspirations. Unable to admit that their goal of a perfectly just society was unattainable, Robespierre and his followers blamed all those who refused to accept their leadership; incapable of admitting that differences of opinion could be legitimate, they classified all opponents as enemies and felt justified in condemning them to death. Robespierre's personality—his tendency to think in abstractions, his absolute faith in his own righteousness, and his suspicion of others' motives—made him especially prone to resort to punitive measures and to ignore their human cost. Supporters of the Revolution at the time and a long line of subsequent historians, including both liberals and Marxists, have countered this analysis by blaming the Terror primarily on the difficult circumstances the revolutionaries had to face. From the outset, the Revolution's enemies were themselves ready to resort to force to oppose the movement. Furthermore, the revolutionary leadership had to take forceful measures to prevent even bloodier outbreaks of popular violence; the legalized Terror was an effort to forestall massacres such as those of September 1792. Historians who see the Terror as explicable in these terms recognize Robespierre's central role in its dangerous expansion in 1794 but see him as a complex personality, whose humanitarian instincts were as genuine as his hatred of opponents. Some see signs that he was looking for a way to bring the uncontrolled killing to an end, perhaps by using the Law of Suspects against the most violent advocates of the guillotine. If so, however, he was unable to achieve his purpose before he himself fell victim to the deadly political rules he had helped establish.

THE REVOLUTION VICTORIOUS

The Great Terror peaked just as the real dangers to the republican government's security were fading. Even before the last of the federalist uprisings in the south had been defeated, the French armies on the frontiers, their numbers swollen by the levée en masse, had regained the initiative against the Austrians and their allies. To replace the many noble commanders who had fled abroad, the Convention promoted patriotic officers from the lower ranks who had demonstrated their abilities, creating a group of young, daring generals devoted to the republican cause. The Committee of Public Safety took charge of overall strategy. From Paris, Carnot sent orders to the field armies and ruthlessly weeded out the timid and incompetent, executing defeated commanders and even some generals who won battles but failed to pursue the beaten enemy with sufficient vigor. Deputies on mission made sure the Committee's orders were carried out. The troops were formed into new units under a policy known as the *amalgame*, in which the separate units of veteran soldiers from the old royal army and draftees and volunteers of the new citizen force were melded together. The new mixed units thus combined experience and patriotic enthusiasm.

By late 1793, the French armies had learned to make good use of the modernized, mobile artillery developed at the end of the Old Regime to

VUE DE LA MONTAGNE ELEVÉE AU CHAMP DE LA REUNION

pour la fête qui y a été célébrée en l'honneur de l'Être Suprême le Décadi 20 Prairial de l'an 2.⁰ de la République Française

A Paris chez Chéreau Rue Jacques, aux deux Colonnes, vers la Fontaine Sveurin. N.° 25.

Festival of the Supreme Being

On June 8, 1794, Robespierre presided over an elaborate "Festival of the Supreme Being," staged by Jacques-Louis David, the leading revolutionary artist. An artificial mountain, topped by a liberty tree, was constructed on the Champ de Mars to represent the triumph of the Montagnards in the Convention; a giant statue of Hercules on a pillar stood for the French people. Other symbols conveyed the message that the Revolution had restored French society to harmony with nature. Two days after this celebration of harmony, the Convention passed the drastic law of 22 prairial II, allowing the excesses of the Great Terror.
Photo credit: Library of Congress.

support the spirit and courage of their citizen soldiers. The hastily recruited soldiers could not execute the elaborate maneuvers customary in eighteenth-century warfare, but they proved successful when they were deployed in loose formations or assembled into large columns for charging enemy lines. In September 1793, the French victory at Hondschoote forced the English to lift the siege of Dunkirk. The following month, a victory at Wattignies drove the Austrians back into Belgium. The Spanish drive into Roussillon was beaten off, and in December, a young artillery officer named Napoleone Buonaparte distinguished himself by ousting the English from Toulon. French successes continued in the spring of 1794, and at the battle of Fleurus on 26 June 1794, the French armies in the north decisively defeated the Austrians, who withdrew from Belgium. The danger of foreign invasion could no longer be used to justify the policy of terror.

THERMIDOR

As the crisis atmosphere of 1793 faded, a number of deputies in the Convention and even within the Committee of Public Safety began to turn against Robespierre's terror policy. Some were cautious moderates who had hesitated to speak out when the fate of the Revolution seemed in suspense, but the most active were former terrorists or friends of the Dantonists who feared that Robespierre planned to have them arrested. When Robespierre gave a speech on 8 thermidor (eleventh month of the Revolutionary calendar) denouncing a plot which he said was directed against him, these deputies decided they had no time to lose. On the next day, 9 thermidor, their leaders unexpectedly took the floor in the Convention to accuse Robespierre of plotting to make himself dictator. The Convention shouted Robespierre down when he tried to reply. The deputies then voted overwhelmingly for the arrest of Robespierre and several of his supporters. Robespierre and his fellow arrestees briefly escaped from their captors and rallied some supporters at the Hôtel-de-Ville, the seat of Paris's city government. They appealed to the Paris sections to back them. But the mass of the Paris sans-culottes, alienated from the Montagnards by the execution of the Hébertists and the repression of the popular movement, made no effort to support them. Early the next day, the Convention's troops captured the escaped prisoners and hustled Robespierre, Saint-Just, and several dozen of their supporters to the guillotine. Once again, the mechanism of the Revolution had turned against those who had set it in motion. But 9 thermidor marked a turning point: instead of intensifying the revolutionary process, the victors, no longer pushed along by organized popular protest, began to dismantle the machinery of revolution.

NOTES

1. Cited in David Jordan, *The King's Trial* (Berkeley: University of California Press, 1979), 136.

2. Ibid., 172.

3. Cited in Michael Walzer, ed., *Regicide and Revolution* (New York: Columbia University Press, 1992), 212.

4. Saint-Just, *Oeuvres choisies* (Paris: Gallimard, 1968), 76.

5. Cited in William Sewell, *Work and Revolution in France* (Cambridge: Cambridge University Press, 1980), 110.

6. Cited in George Rudé, ed., *Robespierre* (Upper Saddle River, N.J.: Prentice Hall, 1967), 59.

7. Cited in Rudé, *Robespierre*, 69.

8. Cited in Louis Trénard, *Lyon de l'Encyclopédie au préromantisme* (Paris: Presses Universitaires de France, 1958), 365.

9. Cited in Serge Bianchi, *La révolution culturelle de l'an II* (Paris: Aubier, 1982), 197.

10. Cited in Darline Gay Levy, Harriet B. Applewhite, and Mary D. Johnson, eds., *Women in Revolutionary Paris*, 1789–1795 (Urbana: University of Illinois Press, 1979), 90.

11. Cited in Darline Gay Levy and Harriet B. Applewhite, "Women and Militant Citizenship in Revolutionary Paris," in Sara Melzer and Leslie Rabine, eds., *Rebel Daughters: Women and the French Revolution* (New York: Oxford University Press, 1992), 97.

CHAPTER 6

THE RETURN TO ORDER, 1794–1799

THE "BOURGEOIS REPUBLIC" AND THE SEARCH FOR ORDER

To a remarkable degree, the first five years of the Revolution, from 1789 to 1794, had set the shape of French society for decades to come. The revolutionaries had eliminated corporate privileges and given equal rights to all male citizens. They had established a strong central government, strengthened the position of the property-owning bourgeoisie and of peasant landholders, redefined the gender division between men and women, and made France the first European country to abolish slavery in its colonies. They had established a secular society, and they had created a formidable military machine. By doing all this in just five years, however, the Revolution had shattered the equilibrium of French society. With the fall of Robespierre, the forces of resistance to continual change came to the surface. The dominant theme of the years from 1794 to 1799 was the search for order and political stability, rather than an effort to accomplish further reforms.

The overthrow of Robespierre on 9 thermidor did not immediately result in a change of political regime. The National Convention, elected in September 1792, continued to govern the country for another 15 months. In October 1795, the deputies of the "thermidorian" Convention, as the legislators who survived Robespierre have come to be known, transferred power to two new legislative councils and a five-man executive committee known as the Directory. The political leaders of the Directory, which governed

France until 1799, were mostly former Convention deputies, and the policies they followed largely continued those adopted after thermidor, so that the period from 1794 to 1799 is usually treated as a unit.

The thermidorian and Directory governments both claimed to be consolidating the essential achievements of the Revolution while avoiding the excesses committed during the Reign of Terror. Liberty and equality were still official slogans, the government remained republican in form, and the revolutionary calendar, which glorified the Convention's proclamation of the Republic in September 1792, remained in use. The postthermidorian Republic carried on the war against Europe begun in 1792 and kept up the struggle against the Catholic Church. The biggest difference in policy between this period and the one that preceded it was in the relationship between the government and the lower classes. The thermidorian Convention revoked almost all the measures taken in 1793 and 1794 in response to pressure from the sans-culotte movement. The new constitution adopted in 1795 drastically curtailed the political rights of poorer citizens. Sobered by what they saw as the consequences of unlimited democracy, the thermidorians openly worked to establish a political regime dominated by the wealthy and educated. Only in this way, they believed, could social order be reconciled with a republican form of government. The "bourgeois Republic" of 1794–1799 was thus the forerunner of the liberal constitutional societies of nineteenth-century Europe, in which hereditary privileges were curtailed but the masses were still excluded from voting.

THE THERMIDORIAN REACTION

Initially it was not clear whether the Convention deputies who had overthrown Robespierre also meant to eliminate his methods. Many of the leading thermidorian conspirators, such as the ex-priest Fouché, one of the most prominent activists in the de-Christianization movement of 1793, had been active in the Terror. But thermidor unleashed a reaction against the Terror and the radical Revolution that soon escaped the plotters' control. For the next five years, the question of how to repudiate the worst excesses committed in 1793–1794 without endangering the Revolution as a whole and all of those who had participated in the revolutionary government of those years remained a major issue.

Since they had overthrown Robespierre because he had tyrannized the Convention and the people, the thermidorian plotters found themselves compelled to dismantle the dictatorial apparatus of the Terror. Thousands of prisoners arrested under the Law of Suspects were released from prison, and several of the most prominent architects of the Terror, including Carrier, who had overseen the massacres of rebels in Brittany, and Fouquier-Tinville, the prosecutor of the Revolutionary Tribunal, were tried

Robespierre Guillotining the Executioner
After his overthrow on 9 thermidor Year II, Robespierre and the guillotine were linked together as symbols of how the radical Revolution had swallowed up the movement's earlier supporters. In the original caption to this engraving, each of the scaffolds represented a different group of former revolutionary leaders executed during the Terror.
Source: Photothèque des Musées dela Ville de Paris.

and executed, despite their protests that they had simply carried out policies approved by the Convention as a whole. In November 1794, the Convention ordered the closing of the Paris Jacobin Club. In Paris, bands of elegantly dressed middle-class youths, the *jeunesse dorée* or "gilded youth," chased down former sans-culotte activists and destroyed symbols of the radical Revolution, such as the busts of Marat that had been placed in all public buildings after his assassination. In the provinces, similar groups were even more violent; a "white terror" took the place of the "red terror" of 1794 as former Jacobin militants were killed in Lyon, Marseille, and other areas where counterrevolutionary sentiment was strong.

THE DEFEAT OF THE SANS-CULOTTES

The "thermidorian reaction" also turned against the Revolution's social and economic policies. The Convention dismantled the maximum system and left prices free to find their own levels. Without the threat of the guillotine to sustain it, the assignat rapidly lost all value. This runaway inflation benefited peasants with grain reserves and middle-class speculators, who scooped up national lands at bargain prices, but it was devastating to the poor, whose wages lagged far behind the skyrocketing price of bread. An exceptionally harsh winter added to their misery. Food prices soared and supplies of grain and firewood ran short as the frozen Seine shut down transportation to Paris.

As winter turned into spring, the Paris sans-culottes reacted to their situation by staging two massive protest demonstrations, the journées of 12–13 germinal III (1–2 April 1795) and 1–4 prairial III (20–23 May 1795). On both occasions, large crowds of men and women from the working-class faubourgs on the edge of the city surrounded the thermidorian Convention's meeting hall. They demanded "bread and the Constitution of 1793," the democratic constitution approved by the Montagnard Convention but never put into effect. These demonstrations showed that neither the repression of the sans-culotte movement during the Terror nor the thermidorian reaction had suppressed lower-class activism. But the repeated purges of the movement had deprived the sans-culottes of effective leadership, and few members of the thermidorian Convention were willing to ally themselves with a popular protest.

The prairial insurrection proved to be the last major episode of popular activism during the revolutionary period. On 1 prairial III, a huge crowd invaded the Convention and massacred one of the deputies. Under this pressure, a handful of former Montagnard deputies urged the Convention to take action to satisfy the sans-culottes' demands. The majority of the deputies remained silent, however, and outside the Convention, troops and National Guards from the middle-class districts, assisted by members of the

jeunesse dorée, eventually drove the demonstrators back. The city was finally pacified three days later, several crowd leaders were executed, and in the
repression that followed, most sans-culotte activists were forced to give up
the weapons they had used in protest marches and were deprived of their
political rights. The Montagnard deputies who had sided with them were
tried and sentenced to death. Four of them succeeded in committing suicide
before they could be guillotined, winning fame as the "martyrs of prairial."
The defeat of the prairial uprising eliminated both the organized popular
movement in Paris that had played such a major role in revolutionary politics and the last deputies willing to identify themselves with its demands in
the Convention.

The defeat of the popular movement accelerated the reaction against
everything associated with the radical phase of the Revolution. Instead of
dressing to look like sans-culottes, the wealthier classes reverted to elegant,
sometimes extravagant costumes that emphasized their special status, such
as the provocative see-through dresses worn by some fashionable Parisi-
ennes. While the poor continued to struggle to afford bread, the wealthy
crowded cafés, restaurants, and theaters where they applauded plays that
denounced the horrors of Robespierre's reign and presented the sans-
culottes as bloodthirsty monsters. In the streets, the honorific term "Monsieur" ousted the revolutionary "Citizen" as the preferred form of address,
and the polite form "vous" regained its ascendancy. Objects of sympathy
during the early revolutionary years, the poor were now seen as violent and
dangerous, needing to be disciplined by the rigorous workings of economic
laws.

COUNTERREVOLUTION
AND THE CONSTITUTION OF 1795

By this time it was clear that the Convention would never put the radical
democratic constitutional plan of 1793 into effect. The discrediting of revolutionary radicalism raised the hopes of counterrevolutionaries, both those
inside France and the emigrés abroad. In Paris, even some Convention
deputies toyed with the idea of proclaiming Louis XVI's young son as king
and setting up a regency council chosen among themselves to govern the
country until he reached adulthood. The boy's death on 8 June 1795 scuttled
this project, however. Louis XVI's brother, the Comte de Provence, who had
fled the country in 1789, proclaimed himself the rightful heir to the throne,
taking the title of Louis XVIII. From his Italian refuge, he issued the Declaration of Verona, announcing that he intended to restore the privileges of the
nobility and the Church and punish all those who had taken part in the Revolution since its inception. His intransigent position ruled out any possible
compromise with the thermidorian deputies.

In western France, the fall of Robespierre had allowed the chouan guerrilla forces that had become active during the Vendée rebellion to reorganize themselves. In the spring of 1795, their leaders established contact with the British government and French royalist emigrés across the Channel. The British promised to land an emigré army if the rebels could seize a port on the French coast. Misunderstandings between the French monarchists and their country's traditional enemy crippled this alliance from the start. The British did transport 4,500 French emigrés to the Quiberon peninsula in Brittany at the end of June 1795, but promised reinforcements never arrived. Republican forces under General Hoche quickly surrounded the royalists and forced them to surrender. Under a law requiring the execution of emigrés captured bearing arms, 748 royalist officers were immediately put to death. The Quiberon disaster devastated the emigrés, who came to suspect a British plot to kill them off, and weakened the chouan resistance. By mid-1796, Hoche's forces had pacified Brittany and the Vendée and ended armed resistance to the republican government's authority in the region.

While the royalist insurrection in the west was being crushed, the thermidorian Convention voted to scrap the 1793 constitution and draft a new document. In this new Constitution of 1795 (also known as the Constitution of the Year III, according to the republican calendar), the deputies sought to prevent the rise of another dictatorial government. To do this they believed they needed to exclude the common people from politics. The new Constitution of 1795 limited the right to vote and to hold office to the wealthiest taxpayers: only about 30,000 met the requirements to serve in the departmental electoral colleges, where deputies were to be chosen. All references to social rights were eliminated from the constitution, and the deputies added a "declaration of duties" designed to remind the poor of their obligation to respect the rights of property and the authority of the law. (See Document J.)

The administrative system remained highly centralized, but the powers of the central government were carefully divided. The deputies took to heart the abbé Sieyès's warning that the Terror had turned the French government into a "Re-Total," invading all aspects of life, rather than a "Re-Public," limited only to those matters that were truly of general concern. To prevent the creation of an all-encompassing central power, the five-member Directory, the executive branch of the new constitution, was held in check by a two-house legislature, made up of a Council of 500 and a smaller Council of Elders, limited to deputies over forty years of age.

The announcement of a popular referendum to approve the new constitution inspired one more counterrevolutionary assault. In Paris, the sectional assemblies, purged of sans-culotte activists, had fallen into the hands of men who had participated in the jeunesse dorée's activities during the thermidorian reaction. The Convention gave this movement a target by passing a decree requiring voters to choose two-thirds of the deputies for the new Councils from the outgoing members of the Convention. The

Document J

A Justification of the Constitution of 1795

F.-A. Boissy d'Anglas had been a deputy to the National Assembly and then a conservative member of the National Convention. After the overthrow of Robespierre, he chaired the committee that drafted the socially conservative Constitution of 1795 and presented the draft to the thermidorian Convention in July 1795. In this passage, he justifies provisions that excluded the common people from voting or holding political office.

"We must be governed by the best; the best are those who are best educated and most interested in the maintenance of the laws: now, with very few exceptions, you find such men only among those who, owning a piece of property, are devoted to the country that contains it, to the laws that protect it, to the tranquility that maintains it, and who owe to this property and to the economic security it provides the education that has made them capable of discussing with wisdom and exactitude the advantages and inconveniences of the laws that determine the fate of their native land. The man without property, on the other hand, requires a constant exercise of virtue to interest himself in a social order that preserves nothing for him, and to resist actions and movements that hold out hopes to him. One must assume him to be possessed of very sophisticated and profound conceptions for him to prefer genuine good to apparent good, and future interests to immediate interests. If you give men without property political rights without reservations, and if they ever find themselves on the benches of the legislature, they will excite unrest or allow it to be excited without fearing its effects; they will establish or allow to be established taxes disastrous for commerce and agriculture, because they will not have appreciated, or feared, or foreseen the deplorable results; they will precipitate us, finally, into violent convulsions like those from which we are barely recovering, the woes of which will be felt for so long everywhere in France." (From Paul Beik, ed., *The French Revolution* [New York: Harper and Row, 1970], p. 318. Reprinted with permission.)

Convention's intention was to prevent any widespread purge of republicans—exactly what the Paris activists were determined to accomplish. When the Convention refused to count most of the votes cast in Paris against this "two-thirds" decree and declared it approved, the section assemblies mobilized an armed insurrection in protest.

To suppress this uprising of 13 vendémiaire IV (5 October 1795), the Convention called on troops from the regular army. This use of the army to maintain the regime set a dangerous precedent, particularly since one of the officers employed was the young general Napoleon Bonaparte, who thus brought himself to the attention of government leaders; he was duly rewarded with his first independent military command. The defeat of the vendémiaire uprising demonstrated that even an unpopular revolutionary government could now count on the army to put down a challenge from the streets. Ironically, a counterrevolutionary movement aimed at restricting popular participation in politics thus proved to be the last mass insurrection of the revolutionary period.

THE DIRECTORY

A French journalist once remarked that the Directory was the only regime in the country's history that no one ever expressed nostalgia for after it fell. It has been remembered as a period of flagrant corruption, unscrupulous intrigue, and fruitless confrontation, the history of which lacked the dramatic high points that dominated the earlier years of the Revolution or the Napoleonic period that followed it. Recent historians have demonstrated that the Directory years were not as chaotic as this stereotype suggests. The period saw the consolidation of important institutions that continued to structure French life in the nineteenth century and saw crucial developments in the relationship between revolutionary France and its European neighbors. Perhaps the regime's greatest weakness was that it failed to inspire loyalty even among its own leaders: their betrayal eventually destroyed it.

The political leaders of the Directory lacked the stature of their predecessors under the National Assembly and the Convention. Paul Barras, a corrupt thermidorian Convention deputy who served on the five-man Executive Directory throughout its existence, symbolized their shortcomings. Barras had no commitment to revolutionary ideals, but he had a single-minded devotion to keeping himself and men like him in power, even at the cost of disregarding the republican constitution he had helped to create. Most of his fellow politicians were less flamboyant than Barras. The majority were successful members of the bourgeoisie who had been active in local affairs during the early years of the Revolution. Having held public office after 1789 and often having invested in national lands, they had good reason to support the republican regime against any counterrevolution. In general, however, they had avoided taking strong positions on controversial issues prior to 1794. Their caution enabled them to survive the Terror, but the result was that France was governed during the Directory years primarily by men concerned not to stick their necks out. In a crisis, these men were easily pushed aside by cynical revolutionary veterans like Barras.

Despite this weakness at the top, the Directory succeeded in restoring a certain degree of order to a country racked by six years of revolutionary upheaval. The regime benefited from a favorable economic climate, due to a series of good harvests. After an unsuccessful effort to replace the worthless assignats with *mandats*, another form of paper money that also soon lost all value, the Directory in 1797 reverted to metallic currency. By 1798, monetary stability had been achieved and economic growth resumed. The Directory also resolved the government debt problem that had forced the calling of the Estates-General in 1789 and that had dogged every subsequent revolutionary government. In 1797, it "consolidated" the public debt, writing off two-thirds of it. This partial bankruptcy freed subsequent governments from a painful burden. To put the government on a sound financial footing, the Directory systematized the collection of the taxes on land and on business activity imposed by the National Assembly and added new taxes on luxury items and a real-estate tax calculated according to the number of doors and windows in each taxpayer's house. Easier to collect than the multitude of Old Regime taxes, these four taxes remained the main bases of French government revenue for a century. To enforce its policies, the Directory continued the centralization of authority begun during the Terror, sending appointed officials, called commissioners of the executive power, to oversee departmental administrations. The apparatus of the central government continued to grow throughout the period, but its increased effectiveness was masked by the government's inability to get rid of armed counterrevolutionary groups and bandit gangs in many rural areas.

An important aspect of the Directory period was the consolidation of a set of institutions that gave the country a new kind of bourgeois elite. The Convention had already begun to replace the aristocratically dominated royal academies of the old regime with more professionally oriented institutions for research and teaching, such as the Museum of Natural History, founded in 1793, the *Ecole normale* for teachers, and the *Ecole polytechnique* for engineers, both set up to teach an elite of outstanding students from all over the country in 1794. New medical schools, organized along scientific lines, were also opened that year, and the Institute, an organization intended to bring together France's leading scientists and philosophers, replaced the abolished academies in 1795. In contrast to the academies of the old regime, members of these new institutions were supposed to be recruited strictly on the basis of merit. In practice, they served to elevate the status of a largely bourgeois intellectual elite recruited on a national scale. Modified somewhat during the subsequent Napoleonic period, these schools and institutes formed the basis for the highly competitive and centralized educational and scientific system that still characterizes France today.

These new institutions served to make Paris the world's center in science and medicine for the next several decades. They also reflected the fact that professors and scientists held more positions of political responsibility under the Directory than in almost any other French regime. The majority of the period's intellectuals hailed the Revolution for having cleared the way for the triumph of rationalism by its destruction of the old academies and the

Church, and the Directory period saw the publication of important works that summed up the Enlightenment's worldview in a new, more rigorously scientific manner, such as the astronomer Laplace's *Exposition of the System of the World*. Leading philosophers and social thinkers formed a group known as the *Idéologues* and elaborated the science of *idéologie*, the analytic study of human thought. Taking new advances in medicine and anatomy into account, the Ideologues tried to provide a purely scientific explanation of the functioning of the mind and the laws governing human society.

THE DIRECTORY AND EUROPE

While the Directory thus took some important steps to stabilize conditions inside France, its most striking achievements were military and diplomatic. Even before the fall of Robespierre, the French had regained the initiative in the war. In the second half of 1794, the revolutionary armies swept through Belgium and the Rhineland. In the first months of 1795, they occupied the Netherlands, where they sponsored a "Batavian revolution" in which the old ruler, the Stadholder, was expelled, and a republican constitution on the French model was drawn up. The Netherlands became the first of the several "sister republics" established during the Directory period. The "sister republics" were established by natives of their countries, but, unlike the French Republic, they did not have a strong base of popular support and were dependent on French military support. For their services in liberating the country and protecting its new government, the French imposed a heavy indemnity on the Dutch, a policy they repeated in other territories in following years. The revolutionary war began to change into a war of conquest, undertaken for the profit of republican France.

France's military successes had important repercussions on the European balance of power. In April 1795, republican France and monarchist Prussia signed the Peace of Basel. The Prussians, preoccupied with the recent uprising in Poland and the need to limit Russian expansion there, became the first Old Regime government to treat the French Republic as a regular participant in the European state system. And the French increasingly acted like a "normal" European power. By 1795, their expectations that foreign populations would welcome French troops as liberators had evaporated. The brief French occupation of Belgium and the region around Mainz in 1793 had shown that revolutionary principles were welcomed by a small minority but often resisted by peasant and urban populations attached to their traditional privileges and to Catholicism. In response, the French themselves came to treat the territories they occupied as conquests, to be exploited from the point of view of France's national interest. In October 1795, France annexed Belgium, enlarging its borders in the same way that Prussia, Austria, and Russia had by completing the partition of Poland.

Under the Directory, France continued to expand. In 1796 and 1797, French armies penetrated deep into Germany and Italy, where the young general Bonaparte scored spectacular successes, occupying the peninsula as far south as Rome. He applied the policies pioneered in the Netherlands, backing local movements to set up "sister republics," which were required to pay heavy indemnities to their liberators. The French raided Italian churches and palaces and sent many of the country's artistic masterpieces back to Paris, outraging Italian cultural sensibilities. These exactions alienated the local populations, which came to consider French-style reforms a smokescreen for exploitation. Anti-French uprisings in some parts of Italy and resistance to occupation in the Rhineland helped confirm the French impression that they needed to keep the territories they occupied under tight control. But heavy-handed military rule only widened the gap between the French and the foreign populations under their domination.

France's expansion had important consequences for the army's place in French society and politics. The citizen-soldiers of 1792–1793 turned into battle-hardened professionals who lost contact with the civilian population at home. The soldiers also came to have strong personal loyalties to their commanders. For their part, the leading generals became less and less patient with interference from the government in Paris. Financially independent because of the money they extracted from the regions their armies conquered, they developed their own policies and became important influences in domestic politics. The various political factions in Paris cultivated generals sympathetic to their views, encouraging the growth of army influence.

No other general profited more from this situation than the young commander of the Army of Italy, Napoleon Bonaparte. By the summer of 1797, with his army having crossed the Alps and threatening Vienna, the Austrians seemed ready to make peace, as Prussia had done in 1795 and Spain in 1796. Bonaparte, acting on his own without approval of the Directory, negotiated a treaty in which Austria ceded its claims to Belgium and recognized the French-sponsored republics in Italy; in exchange, he presented them with Venice, which his troops had conquered. This exchange of territories, carried out without any regard for their inhabitants' wishes, showed how completely France had abandoned any pretense of extending the principle of national self-determination to other peoples.

With Austria out of the war and Britain limited to naval operations and the capture of France's overseas colonies, the French tide of conquest rolled on. In 1798, Switzerland, renamed the Helvetic Republic, was added to the belt of satellite states surrounding the "Great Nation," as the French referred to themselves, and in early 1799 a short-lived Parthenopean Republic replaced the Kingdom of Naples in southern Italy. The Directory, fearful of its leading general's growing popularity, had been happy to send Bonaparte on an expedition to Egypt in 1798. He landed and defeated the Turks in the Battle of the Pyramids, but British admiral Horatio Nelson's destruction of the French fleet at Aboukir cut him off from France. With its forces spread over half of Europe and its best general trapped at the far end of the Mediterranean, the Directory's position was shakier than it appeared.

THE "POLITICS OF THE BALANCE"

Although it expanded French power abroad, the Directory could not achieve political stability at home. The popular sans-culotte movement had been crushed in the spring of 1795, and peasant discontent had died down, but the vendémiaire uprising in October 1795 showed that the new regime could not trust the middle-class landowners, businessmen, and professionals to whom the constitution-makers of 1795 tried to appeal. Many of these men, including a number who had profited from the Revolution by buying national lands, had been deeply shaken by the Terror and remained hostile to the republican government. They supported politicians who hinted broadly at the restoration of the monarchy and a purge of all those who had held important political positions during the radical phase of the Revolution. On the other hand, a significant number of former Jacobins remained politically active, denouncing the Directory government for being insufficiently dedicated to the principles of liberty and equality. The religious issue remained divisive: militant republicans and Idéologue intellectuals continued to identify Catholicism with counterrevolution and obscurantism, while the faithful denounced the regime's restrictions on worship and religious education.

Rather than following a clear policy in either direction, the government of the Directory strove to remain above politics. Its policy consisted of a series of alternating blows aimed against the royalists and the neo-Jacobins. This "balance-beam policy" multiplied the regime's enemies without gaining it substantial support. In May 1796, the government attacked the radical left. It arrested the agitator Gracchus Babeuf, an agrarian radical who advocated communal ownership of property, along with a number of former supporters of Robespierre. Babeuf had absorbed the lesson of the defeated sans-culotte uprisings in 1795, concluding that the regime could not be overthrown by a spontaneous popular insurrection. Instead, he tried to organize a conspiracy to overthrow the Directory and install a dictatorship that would carry out his communist program. His plan never had much chance of success, but his arrest presented the Directory with a chance to pose as the firm defender of social order and the rights of property. The arrest of a group of royalist conspirators in February 1797 allowed the government to show that it was equally opposed to any return of the Old Regime.

Rather than rewarding the Directory for its balanced policy, voters in the first regular parliamentary elections in April 1797 elected conservative deputies who promised to continue the purge of politicians who had been involved in the radical phase of the Revolution. Divided about whether to work for a constitutional monarchy or to achieve what they could within the republican constitution, these new deputies spent the summer of 1797 arguing among themselves. The five-man Directory was also divided. Two of its members favored an attempt to work with the more moderate right-wing deputies. The other three, led by Barras, rejected this idea and decided to use force to halt the spread of counterrevolutionary tendencies.

The prorepublican "triumvirate," headed by Barras, arranged for military support. Napoleon Bonaparte sent one of his aides to command the troops used to back the plan and had his soldiers sign proclamations threatening to march on Paris if the right-wing election results were allowed to stand. On 18 fructidor V (4 September 1797), Barras and his colleagues staged a carefully planned coup, expelling their two more moderate colleagues from the Directory and purging the prominent right-wing deputies from the Councils. They also silenced the right-wing press, banning more than thirty daily papers. Despite ample warning, the right-wing deputies and journalists put up no resistance. They had attempted to use the legal means provided by the 1795 Constitution to undermine the regime; they failed to understand that their republican opponents would resort to force to keep themselves in power.

The "Second Directory"

The coup d'état of fructidor marked a turning point in the Directory's policies. The "Second Directory" formed by the "triumvirate" and their two new colleagues reverted to the militant republican rhetoric of 1793. Pro-government deputies clamored (unsuccessfully) for a law expelling all former nobles from the country, and the government did take drastic measures against "refractory" Catholic priests, many of whom had been quietly allowed to resume their posts after thermidor. The Directory ostentatiously supported the celebration of the *décadi*, the tenth day of the republican week according to the new calendar, in place of Sunday. It encouraged writers like the poet Parny, whose *La Guerre des Dieux* ("The War of the Gods") ridiculed Christian beliefs in elegant but often blasphemous lyrics. Outside of France, the "Second Directory" encouraged fructidor-style coups in the "sister republics" that turned their political policies in a more radical direction.

In France, the new atmosphere encouraged the militant republicans or neo-Jacobins, who scored important gains in the elections of April 1798. But the Directory was no more willing to have its policies shaped by an autonomous neo-Jacobin movement than it had been to accept the influence of the conservatives elected in 1797. It responded by "correcting" the voters' decisions in the coup of 22 floréal VI (11 May 1798), installing its own henchmen in contested races. The fructidor and floréal coups showed that politi-

The Great Monster Republican

Although the Directory adopted conservative social policies at home, its conquests contin-
ued to spread the Revolution abroad. This British cartoon from 1798 shows the fears French
republican expansionism caused in other countries. The British lion prepares to give the
figure representing France a "proper reception."
Source: Library of Congress.

cal power had become concentrated in the hands of a self-appointed group
of professional politicians who identified the survival of the Republic with
their own tenure in office.

Whether a regime with such a narrow base of support could have survived thanks to economic prosperity and military success is hard to say. But
the Directory was certainly poorly placed to cope with a crisis, and, by the
end of 1798, it was confronting one. A new foreign coalition had assembled
against France. It included the intransigent British, the Austrians, who
hoped to reverse the unfavorable treaty of Campo-Formio of 1797, and the
Russians, whose new ruler, Tsar Paul, harbored a fanatical hatred for the
Revolution. In the first half of 1799, the French armies reeled backward on
every front. The sudden military collapse discredited the Directory at home.
The Directors once again failed to control the spring parliamentary elections, and a broad coalition of discontented deputies reversed the procedure
of the coups of fructidor and floréal, purging the Directory itself in the coup
of 30 prairial VII (18 June 1799).

THE FALL OF THE DIRECTORY

The prairial victors represented two tendencies. Some were neo-Jacobins who believed that the military crisis required a revival of the emergency measures and the patriotic spirit of 1793. Others, led by Sieyès, who was now a member of the Directory, intended to "revise" the Constitution of 1795 so that it would no longer be vulnerable to periodic challenges from either right or left. At first, the neo-Jacobins seemed to hold the upper hand. They pushed through a new draft law to fill the ranks of the army, a forced loan to levy money from the rich, and the "law of hostages," which allowed local officials to deal with counterrevolutionary unrest by arresting relatives of nobles and emigrés. These measures revived unhappy memories of the Terror and provoked considerable resistance. Meanwhile, Sieyès and his group conspired to rid themselves of their neo-Jacobin allies. Recognizing their lack of organized public support, the plotters looked for a popular military figure to serve as their figurehead.

As Sieyès was casting around for a suitable general, the most celebrated of the Directory's commanders unexpectedly reappeared in Paris. Having learned of France's defeats in Europe and alarmed by letters about his wife's infidelities, Napoleon Bonaparte abandoned his stranded army in Egypt and arrived in France at the beginning of October. Large crowds turned out to cheer him as he traveled from the Mediterranean to Paris; his remarkable military accomplishments had made him genuinely popular. Napoleon had abandoned the revolutionary radicalism that had once made him a friend of Robespierre's younger brother and had led to his arrest after thermidor. During his years in Italy, he had supported pragmatic, socially conservative republicans rather than passionate idealists. He quickly cast his lot with the Sieyès group, who arranged for his appointment as commander of the troops in Paris. In three weeks, the coup plan was completed; on 18 brumaire VIII (9 November 1799), it was put into effect.

Deputies sympathetic to the brumaire plotters invoked a constitutional provision allowing for convocation of the legislature outside of Paris in case of a crisis. By the time the two Councils met in the Parisian suburb of Saint-Cloud on 19 brumaire, however, many deputies had become suspicious of the claim that there was an emergency. When Napoleon Bonaparte addressed the Council of 500, members accused him of seeking to become dictator. The shaken general retreated from the meeting hall and the entire plan threatened to collapse. It was saved by Napoleon's younger brother Lucien, who persuaded the soldiers surrounding the legislators to occupy the meeting room. Most of the deputies fled. Those who remained voted to give full powers to Sieyès and his group to prepare a new constitution. The members of the Directory were pressured into resigning. The lack of public reaction showed how little support the Directory had had.

CHAPTER 7

THE NAPOLEONIC CONSULATE, 1799–1804

The conspirators who overthrew the Directory in November 1799 claimed to be protecting the achievements of the Revolution. For the first five years after the brumaire coup, France officially remained a republic. The motto "Liberty and Equality" continued to appear on coins and government documents, and the country was governed by men who had established their careers since 1789. But it quickly became obvious that the brumaire coup had produced a fundamental change. The participatory politics inaugurated in 1789, already robbed of much of its substance, first by the Jacobins, then by the Directory, disappeared, and one man concentrated all real power in his own hands.

From 1799 until his coronation as Emperor in 1804, Napoleon Bonaparte exercised his personal power within the framework of apparently republican institutions. He held the title of First Consul, and the regime was known as the Consulate. Whereas the preceding period of the Directory has gone down in French history as an ineffective and disreputable regime, the period of the Consulate has often been seen as one of the most brilliant eras in the country's history. Backed by genuine popular support, and profiting from the unpopularity of the preceding regime, Bonaparte successfully reconciled the warring political factions of the previous decade. He oversaw the creation of an efficient administrative machine, consolidated many of the positive achievements of the Revolution, ended the conflict with the Catholic church, and compelled all of France's enemies to make peace on favorable terms.

There is some substance to this positive assessment of the Consulate years. Critics have long pointed out, however, that these accomplishments were achieved by abandoning the revolutionary movement's goal of a government based on genuine popular participation and by curtailing many of the liberties enshrined in the Declaration of the Rights of Man. More recently, modern historians have stressed the many continuities between the preceding revolutionary regimes, especially the Directory, and the Consulate. Many of the achievements Napoleon claimed credit for had in fact been initiated before he took power.

THE CONSUL AND THE CONSULATE

The coup of 18 brumaire, which brought Napoleon Bonaparte to power, was more the work of Sieyès, the veteran politician who had done so much to launch the Revolution ten years earlier, than of the man who reaped the main benefit from it. Sieyès's intentions were the same as those of the authors of the 1795 Constitution: to consolidate the power of moderate republican politicians and bourgeois property holders and to prevent any revival of either royalism or Jacobinism. The main innovation in Sieyès's scheme was the abolition of the parliamentary elections which had troubled the Directory so much. Instead, he proposed a system of cooptation, in which politicians already in power would pick their own successors from lists of property-owning "notables" drawn up by local electoral assemblies. Before Sieyès could implement his ideas, however, he had to negotiate with the young general he had been forced to bring into the coup plan. He quickly discovered that Napoleon Bonaparte had definite ideas of his own about how France should be governed. The rest of France soon learned the same lesson: the coup of brumaire had brought a dominating new leader to the fore.

More has been written about Napoleon Bonaparte than about any other figure in France's long history. He has been hailed as a political and military genius and condemned as the first modern totalitarian dictator, credited with consolidating the achievements of the Revolution and damned for destroying it. In the nineteenth century, with its cult of romantic genius, Napoleon was often seen as a colossus, a unique figure who changed the course of his era. More recent historians have tended to downplay both his personal impact and the importance of the changes that occurred in France during the fifteen years of his rule. Regardless of how one evaluates the impact of Napoleon's actions, however, he has certainly haunted France's collective memory. The "Napoleonic legend," planted in Napoleon's own propaganda and memoirs and cultivated by a host of subsequent artists, historians, and memoirists, has been an essential part of French culture.

TABLEAU HISTORIQUE

DES CAUSES QUI ONT AMENÉ LA RÉVOLUTION DU DIX-HUIT BRUMAIRE.

Mauvaise conduite du Directoire. — Motion incendiaire de la faction dominante au Conseil des 500. — Poignards tirés sur Buonaparte, parés par un grenadier. — Courage de ce Général pour disperser les factieux, et empêcher les soldats de les passer à la bayonnette. — Nomination de deux Commissions pour reviser la constitution — Entrevue des Consuls de la République française et d'un Parlementaire anglais. — Ouverture et communications qui ont été faites dans cette conférence. — Détermination prise par ces mêmes Consuls à la suite de cette entrevue. — Déclaration du roi de Prusse de faire marcher 70 mille hommes contre les puissances qui refuseraient de faire la paix. — Annonce d'une suspension d'armes. — Convocation d'une séance extraordinaire pour la ratification de la paix générale. — Prochaine rentrée des réquisitionnaires et des conscrits dans leurs foyers.

LA révolution du 18 Brumaire, entraîne les derniers | le ranivement du commerce, la restauration de finances, soupirs des tirans désorganisateurs, elle nous fait espérer | et déjà plusieurs millions versés dans les caisses nationa-

Broadsheet Celebrating 18 Brumaire

The plans for the coup of 18 brumaire Year VIII (9 November 1799), which brought Napoleon to power, included preparation of printed propaganda like this illustrated broadsheet. Text and illustration were used to preach the message that the Directory had damaged France's interests and that the new regime would bring France peace, political stability, and economic prosperity after ten years of revolutionary upheaval.

Source: Bibliothèque Nationale, Paris.

NAPOLEON'S CAREER

Napoleon, it has often been said, was a "child of the Revolution," who owed his rise to the upheaval of 1789. Born in 1769 to a poor noble family on the island of Corsica, a territory annexed to France just a year earlier, the young Bonaparte had been educated as an artillery officer. Teachers and fellow cadets had noted the young man's intelligence and fierce will power, but because of his modest background, his prospects for promotion in the prerevolutionary army were not dazzling. A young lieutenant at the time of the Revolution, he enthusiastically embraced its promise of "careers open to talent."

The emigration of many aristocratic army officers after 1789 and the outbreak of war in 1792 turned those possibilities into realities. By 1793, Bonaparte had been promoted to captain. The federalist revolt gave him the opportunity to show his mettle. His skillful use of artillery at the siege of Toulon won the day for the Convention's forces and brought him promotion to the rank of general. Augustin Robespierre, a deputy on mission in the area and the younger brother of the Montagnard leader, became his patron and had him draft plans for an invasion of Italy. As a result of this association, Napoleon nearly fell victim to the purge that followed 9 thermidor. Briefly imprisoned, he remained unemployed until the Convention called on him for help in putting down the counterrevolutionary uprising of 13 vendémiaire in October 1795. This gained him entry to Barras's political circle, where he met and hastily married Josephine Beauharnais, the attractive widow of an officer executed during the Terror. As a reward for his services on 13 vendémiaire, he was given command of France's most demoralized troops, the Army of Italy.

In the Italian campaign of 1796, Napoleon immediately demonstrated the qualities that were to carry him to glory. With his determined personality, he succeeded in imposing his authority on his troops and on subordinate officers who were often older and more experienced than he was. He had a remarkable ability to sense the decisive point where victory could be obtained, and he acted quickly and boldly to achieve it. Outnumbered by the combined Austrian and Piedmontese forces opposing him, Bonaparte succeeded in splitting his foes and overwhelming them separately. In two months, he had knocked the Piedmontese out of the war, chased the Austrians from Milan, and established himself as the most brilliant of the French Republic's generals. As commander of the French occupation forces in northern Italy, he showed himself an adept politician as well. He stage-managed the creation of carefully controlled sister republics, enriched both himself and the Directory from the levies he raised, and successfully courted the Catholic church, avoiding the religious conflicts that had dogged the Revolution at home.

The Directory recognized Bonaparte's driving ambition and kept him at arm's length after he negotiated his own peace treaty with the Austrians in 1797. Inspired by memories of the glory that great conquerors like Alexander had won in the Middle East, Bonaparte had eagerly taken on the command of an expedition to Egypt in 1798. His victories in that exotic locale added to his fame, but his attempt to win the local population over to French-style republicanism was defeated by the vast cultural difference between Europe and the Islamic world. Cut off from France by the British navy, he lost touch with Paris politics and only belatedly learned about the military defeats of the first half of 1799. Together with worries about his wife Josephine's infidelities, reported in letters from his brothers, the fear that the Republic might collapse and destroy his own career prompted Bonaparte to abandon his army in Egypt and sail back to France.

THE CONSTITUTION OF THE CONSULATE

On arriving in Paris, Bonaparte quickly realized that his popularity gave him the chance to play a major political role. But the planning for the brumaire coup was largely carried out by Sieyès and his allies, and Bonaparte's stumbling performance in front of the Council of 500 at Saint-Cloud on 19 brumaire left the impression that he lacked real political ability. As the successful plotters set out to remake the constitution, Sieyès intended to shunt Bonaparte aside with a high-sounding title but little real power. But the general quickly proved that he had more political acumen than his performance on 19 brumaire had suggested.

Despite his lack of political experience, Bonaparte proved more than a match for Sieyès in the constitutional negotiations. He was unconcerned with most of the document's details—a constitution, he remarked, should be "short and obscure"—but he insisted that real power, instead of being carefully divided, should be concentrated in the hands of a single official. He accepted those parts of Sieyès's draft that weakened parliamentary government, as well as the elimination of a declaration of rights such as the three previous revolutionary constitutions had contained. But he insisted on the creation of a strong executive body of three Consuls. The First Consul was to have much greater powers than his two colleagues and, in case of a disagreement among them, his decision would prevail. Once Bonaparte's definition of the First Consul's role was accepted, it was inevitable that he would be entrusted with the office; no one else had the prestige and popularity to fill it. Two relatively unknown political figures were appointed as the other Consuls, and Sieyès found himself relegated to the presidency of the largely powerless Senate that he had designed.

The brumairian plotters submitted this hastily drafted Constitution of the Year VIII to the voters for ratification. This plebiscite enabled the new strong man to maintain that he had a popular mandate to govern. The frequently quoted story of the voter who, asked what was in the constitution he was approving, said it was enough for him that "there is Bonaparte" was a creation of the new leader's propaganda machine. But few citizens stepped forward to object to the abolition of meaningful elections and many of the public liberties enshrined in the previous revolutionary constitutions. Although electoral participation was low, fewer than 1,500 voters risked casting a negative vote. Bonaparte understood, however, that his support was less overwhelming than it seemed. Government officials had been ordered to pad the totals to make the plebiscite look like a success. France was weary of political turmoil and disenchanted with revolutionary ideals, but it remained up to him to show that he could do better.

CONSOLIDATION OF POWER

To consolidate his power, the new First Consul, increasingly referred to as Napoleon, rather than by his family name of Bonaparte, moved quickly to break up the political factions created by the Revolution. He muzzled the political press and used the police to harass prominent neo-Jacobins and die-hard royalists. But all those political figures between the extremes were welcomed into the system. By choosing collaborators regardless of their attitude to the Revolution, Napoleon did much to defuse the bitter conflicts of the previous decade.

Another feature of the Napoleonic system was the creation of a stream-lined government that could act swiftly and effectively. Napoleon strength-ened the already centralized bureaucracy by the creation of the prefects, administrators appointed in Paris and dispatched to the departments to oversee local administration. The prefects bore some resemblance to the pre-revolutionary intendants and to the Directory's commissioners, but they had more extensive powers in the field, while being more strictly controlled from Paris. Thanks to the Revolution, they faced no institutional opposition in their local regions: the reforms of 1789 had abolished all the traditional privileged bodies that had obstructed the monarchy's officials. Appointed from Paris and rotated from post to post after a few years to keep them from developing too many attachments to local interests, the corps of prefects, which included men drawn from a variety of political backgrounds, gave the central government a powerful mechanism for imposing its will on the country.

The laws the prefects enforced were no longer the result of stormy public legislative debates, as they had been throughout the Revolution. Napoleon concentrated real lawmaking powers in a new body, the *Conseil d'Etat* or Council of State, to which he appointed himself, and the meetings of which were held in private. To it, Napoleon appointed competent and articulate councillors drawn, like the prefects, from diverse political camps, whom he urged to engage in free-wheeling debate. Once he had approved a proposal hammered out in the council, however, public debates were largely a formality. The deputies, divided under Sieyès's complex scheme into a Tribunate, which debated proposals without voting on them, a Legislative Body, which listened to the debates and voted without speaking, and a Senate supposedly charged with preventing violations of the constitution, generally accepted the government's proposals.

With all real power in his own hands and with the new administrative and law-making machinery at his control, Napoleon was able to govern more effectively than any previous French regime. To carry out his wishes, he had a talented team of ministers. Charles Gaudin served as finance minister throughout Napoleon's reign, successfully keeping the government out of the fiscal problems that had plagued the Old Regime. Napoleon's loyal companion Alexander Berthier oversaw the army, and Jean-Antoine Chaptal held the key post of minister of the interior. In foreign affairs, the ex-bishop Talleyrand retained the office he had held during the Directory, while the efficient but ruthless ex-terrorist Joseph Fouché managed the police.

Under this leadership, the prefects and the courts hunted down robber bands, which had flourished during the Directory years and had spread fear in many rural regions. The economic revival that had begun under the Directory continued, benefiting merchants and manufacturers and providing jobs for workers. The establishment of the Bank of France in 1800 made it easier for the government to borrow money while also supplying credit for private business needs. In 1803, the new government completed the restabilization of France's currency begun under the Directory by issuing new gold coins. These "germinal francs" set the value of France's money for a century to come. Napoleon reassured the purchasers of the national lands sold under the Revolution that their acquisitions would be protected, even though he allowed many of the emigrés whose estates had been confiscated and sold to return to the country. This "Napoleonic settlement," under which properties and positions attained during the Revolution were guaranteed in exchange for acceptance of Napoleon's one-man rule, satisfied much of the population. The spy network set up by Fouché kept grumblers under surveillance.

Napoleon's policies and the efficient centralized government he established did much to make his regime the first one since 1789 that could count on a firm base of support. But his personality also played an essential part in this success. Able to grasp complex issues quickly, Napoleon held his own in discussions with intellectuals and experts in a wide variety of fields. In personal conversations, he could exert a magnetic charm. In dealing with his ministers, Napoleon made sure that his wishes were carried out and kept the behind-the-scenes intrigues that had characterized the Bourbon monarchy to a minimum. Particularly in the Consulate years, his youth and energy made a striking contrast to the indecisiveness of Louis XVI and the apparent ineffectiveness of most revolutionary politicians.

THE PEACE OF AMIENS AND THE CONCORDAT

To complete his policy of liquidating the conflicts engendered by the Revolution, and to silence potential opponents at home, Napoleon needed to resolve two crucial issues: the foreign war and the religious struggle. Even before the brumaire coup, the French armies had stopped the tide of Coalition victories that had threatened France in early 1799, but France had lost much of the territory gained under the Directory. With the Russians having quarrelled with their allies and withdrawn from the war, Napoleon turned his attention to defeating Austria. Leaving Paris behind before his new regime was fully consolidated, he took personal control of a newly formed Reserve Army at Dijon. With Austrian forces tied down by a lengthy siege at Genoa, Napoleon saw a chance to surprise the enemy from the rear. He led his forces through the narrow Alpine passes, and in June 1800 his dramatic victory at Marengo, assured only by the last-minute arrival of reinforcements on the battlefield, restored French control of northern Italy. Sieyès and the Ideologue circle in Paris, alarmed at Napoleon's success in establishing his one-man rule, had barely concealed their hopes that a military defeat would make him vulnerable; the Marengo victory ended their chance of undermining him.

The Austrians continued the fight on the German front until General Moreau's victory at Hohenlinden in southern Germany in December 1800 completed their demoralization. In February 1801, they accepted the treaty of Lunéville, which gave France even greater gains than the 1797 Campo-Formio treaty. In addition to Belgium and Luxemburg, France now annexed the German territories west of the Rhine River that it had occupied since 1795, setting in motion a reshuffling of borders throughout the Holy Roman Empire as rulers who had lost lands to France sought compensation elsewhere. French-dominated regimes loyal to Napoleon were installed in the Netherlands and throughout the Italian peninsula.

With Austria out of the war, Britain, France's most implacable enemy, made overtures for peace as well. In the treaty signed at Amiens in March 1802, Britain made a few colonial gains but had to acknowledge France's continental predominance. With this treaty, Napoleon appeared to have brought the ten years of war with Europe to a glorious conclusion. He could boast that revolutionary France had expanded far beyond the limits dreamed of by its Bourbon kings; the other European powers had had to recognize France's "natural frontiers" along the crest of the Alps and the Rhine River. To free himself to concentrate on maintaining France's hegemony in Europe, Napoleon sold off to the United States France's claims to vast territories in North America in the Louisiana Purchase arrangement of 1803. A military expedition to reclaim the colony of Saint-Domingue, where the revolt against colonial rule that had begun in 1791 had simmered ever since, ended in failure, and France had to leave the young nation of Haiti, which proclaimed its independence in 1804, to follow its own destiny. Napoleon did reestablish the slave system in France's remaining colonies.

At the same time as he negotiated with Britain, Napoleon had undertaken efforts to resolve the split between the Revolution and the Church. Napoleon had no firm religious beliefs of his own. In Egypt, he had made a great show of courting Muslim leaders. But he considered religion a useful instrument of social control. "How can there be any order in a State without religion? Society cannot exist without inequality of fortune, and inequality of fortune cannot exist without religion," he once remarked.[1] He was also determined to end the conflict that had grown out of the Revolution's religious reform efforts. His strategy was to go over the heads of the counterrevolutionary French bishops, most of whom had gone into exile during the 1790s, and deal directly with the Pope, Pius VII, a man who had shown some sympathy for revolutionary reforms during Napoleon's first occupation of Italy.

Negotiations for a *Concordat* or treaty between the French government and the Papacy were successfully completed in July 1801. Under this agreement, Napoleon recognized Catholicism as the religion of the majority of the population in France and authorized the resumption of public worship. The government would pay priests and bishops; as under the Old Regime, it would nominate bishops, who would receive their consecration from the Pope. To end the schism resulting from the Civil Constitution, the Pope called on all French bishops, both emigrés and constitutionals who had remained in France, to submit their resignations and appointed a new hierarchy including some members of both factions. The Church had to accept the permanent loss of its confiscated lands and the legalization of other religions, as well as government control of education and tight regulation of religious orders and charitable activities. Pius VII and many French clergy were offended by the lengthy regulations known as the "Organic Articles" that Napoleon unilaterally added to the Concordat before its publication; they gave the government almost complete control over the internal administration of the Church. Napoleon's behavior foretold future conflicts, but the restoration of regular public worship after April 1802 was a major satisfaction for the Catholic population.

Many prominent ex-revolutionaries objected to the Concordat and blamed Napoleon for abandoning the Revolution's hard-won triumph over what they saw as outmoded superstition. But the majority of the population welcomed the end of the conflict that had begun with the imposition of the Civil Constitution of the Clergy. The Protestant and Jewish religious minorities still enjoyed the legal protection they had been granted after 1789. In 1806, Napoleon took the extraordinary step of convoking an international congress of Jewish religious leaders, the Sanhedrin, to discuss the relationship between French and Jewish law. Together with the granting of citizenship rights to Jews in 1791, the meeting of the Sanhedrin constituted a remarkable departure in the relations between Jews and the world around them, and not even Napoleon's imposition of discriminatory regulations on the Jewish money-lenders of Alsace in 1808 destroyed the impression made by his earlier initiative.

To round out the changes taken to consolidate his regime, in May 1802 Napoleon announced the creation of the Legion of Honor, an award to be given to those who had rendered special service to the country. Giving special distinctions to certain citizens struck many as a violation of the Revolution's promise of equality, but Napoleon maintained that he was not creating a new privileged class. Membership was not hereditary, and any French citizen could earn the coveted cross. To critics of his reliance on "baubles" instead of devotion to the public good, Napoleon responded that "it is with 'baubles' that mankind is governed."[2] In practice, the Legion became composed primarily of military officers; it served to bind them and the small elite of civilian members to their leader. The Peace of Amiens, the Concordat, and the successful restoration of domestic order brought Napoleon to the height of his popularity. He used the occasion to carry out various modifications of the constitution that strengthened his power and silenced virtually all opposition. In a plebiscite in late 1802, more than three-and-one-half million voters approved Napoleon's being named First Consul for life; only 8,000 cast negative votes.

After 1802, Napoleon introduced fewer major reforms. The shift from the Consulate for Life to the hereditary Empire, carried out in 1804 after another plebiscite, dramatized France's return to a system of one-man rule but added little to Napoleon's authority. The introduction of the Civil Code, often known as the *Code Napoléon*, in 1804, was more significant. Since 1792, France's revolutionary legislators had labored to replace the hundreds of prerevolutionary local law codes with a single national system of civil law. The project, carried to completion at Napoleon's urging, implemented a conservative version of the Revolution's major principles at the level of everyday life. It gave property owners the clear right to use their wealth as they saw fit, eliminating the last vestiges of feudal dues on land and guild restrictions on business. In the interests of equality, revolutionary legislators had required parents to divide their property equally among their children, outlawing the system of primogeniture that had kept estates intact before the Revolution. The Civil Code retreated somewhat on this point, allowing one privileged heir to receive an extra portion of parental property. The Code's harsh restrictions on women's rights codified male superiority: husbands had full control of their family's property and the fate of their children. Divorce was sharply restricted, though not completely abolished, and the husband had greater latitude to start proceedings than the wife, a retreat from the 1792 law that had treated men and women equally. The Civil Code provided a clear and systematic framework for the society of autonomous individuals and private families that the Revolution had created: with modifications, it has remained the basis of French civil law down to the present. Introduced in most of the territories the French occupied during the Napoleonic era, including the state of Louisiana, it proved to be one of the most influential results of the French Revolution.

ELEMENTS OF OPPOSITION

As long as Napoleon marched from victory to victory, there was little visible opposition to him at home. Under the surface, however, there was quiet resistance to the regime's increasing authoritarianism. Small circles of devoted royalists and disgruntled republicans continued to exist. Napoleon could hire artists to glorify him and pamphleteers to praise him, but he was unable to win over the country's major thinkers. The leading members of the rationalist Ideologue group that had formed during the Directory period became the hard core of the opposition to him during the Consulate. Convinced that republican institutions reflected the dictates of reason, the Ideologues and politicians close to them objected to Napoleon's subversion of legislative autonomy, his abolition of genuine elections, and his restoration of the Catholic church, which they condemned for teaching irrational dogmas.

In 1802, Napoleon eliminated the Ideologues' supporters from the legislative councils, and, in 1803, he suppressed their institutional stronghold, the Third Section of the Institute, but he remained uneasily aware of their silent disapproval of the regime. Paris continued to be a center of scientific activity, but imperial policy favored applied research over theoretical investigations, and leadership in this area began to shift from France to the less restricted universities in Germany. Napoleon maintained the grandes écoles, such as the Ecole polytechnique, set up during the revolutionary decade to train the nation's intellectual elite, but he imposed a quasi-military discipline that the most independent-minded students resented.

Napoleon himself thought for a time that he might find support among the thinkers associated with the revival of Catholicism that had begun even before the Concordat. As a result of the controversy over the Civil Constitution of the Clergy and the de-Christianizers' attacks on the Church, those priests who lacked a real commitment to the faith had left the Church. Those who stayed formed a clergy far more serious about its beliefs than the common run of their prerevolutionary predecessors. The laity's faith had also been renewed. During the Terror, many formerly free-thinking nobles and other victims of persecution had embraced Catholicism, and many of the emigrés had found consolation in religion during their years in exile. It was one of them, François-René de Chateaubriand, who captured this mood of religious revival in his two-volume *Genius of Christianity*, which appeared in April 1802, just at the moment of the first

Easter celebration in Paris's Notre-Dame Cathedral since 1793. Chateaubriand's lyrical evocation of religion's aesthetic and emotional appeal made Catholicism fashionable, particularly among the upper classes, who had frequently distanced themselves from it before 1789. The success of Chateaubriand's book marked a shift in the intellectual climate. He and other apologists for religion challenged the representatives of the rationalist Enlightenment tradition that had dominated French public life since the time of the Encyclopédie in the 1750s.

Chateaubriand marked a break with the Enlightenment not only because of his embrace of Catholicism but also because of his emphasis on the superiority of sentiment and emotion over reason. He was one of the first writers of the French romantic movement; his novel *René* was one of the first to sound the characteristic romantic themes of introspection and melancholy. Romanticism was not a monopoly of conservative writers during the Napoleonic period: Liberals frustrated with the stifling of public life under Napoleon, such as Benjamin Constant and Madame de Staël, also wrote novels exploring psychological issues, implicitly suggesting that private life was more important than what went on in the regimented public sphere.

Like the romantic artists, the social thinkers of the period were united only by their distaste for the imperial regime. The thinkers of the Ideologue tradition continued to defend the rationalist individualism of the Enlightenment, implicitly condemning the Concordat and the Empire's tight controls on intellectual activity. The economist Jean-Baptiste Say was a typical representative of this tradition. His *Treatise of Political Economy*, published in 1803, adapted and systematized Adam Smith's doctrines of economic liberty, which were in sharp contrast to Napoleon's policies of state intervention.

More original was the conservative Catholic thinker Louis de Bonald. During his years as an emigré, this provincial nobleman had elaborated a far-reaching critique of rationalism and individualism, which he blamed for the horrors of the Revolution. He argued that society needed an unquestioned principle of authority, which he found in the Catholic church. The truth of its doctrines was confirmed, he argued, by the testimony of tradition. A body of beliefs that had endured for 1,800 years was more reliable than the speculations of modern philosophers. Society, according to Bonald, was a living organism that needed to be governed by a single head, not an agreement among private individuals. Until France returned to a society in accordance with divine will, with authority flowing from God through the Pope and the king to the aristocracy and finally down to the common people, it would continue to be racked by turmoil. Bonald's organic conception of society made him one of the ancestors of modern sociology. The authoritarian cast of his doctrines attracted Napoleon, but he could not wean the stubborn marquis away from his loyalty to the Bourbon monarchy.

Bonald was only one of a number of writers who contributed to the revival of royalist sentiment under the Empire. He and many others contributed occasional articles to the *Journal des Débats*, the most widely read newspaper of the period, whose sympathy for the Bourbon monarchy was barely disguised. Unable to raise the issue directly, the paper's contributors turned to literary and theatrical criticism, condemning the writings of Voltaire and the philosophes and glorifying the classic seventeenth-century works of Corneille and Racine, with their royal heroes. The popularity of this thinly veiled royalist propaganda continued to remind Napoleon that he had not achieved a solid grip on educated French public opinion.

NOTES

1. Cited in J. Christopher Herold, *The Mind of Napoleon* (New York: Columbia University Press, 1955), 104.
2. Cited in Felix Markham, *Napoleon* (New York: Mentor, 1963), 95.

CHAPTER 8

THE NAPOLEONIC EMPIRE, 1804–1815

In 1804, Napoleon decided to abandon the republican facade of the Consulate. By crowning himself Emperor and making his power hereditary, he institutionalized his system of one-man rule and tried to make it permanent. This return to the monarchical principle abandoned in 1792 was an important symbolic step. It meant repudiating one of the major aspects of the Revolution and renewing a link with France's historic past. Propagandists presented Napoleon as the founder of a "fourth dynasty," taking his place alongside the Merovingians, the Carolingians, and the Capetians. The proclamation of the Empire was meant to demonstrate once and for all that the Revolution was over.

At home, the proclamation of the Empire ended all public debate about the form of France's political institutions. Nevertheless, Napoleon remained uneasy about the success of his plan. His marriage to Josephine was childless. The succession law adopted along with the new constitution stated that the throne would pass to one of his brothers, but it was by no means clear that the country would accept this procedure. Nor could Napoleon be assured that the other European powers would tolerate his new system unless he convinced them that it was too powerful to be overthrown. In spite of his past successes, Napoleon continued to feel compelled to be constantly active, reminding the French of his indispensability and the rest of Europe of his invincibility. As a result, the history of the Napoleonic Empire is dominated above all by the history of Napoleon's continuing wars, which have always overshadowed developments in France itself. (See Document K.)

DOCUMENT K
NAPOLEON REFLECTS ON HIS OWN CAREER

Looking back on his life during his confinement on the island of Saint Helena, Napoleon maintained that he had had no choice but to follow authoritarian policies at home and an aggressive military policy abroad.

"When I acquired the supreme direction of affairs, it was wished that I might become a Washington. Words cost nothing; and no doubt those who were so ready to express the wish, did so without any knowledge of times, places, persons, or things. Had I been in America, I would willingly have been a Washington, and I should have had little merit in so being; for I do not see how I could reasonably have acted otherwise. But had Washington been in France, exposed to discord within, and invasion from without, I would have defied him to have been what he was in America; at least, he would have been a fool to attempt it, and would have only prolonged the existence of evil. For my own part, I could only have been a crowned Washington. It was only in a congress of kings, in the midst of kings yielding or subdued, that I could become so. Then and there alone, I could successfully display Washington's moderation, disinterestedness, and wisdom. I could not reasonably attain to this but by means of the universal Dictatorship. To this I aspired; can that be thought a crime? . . ." (From Count Las Cases, *Life of Napoleon* [1835].)

THE RESUMPTION OF WAR

The brief period of peace inaugurated by the treaty of Amiens with Britain in 1802 had ended even before the proclamation of the Empire. Neither side had been fully satisfied with the 1802 treaty: Napoleon still considered British sea power a threat, and the British were unwilling to accept France's domination of its neighbors and the loss of their European markets. The British furnished Napoleon a pretext for breaking off relations by refusing to carry out their promise to evacuate the island of Malta, as the treaty required, and hostilities recommenced in May 1803. But Napoleon lacked any immediate way to strike at the British. He assembled an army along the Channel coast and trained it to a high pitch of readiness, but he never succeeded in building up a fleet capable of transporting the troops. Cartoonists imagined French soldiers crossing the Channel by balloon, but Britain's naval supremacy foiled Napoleon, even before Admiral Nelson's crushing victory at Trafalgar in October 1805 permanently ended any hopes of a seaborne invasion.

The resumption of the war was linked to Napoleon's decision to establish the Empire. After the collapse of the peace of Amiens, French royalist emigrés, backed by the British, had launched a conspiracy to assassinate Napoleon. A double agent betrayed the plan to the French police, and the conspirators were arrested before they could strike. But Napoleon, who had narrowly escaped a previous royalist assassination attempt in December 1800, became convinced that his life would remain in danger as long as it appeared that his death would bring the end of his regime. By making his rule hereditary, he hoped to convince opponents that his system would outlive him. Similar reasoning led him to approve a retaliatory strike against the Bourbon family. French troops invaded neutral Baden to capture the Duke d'Enghien, a Bourbon prince Napoleon thought was implicated in a plan to restore the monarchy. Napoleon had the Duke tried in secret and executed. Although the execution of the Duke d'Enghien apparently deterred further royalist plots against Napoleon's life, it had an unfavorable effect on French public opinion. Even many of the former emigrés who had reconciled themselves with the Napoleonic regime never forgave this direct assault on the Bourbon family. Napoleon's foreign minister, Talleyrand, said, with reason, "it is worse than a crime, it's a blunder."

The elaborate coronation ceremony held on 2 December 1804 was carefully prepared to emphasize Napoleon's glory and power. After lengthy negotiations, Pius VII agreed to come from Rome, although Napoleon decided to crown himself rather than make it appear that he had received his title from the Church. Elderly courtiers who remembered the rules of etiquette from Versailles were sought out to advise the dignitaries of the new regime, many of them originally from humble backgrounds, on proper ceremonial behavior. Although Napoleon intended the coronation to serve the serious political purpose of consolidating his reign once and for all, he was conscious of the theatrical element in the show he was arranging. "If only our father could see us now," he whispered to his brother Joseph.[1] And he remained keenly aware that, in the absence of any traditional claim to the throne, he had to keep French society under firm control and foreign enemies at bay to stay in power.

FROM ULM TO TILSIT

At the moment of his coronation, Napoleon's only active military foe was Britain. Britain's ability to defeat France depended on finding allies on the Continent to challenge Napoleon's land forces. The obvious candidates were Austria, which had lost both territory and prestige in its previous campaigns against France, and Russia, which had never accepted France's revolutionary conquests. British subsidies helped draw them back into the fight in August 1805, the start of a renewed round of war on the Continent that was to last until 1807. As soon as he learned of the Austro-Russian declaration of war, Napoleon marched the forces he had been training for a possible invasion of England toward the Danube. By this time, he had turned his Grand Army into a magnificent fighting machine. Like the generals of the revolutionary period, he continued to combine the mobile artillery developed after the Seven Years' War with the mass attacks made possible by the size and enthusiasm of the revolutionary citizen armies. But the soldiers of 1805 were no longer raw recruits. The core of the army had over ten years' experience, which allowed Napoleon to rely on them to execute complicated maneuvers on the battlefield. Over a decade of campaigning had given him a galaxy of combat-tested generals.

On 20 October 1805, Napoleon's fast-moving troops encircled the main Austrian army at Ulm in southern Germany and forced its surrender. Six weeks later, at Austerlitz, close to Vienna, Napoleon won perhaps his most celebrated battle, completely crushing the Austrian and Russian forces. The Austrians hastened to make peace, ceding even more territory to France and its satellite states. The following year, Prussia, which had remained neutral during the Austerlitz campaign, unexpectedly joined Russia in the fight against Napoleon. The Emperor moved his forces into central Germany, and at the battles of Jena and Auerstädt, the French annihilated the famous Prussian army. Napoleon occupied Berlin. The Russians continued the war in 1807, as Napoleon advanced into Poland. At Eylau, in February, the two armies fought to a bloody draw, but in June 1807 Napoleon caught the Russian forces in a trap at the battle of Friedland and inflicted decisive casualties on them. Russia, too, sued for peace.

Napoleon met the young Russian emperor Alexander I personally at Tilsit, in Poland, to conclude a settlement to end the round of fighting that had begun two years earlier. The Peace of Tilsit of 1807 went well beyond a mere end to hostilities. The charismatic French emperor persuaded Alexander to become his partner in a grand plan by which the two powers would divide Europe and Asia into spheres of influence and work together to defeat Britain. With Russia on his side, Napoleon appeared to have achieved total control of the European continent. He had already converted the sister republics established in the Directory period into satellite kingdoms, ruled by members of his family. Hapless Prussia and Austria had to accept Napoleon's decrees.

THE CONTINENTAL SYSTEM

The defeat of Austria and Prussia and the peace of Tilsit gave Napoleon the opportunity to pursue a grandiose program intended to cripple his last major enemy, Britain, and to make France the dominant economic power on the Continent, as well as its leading political force. Unable to directly challenge Britain's naval power, Napoleon planned a program of economic warfare that he called the Continental System. In essence, this amounted to a boycott of trade with Britain, whose rapidly industrializing economy depended on overseas outlets to sell its goods. The Continental System was also aimed at promoting the growth of French industry, which Napoleon hoped would capture the European markets Britain would lose. With his encouragement, cotton-spinning plants sprang up in Paris, which became France's largest industrial center, and in Alsace, whose location along the Rhine was favorable for export to Germany and central Europe. To replace cane sugar, previously imported from the West Indies, the Napoleonic regime encouraged the planting of sugar beets in northern France and the Belgian departments and sponsored the growth of a refining industry. Coal mining and iron making boomed, too, although much of the growth in this area took place in the Belgian departments that were to be separated from France after Napoleon's fall.

French manufacturers benefited from the hothouse atmosphere of the Continental System, but the port cities, cut off by the British naval blockade, suffered. Those in France itself could do little more than grumble, but in the French-occupied areas, illegal trade with Britain flourished, undermining the boycott and driving the authorities to ever-harsher measures against the local population. To stop up the leaks, Napoleon felt driven to impose tight controls on one territory after another. Spain, with its long coastline and its proximity to southern France, was one of his main concerns. In 1808, he replaced Spain's Bourbon king with his brother Joseph. This insult to Spanish national pride triggered a guerrilla insurrection that tied down considerable French forces. The following year, Napoleon took over the Papal States in Italy, starting a test of wills with Pius VII that lasted until the Emperor's downfall. In 1810, Napoleon annexed northern Germany, the Netherlands, and Italy as far south as Rome directly to France, installing French prefects and French police.

THE EMPIRE AT HOME

The counterpart to Napoleon's bid for control over Europe was a steady expansion of government authority in France itself. Much of the country had welcomed the installation of an efficient system of administration during the Consulate period, when memories of the often-chaotic revolutionary decade were still fresh. But the relentless extension of government power into every area of national life under the Empire was less popular. Even today, the legacy of this overgrown Napoleonic bureaucracy is often cited to explain why French citizens continue to both expect and resent state involvement in almost every aspect of social affairs.

The increasing power of the bureaucracy went along with a further decline in the importance of the legislative branch of government. The three legislative chambers remained in existence after the declaration of the Empire in 1804, but their powers were still further curtailed. The Tribunate, ostensibly charged with debating laws, ceased to meet in public after 1804. In 1807, Napoleon abolished it altogether. The Imperial Senate, supposedly responsible for maintaining the constitution, became a convenient tool for changing it. Napoleon had little trouble getting the well-paid senators to pass special resolutions, called *senatus-consulta*, that avoided the necessity of calling plebiscites to approve constitutional alterations. The continued existence of the Senate and the Legislative Body served as a facade to keep the regime from looking like a straightforward revival of absolute monarchy. In 1814, however, at the moment of Napoleon's defeat, the fact that he had never entirely suppressed the legislature would give his enemies a foothold from which to challenge him.

With the legislature neutralized, Napoleon was able to extend centralized government control to almost every aspect of French society. One of his main concerns was education. In 1808, Napoleon created the Imperial University, a bureaucratic arrangement giving the government a monopoly over secondary and higher education throughout the country. The secondary schools, or *lycées*, descendants of the écoles normales established during the Directory period, were turned into strictly disciplined training grounds for future bureaucrats, and the students had to wear military uniforms. The regimented atmosphere alienated many of the brightest students, such as the future romantic poet Victor Hugo, and prepared them to welcome the collapse of the regime when it occurred. (See Document L on page 131.)

Napoleon used the Concordat to turn the Catholic church into an instrument of political indoctrination. Just as he installed his brothers as rulers of his satellite states, he arranged the nomination of his uncle, Cardinal Fesch, as head of the French Church hierarchy, ensuring its loyalty even during the years when he was locked in combat with the Pope. The Imperial Catechism, issued in 1807, required priests to teach that loyalty to the Emperor and military service were religious obligations. As in the case of the schools, this heavy-handed regimentation generated a spirit of resistance. Young seminarians like the Breton Félicité de Lamennais secretly dreamed of a church freed from government control. After Napoleon's fall in 1814, this new generation would bring a new spirit of devotion to French Catholicism.

Determined to prevent the emergence of lower-class protest, Napoleon strengthened employers' powers over their workforce. An 1803 law required every worker to have a *livret*, or work book. Workers needed their employer's signature to change jobs, and, in case of conflicts, the employer's testimony was to be accepted in court. The ban on the formation of trade

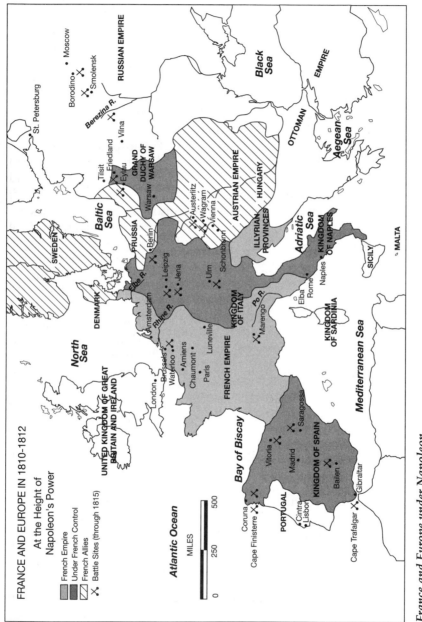

FRANCE AND EUROPE IN 1810–1812

At the Height of Napoleon's Power

French Empire
Under French Control
French Allies
✕ Battle Sites (through 1815)

MILES

0   250   500

Atlantic Ocean

Bay of Biscay

North Sea

Baltic Sea

Black Sea

Adriatic Sea

Aegean Sea

Mediterranean Sea

UNITED KINGDOM OF GREAT BRITAIN AND IRELAND

London

SWEDEN

DENMARK

St. Petersburg

RUSSIAN EMPIRE

Moscow

Borodino
Smolensk

Berezina R.

Vilna

PRUSSIA

Tilsit
Friedland
Eylau

GRAND DUCHY OF WARSAW

Warsaw
Berlin

Amsterdam
Brussels
Waterloo
Rhine R.
Amiens
Paris
Chaumont
Luneville

FRENCH EMPIRE

Elbe R.
Leipzig
Jena
Ulm
Schönbrunn

Austerlitz
Wagram
Vienna

AUSTRIAN EMPIRE

HUNGARY

OTTOMAN EMPIRE

ILLYRIAN PROVINCES

KINGDOM OF ITALY

Po R.
Marengo

Elba
Rome

KINGDOM OF SARDINIA

Naples

KINGDOM OF NAPLES

SICILY

MALTA

PORTUGAL
Cintra
Lisbon

KINGDOM OF SPAIN

Coruna
Cape Finisterre
Vitoria
Madrid
Saragossa
Bailen
Gibraltar
Cape Trafalgar

France and Europe under Napoleon

At the height of Napoleon's power, France's borders stretched from Rome in Italy to Hamburg in Germany. Satellite states ruled by Napoleon's relatives copied French institutions and contributed soldiers to the Imperial army. Controlling this vast area was a constant struggle for Napoleon.

DOCUMENT L
THE ATMOSPHERE OF THE NAPOLEONIC EMPIRE

In his memoirs, François Guizot, a leading nineteenth-century French liberal politician, recalled the stifling atmosphere of the Napoleonic Empire.

"When I began my career in 1807, the chaos [of the revolutionary years] had long since blown away. The intoxication of 1789 had completely dissipated. Society, absorbed in reconsolidating its foundations, was no longer interested in improving itself through its amusements. Violent spectacles had replaced its earlier desires for liberty. A lack of interest, a coldness, an isolation of feelings and of private interests, is the ordinary state of things. France, tired of illusions and bizarre excesses, eager for order and ordinary common sense, had fallen back into that morass . . .

"Minds elevated above the common run and sensitive to human dignity had good reason not to like this regime, and to foresee that it would provide neither happiness nor lasting glory for France. At the time, however, it seemed so solidly supported by the general sentiment of the country, everyone was so convinced of its strength, there seemed so little possibility of a future change, that even in those exclusive circles where the spirit of opposition dominated, it seemed perfectly natural that young men should take government jobs, the only public career open to them." (From F. Guizot, *Mémoires pour servir à l'histoire de mon temps* [Paris: Michel Lévy fréres, 1858], vol. 1, pp. 7, 13. *Translation by Jeremy D. Popkin.*)

---

unions, enacted in 1791, was reasserted in 1803. Workers did have some representation, but not an equal voice, on the *conseils de prud'hommes*, or arbitration panels, set up after 1806 to resolve conflicts between employers and employees in different trades.

In general, merchants and manufacturers managed to retain more independence from the state; the complex of government-backed regulations characteristic of the Old Regime was not restored. But some trades considered particularly important for the maintenance of public order were tightly controlled—butchers and bakers, whose prices had the potential to incite popular protests, and printers, who had to have a license to operate in order to prevent the publication of subversive works. The Napoleonic regime created a state monopoly on the sale of tobacco products as a way of adding to government revenue. Attempts to enforce the Continental Blockade also increased government involvement in the economy, as customs agents raided warehouses looking for contraband British goods.

CULTURE UNDER THE EMPIRE

Napoleon intended to make art and culture serve the purposes of the state. The "Empire style" that characterized the decorative arts favored heavy pieces of furniture, often using Egyptian motifs that recalled Napoleon's expedition of 1798. The Napoleonic government was an active patron, commissioning numerous paintings glorifying the Emperor and his accomplishments. Jacques-Louis David, once an enthusiastic supporter of Robespierre, now put his talents in the service of the new regime, painting several famous portraits of Napoleon, including a fanciful depiction on horseback and a huge canvas representing the Emperor's coronation.

A generation of younger artists, most of them David's students, competed for commissions to immortalize the high points of Napoleon's career. Antoine-Jean Gros painted a Christlike Napoleon visiting plague victims during his Egyptian campaign. His "Battlefield of Eylau" commemorated a victory over the Russians in 1807, although it also vividly portrayed the suffering of the wounded and dying soldiers from both armies. J.-A.-D. Ingres, perhaps David's most famous disciple, began his long career with an elaborate portrait of the Emperor in his coronation robes. The revival of the art market after the disruptions of the revolutionary decade did allow painters to pursue other projects besides the glorification of the ruler, however. Recent art historians have noted a growing interest in scenes from exotic lands, subjects from medieval literature and history, and portraits and allegorical scenes with psychological overtones. These developments pointed toward the more fully developed romantic art that would flourish after Napoleon's fall.

Napoleon's ideas about how art should serve the state were exemplified by his plans to make Paris a monument to his glory. A long, straight boulevard, the rue de Rivoli, was to traverse the city, and Roman-style monuments, including a column surmounted with a statue of the Emperor in the Place Vendôme and two Arches of Triumph, were to mark his conquests. Only the smaller of these, the Arch of the Carousel, located between the Louvre and the Tuileries gardens, was completed during his reign. The great Arch of Triumph at the Etoile, still one of Paris's best-known monuments, was finally finished in the mid-nineteenth century, serving as a monument to the French nation rather than to Napoleon alone.

The imperial period was less favorable for French writers. Madame de Staël, alienated from Napoleon during the Consulate period, spent most of the Empire in exile. Her book *On Germany*, published in 1810, glorified the independent spirit of the early romantic philosophers and poets in Germany. It was an implicit criticism of the atmosphere in France, where heavy-handed censorship prevented the publication of anything smacking of dissidence. The government found ingenious ways to muffle potential criticism, such as forcing the editors of the pro-Catholic *Mercure de France* and the rationalist Ideologue journal *La Décade philosophique* to merge their two publications. The leading daily newspaper of the Consulate period, the *Journal des Débats*, which had represented a moderate conservative viewpoint, was forced to change its name to *Journal de l'Empire* and compelled to follow the official line. Not surprisingly, writers and intellectuals of almost every persuasion reacted against the Empire's stifling atmosphere by welcoming its downfall in 1814.

THE SOCIAL BASES OF THE EMPIRE

Although his Continental System aimed to promote the growth of French manufacturing, Napoleon continued to envisage France as primarily an agricultural society. Modifications to the process for selecting local government officials were intended to put power in the hands of large landowners, the "masses of granite" whom Napoleon regarded as the natural leaders of society. This elite included both members of the prerevolutionary aristocracy who had preserved or restored their holdings and a new nobility that Napoleon himself created after 1808 by rewarding his loyal followers with titles and land grants. Members of the bourgeoisie consolidated their hold on the government posts opened up to them after 1789. State licensing of physicians, imposed in 1803, and the restoration of the bar in 1811 recreated the professional monopolies of bourgeois doctors and lawyers, which had been threatened during the revolutionary period. As under the Old Regime, the bourgeoisie continued to invest much of its acquired wealth in land, imitating the behavior of the aristocracy rather than adopting a new set of values.

It has often been argued that the Napoleonic regime had a special appeal for the country's peasants, who still made up the overwhelming majority of the population. The Napoleonic land settlement guaranteed that peasants who had purchased land from church and noble holdings during the 1790s could keep it. Prosperous peasants continued to acquire property during the Napoleonic period, as bourgeois investors who had bought large estates during the Revolution sold them off piecemeal. The Napoleonic armies provided an outlet for surplus population and an opportunity for social advancement for many young peasants. They shared in the plunder from successful campaigns, and outstanding soldiers could still hope for promotion from the ranks. France became more than ever a country of small family farms, in contrast to England where large landowners had used the process of enclosure to drive less prosperous neighbors off the land. While peasants counted on Napoleon to protect them against the loss of Church and noble lands purchased during the Revolution, they did resent Imperial taxes and the heavy burden of military conscription, both of which increased in the last years of the regime. This resentment helps explain why there would be no peasant movement to support Napoleon when military defeats drove him from the throne.

The urban working classes' situation in this period is harder to characterize. Police supervision prevented any visible agitation among the population, and former sans-culotte activists faded back into the anonymity of private life. Urban poverty was still widespread. The large numbers of prostitutes active in Paris testified to the number of poor women who remained unable to make a living in any other way. But even the sharp economic crisis of 1811 saw no repetition of the mass protests that had marked the revolutionary decade. Not until the July Revolution of 1830, fifteen years after the end of the Napoleonic era, did France's urban poor reappear as an active force in public life.

As long as Napoleon continued to achieve military success abroad and provide economic prosperity at home, no broad-based protest against his regime developed. Even the continuing demand for troops stirred little protest. By allowing draftees to pay someone to take their place, the Napoleonic administration defused protests against conscription from wealthier families. Between 1803 and 1811, the total number of soldiers from the territories making up pre-1789 France who died, were captured, or were seriously injured never exceeded 80,000 per year. By recruiting a large proportion of his troops from his non-French territories and his satellite kingdoms, Napoleon kept the human cost of his wars to France down. The French population continued to grow throughout the Napoleonic period. The Emperor also succeeded in paying for his war-making without incurring the debts that had crippled the old monarchy. He financed his conquests from tribute levied on his defeated foes; even after his final defeat in 1814, he left his successors a healthy treasury.

THE DECLINE OF THE EMPIRE

The year 1810 marked a turning point for Napoleon's regime. Although he faced little apparent opposition at home, the Emperor found himself bogged down in a growing number of foreign conflicts that seemed to defy resolution. His efforts to resolve them by force eventually widened the war to the point where France could no longer hold its own against the coalition of enemies Napoleon's policies had inspired.

Even at the height of Napoleon's reign, from 1807 to 1810, his hold on Europe was never completely secure. The "Spanish ulcer," the revolt against French domination that had begun in 1808, turned into a bloody peasant war, as brutal as the Vendée rebellion. It ate up increasing numbers of French troops and provided an opening for the British, who landed an expeditionary force under General Wellington in Portugal in 1809. Except for a few months, Napoleon never gave the Spanish front his personal attention.

Second-rate French commanders were left to deal with the widespread guerrilla resistance, which could not be put down by the kind of knock-out punch in which Napoleon specialized.

The fact that so many French troops were tied up in Spain encouraged the Austrians to make a new bid to shake off French domination in 1809. Napoleon won another memorable victory at Wagram that smashed Vienna's military hopes, but he himself was well aware of how thin his forces had been stretched. He no longer had the luxury of commanding a thoroughly trained veteran army, as he had in 1805. His forces now included a much larger proportion of hastily recruited non-French soldiers, and he had to simplify his battle tactics and put increasing reliance on his elite striking force, the Imperial Guard. A peasant uprising in the Tyrol and scattered outbreaks of resistance in Germany showed that the kind of popular unrest that bedeviled him in Spain simmered just below the surface in many other parts of Europe. Napoleon also faced an open conflict with Pope Pius VII, who refused to integrate his territories into the Continental System and excommunicated the Emperor when he seized them by force. An exasperated Napoleon had the Pope put under house arrest in a small Italian town; he was later brought to France. This rupture with the Papacy alienated Catholics in many parts of the continent. Napoleon's decision to divorce Josephine and his punishment of French cardinals who refused to accept this violation of Church law worsened the conflict. The Pope retaliated by refusing to consecrate bishops nominated to fill vacancies in France, leading Napoleon to try to force the French clergy to agree that bishops could be installed without Papal approval after a six-month delay. This proposal threatened to revive the religious divisions of the 1790s, but before a complete rupture occurred, military defeats forced Napoleon to turn his attention elsewhere.

Napoleon tried to counter these mounting difficulties by strengthening his ties with other European rulers. In 1810 he divorced the childless Josephine and married an Austrian princess, Marie-Louise, who bore him a son in 1812, thus raising hopes for the permanence of the dynasty. Napoleon's rapprochement with Austria failed to solve his mounting problems. The Continental System had begun to unravel; Napoleon himself connived at violations of it, selling licenses for trade with Britain as a means of raising money. In December 1810, Russia abruptly withdrew from the System and resumed trade with Britain, convincing Napoleon that Alexander intended to turn against him. At home, the year 1810 was marked by the beginning of a sharp economic crisis that persisted into 1811. French manufacturing slumped, and factory owners joined the merchants of the port cities in blaming the regime for their troubles. Peasants showed increasing resentment about the weight of taxes and the growing draft calls needed to keep the army up to strength.

THE INVASION OF RUSSIA

Napoleon responded to his mounting difficulties with his tried-and-true formula: a daring military campaign to silence his foes. But this time his gamble—an invasion of Russia to force it back into the Continental System—failed. With an army of nearly 1 million men, most of them recruited from territories outside of France, he crossed the Russian border in June 1812, hoping to win a quick victory and bring Alexander to the bargaining table. But his huge *Grande Armée* was too cumbersome to employ the tactics of rapid movement and maneuverability that had brought Napoleon success in previous campaigns. The Russians took advantage of their country's vast size to draw Napoleon further and further from his supply bases, all the while avoiding a decisive engagement. At Borodino, near Moscow, the two armies fought to a draw, but the Russians then slipped away again, leaving Napoleon to occupy their capital without opposition.

The conquest of Moscow proved to be a hollow victory. The Russian forces remained intact, and Alexander refused to negotiate. Most of the city burned down in a fire shortly after the French moved in, leaving the army without supplies or shelter. Napoleon finally had to begin a retreat in the harsh Russian winter. Cold, hunger, and Russian harassment decimated his troops; less than one-tenth of the men who had set off for Moscow returned. In Paris, conspirators spread the rumor that Napoleon himself had been killed in Russia. In the hours of confusion caused by the coup attempt, Napoleon's top officials failed to put into effect plans to declare his infant son Emperor, revealing how shaky the regime's support had become. Napoleon abandoned his shattered forces and hurried back to Paris to restore order.

Even after the defeat in Russia, Napoleon still thought that his own military genius and the potential divisions among his foes would allow him to reverse the situation. In 1813, he pulled together a new army, made up mostly of raw recruits and men previously rejected as unfit. This greatly increased demand for conscripts revived unhappiness with the regime at home. Abroad, one government after another, led by Prussia and then Austria, sensed that the tide had turned and joined forces with the Russians. Even some of the rulers Napoleon had installed as satellites, like the former French general Bernadotte, now king of Sweden, turned against him. In October 1813, the combined allied forces defeated him at the battle of Leipzig, and Napoleon had to retreat across the Rhine; meanwhile, British and Spanish forces under the Duke of Wellington advanced toward the Pyrenees. As the enemy forces penetrated into France in the winter of 1814, Napoleon fought a brilliant rearguard campaign, but he was hopelessly outnumbered. The French population, whose patriotism had enabled the revolutionary armies to fight off invaders in 1792 and 1793, now refused to heed Napoleon's summons to rise to the nation's defense. For too long, he had smothered all real participation in public affairs; ordinary citizens now responded by leaving him to his fate. At the end of March 1814, allied forces reached Paris.

Although military defeat was now certain, it was not clear that the Napoleonic regime would also fall. Royalist conspirators' efforts to set off demonstrations in favor of a Bourbon restoration enjoyed success in some regions, particularly the southwest, but the victorious allies were not convinced that a government hostile to the Revolution could assure stability without becoming totally dependent on them for support. They were therefore receptive to overtures from Napoleon's former foreign minister Talleyrand, who controlled the Imperial Senate that Napoleon had never abolished. Talleyrand and his followers were prepared to reinstate the Bourbons, but on their own terms: Louis XVI's long-exiled brother would be put on the throne as king under the title of Louis XVIII, but he would have to accept a written constitution limiting his power and maintaining the principal features of the "Napoleonic settlement." Those who had obtained high governmental positions under Napoleon would keep them, and purchasers of Church and emigré property would not be disturbed. The opportunistic Talleyrand, who had served every successive French government since the Old Regime, and the much-feared police minister Fouché, a former Convention deputy who had voted for the execution of Louis XVI, retained their offices. Napoleon, warned by his generals that the army would not continue the fight, abdicated his throne on 6 April 1814. Twenty-five years of revolutionary upheaval and Napoleonic rule had brought France back to a system of constitutional monarchy similar to what many reformers had hoped for in the spring of 1789.

THE HUNDRED DAYS

The restoration of the Bourbons in 1814 seemed to mark the end of the revolutionary and Napoleonic era, but Napoleon was still to add an unexpected chapter to his epic story. The victorious allies dealt generously with him, allowing him to retire as ruler of the island of Elba off the coast of Italy. From this observation post, he followed the course of events in France. Despite his willingness to accept the terms offered by Talleyrand and his supporters, Louis XVIII soon encountered major difficulties in consolidating his new regime. His return was followed by an influx of die-hard emigrés who had remained in exile throughout the Napoleonic period. They agitated for the return of their confiscated estates and for the restoration of the prerevolutionary system of privileges. The appointment of emigré military officers who had fought against France to posts in the French army outraged patriotic sentiment, especially since the end of the war had brought massive layoffs at all ranks. The fact that the new Restoration monarchy was propped up by foreign occupying forces made it easy to turn French nationalist sentiment against it.

Emboldened by reports of unrest in France, Napoleon decided to take a dramatic gamble. On 1 March 1815, having slipped past British patrol ships, he landed on the Mediterranean coast. Accompanied by a small band of loyal troops, he began to march north to Paris. Larger military units sent to arrest him, composed largely of veterans of his earlier campaigns, went over to his side as he advanced. On 19 March, Louis XVIII fled Paris, and Napoleon entered the capital the following day, inaugurating the "Hundred Days" of his last bid for power.

The Restoration government's unpopular gestures in favor of nobles and emigrés did give Napoleon a broader base of support than in 1814; a spontaneous movement of volunteers, the *fédérés*, rallied to him and intimidated potential opponents. Napoleon was reluctant to encourage a real resurgence of popular radicalism, however. He made a greater effort to reach out to liberals and members of the middle classes. Benjamin Constant, a longtime critic of the Empire's authoritarianism, drafted an "Additional Act" to the Imperial Constitution, meant to protect individual rights and constitutional government. Napoleon even refrained from punishing the high officials who had betrayed him in 1814. Fouché, the police minister, remained in office, although Napoleon had ample reason to suspect his loyalty. But Napoleon remained uneasily aware that many areas of the country, such as the west, where royalist sentiment had always been strong, still opposed him.

The only chance of consolidating his position was to force the other European powers to accept his return. After fifteen years of almost continual warfare, however, the British, Austrians, Russians, and Prussians had no faith in Napoleon's statements about his peaceful intentions. The allied coalition renewed the war, and Napoleon once again had to risk his regime's fate on the battlefield. Reassembling as much of his Grand Army as he could, Napoleon marched into Belgium, hoping to defeat the British and Prussians separately before the Austrians and Russians could join them. He caught the British at the village of Waterloo, near Brussels, but this time, luck was not with him. Many of his best generals had betrayed him in 1814 or no longer showed the fighting spirit of earlier years. The experienced British veterans under the command of the Duke of Wellington, the architect of France's defeat in Spain, held off even Napoleon's feared Imperial Guard. Napoleon retreated to Paris, but he immediately realized that there was no chance of preserving his power. He surrendered to the British, who packed him off to the remote South Atlantic island of Saint Helena for the six remaining years of his life. Louis XVIII followed the allied troops back to his capital. His second restoration, in July 1815, finally put an end to the long drama of the revolutionary and Napoleonic period.

NOTE

1. Cited in Markham, *Napoleon*, 113.

CHAPTER 9

THE REVOLUTIONARY
HERITAGE

Superficially, Napoleon's downfall seemed to bring France back to the point where the Revolution had started. The Bourbon dynasty was restored and, after spending twenty-five years in exile, Louis XVI's brother was proclaimed as Louis XVIII. However, the Revolution had caused deep and permanent changes in French society. As Alfred de Musset, one of the generation of French writers who grew up in the years immediately following Napoleon's fall, wrote, "the powers divine and human were in fact reestablished, but belief in them no longer existed."[1] The restored king, Louis XVIII, understood this. He made no real effort to reinstate the privileges of the nobility or the Church, and he accepted the necessity of governing according to a written constitution that provided for a legislative assembly, one of whose chambers was elected.

Louis XVIII's acceptance of many of the Revolution's key reforms enabled him to die peacefully in his bed in 1824, but it was not sufficient to protect the restored monarchy. In 1830, a new revolution overthrew Charles X, the last of the Bourbon kings. During the next half century, France repeated in slow motion the revolutionary cycle that had begun in 1789. The liberal constitutional monarchy set up in 1830, the July Monarchy, was overthrown in another revolution in 1848 and replaced with a democratic Second Republic, which was in turn overthrown by Napoleon Bonaparte's nephew in 1851 and succeeded by a second Napoleonic Empire (1852–1870).

France's calamitous defeat by Germany in 1870–71 opened the possibility of a renewed monarchical restoration, but public opinion soon made it clear that the country would only accept a regime based on the democratic and republican principles of the revolutionary era. The establishment of France's Third Republic in 1875 closed the long era of political instability that had started in 1789.

THE POSTREVOLUTIONARY SETTLEMENT

France's political instability in the nineteenth century masked the fact that many of the fundamental changes made during the Revolution were never seriously challenged after 1789. The principles of liberty and equality had sunk deep roots by 1815. The result was a society made up of independent individuals, governed by a greatly strengthened centralized state. Although the various nineteenth-century regimes often curtailed the political freedoms promised in 1789, the belief that male French citizens nevertheless had an equal right to do "all that is not forbidden by the law," as the original Declaration of Rights had stated, survived. Incorporated in the provisions of the Napoleonic Code, which remained the law of the land, this individualistic outlook barred any return to the corporatist society of the old regime, with its numerous restrictions on economic enterprise. The revolutionary and Napoleonic era had also defined the legal and political position of women. Denied political rights by the revolutionary legislators and subordinated to their fathers and husbands by the Napoleonic Code, French women would have a long struggle to gain full access to the new postrevolutionary society.

The revolutionary heritage of egalitarianism prevented any reestablishment of hereditary social status. Noble titles still commanded social prestige, but they no longer carried any legal privileges or tax exemptions. Government jobs—more numerous than ever as a result of the growth of the administration during the revolutionary era—were now open to men from all social classes. As France gradually entered the industrial era after 1815, prosperous bourgeois manufacturers, bankers, and professionals supplanted landowners as the country's wealthy elite. This bourgeois class benefited from the Revolution's protection of property rights, but so did much of the peasantry. The parceling out of the former church holdings and of many noble estates created a rural democracy of small landowners, freed from the collective restrictions that had governed village life before 1789. Together, the strengthened bourgeoisie and the landholding peasantry that emerged from the revolutionary era proved a formidable obstacle both to the return of old privileged groups and to the claims of new ones, such as the propertyless industrial proletariat that developed in the nineteenth century.

Property rights were not the only evidence of the Revolution's extension of individual freedom. The Revolution's secularization of French society also proved permanent. Not only did Protestants and Jews now have the same rights as Catholics, but much of the population also exercised its right not to practice any religion. Although freedom for the newspaper press remained restricted for much of the nineteenth century, censorship of books was not reinstated: the postrevolutionary citizen had access to a variety of ideas and opinions.

The revolutionaries of 1789 had proclaimed that individual rights could only be protected by a written constitution and a government that represented the citizens. These basic principles have been incorporated in all of the country's postrevolutionary regimes, with the exception of the Vichy government established during the German occupation of 1940–1944. Written constitutions have changed frequently since 1815, and elections have not always given voters a true chance to express their wishes, but France has always had some kind of elected assembly to make laws and approve government expenditures. The revolutionary principle of national sovereignty has thus come to be a fundamental feature of the country's political culture.

STATE AND NATION

Like the changes it had made in individual rights, the Revolution's reshaping of France's governmental structure proved to be largely permanent. The elimination of the parlements, the provincial assemblies, and the multitude of local privileges carried out on the night of 4 August 1789 had cleared the way for the creation of an efficient central administration and a national court system, which no subsequent French regime showed any interest in changing. The government kept most of the functions, such as registering births, marriages, and deaths, that it had taken over from the Church after 1789. The equal-sized *départements* which had replaced the old provinces also endured. All these reforms had accentuated the centralization of power in the capital, already evident before 1789 but greatly increased by the Revolution and Napoleon.

The centralized postrevolutionary government ruled over a unified nation. As the legislators of 1789 had intended, a single set of laws now governed the entire country. The tolls and customs duties that had divided the country economically no longer existed, and all parts of the country now paid the same taxes. Experiences such as serving in the revolutionary and Napoleonic armies had taken much of the male population away from home and inculcated a loyalty to the country rather than to native regions. Although it took much of the nineteenth century to establish a national system of elementary schools, the central government now had firm control of secondary and higher education. Schooling, the necessity of understanding laws and regulations issued in Paris, and the habit of following events through the newspapers all favored the spread of a standardized French language at the expense of regional dialects.

Postrevolutionary France still retained some connections with the world of the old regime. Peasants were still a majority of the population throughout the nineteenth century, and farming methods changed only slowly. Regional loyalties remained strong in people's minds, even though the historic provinces had been abolished. But the shared experience of the Revolution had given the country a new set of historical memories that overshadowed what had come before. Throughout the nineteenth century and into the twentieth, the basic issues that divided the French people usually traced their origins to the struggles of the revolutionary period. In 1989, the attempt to organize a national commemoration of the events that had created modern France revived old controversies. François Mitterrand, France's president at the time, proudly reminded his fellow citizens that the Revolution had been "a decisive part of France in the evolution of the world and of human society," but he also acknowledged the "deviations, oppressions, and later derelictions" that had marred its record.[2]

THE BROADER IMPACT

Just as it has continued to affect France for over two centuries, the French Revolution has had a lasting impact in other parts of the world. The French Revolution has inspired many imitators. Among others, the Russian revolutionaries of 1917 saw themselves as the heirs of the Jacobins. The ideals of individual rights, constitutional government, and national sovereignty articulated in 1789 have inspired movements for freedom and democracy throughout the world, from the revolts against Spanish rule in South America at the beginning of the 1800s to student protests in China in 1989. The Universal Declaration of Human Rights, adopted by the United Nations in 1948 as a statement of the principles to which all countries should adhere, drew much of its inspiration from the Declaration of the Rights of Man and Citizen.

At the same time, however, the legacy of the French Revolution has included a warning of how easily revolutionary movements can turn to violence and dictatorship. Violence accompanied every major stage of the Revolution, indicating the difficulty of making radical social and political changes without raising passions to dangerous levels. In its efforts to defend itself against real and imagined foes, the French Revolution provided the first model of the totalitarian state, silencing all opposition and sometimes aspiring to efface all diversity in the name of the public good. The revolutionary government of the Terror also showed how such a regime could mobilize the entire force of a large country for military purposes. The French Revolution inaugurated the age of ideological and nationalistic warfare, foreshadowing the horrendous conflicts of the twentieth century.

The legacy of the French Revolution is thus a complex one. It provokes continuing controversy because it raises the most fundamental issues about how societies should be structured. In our own age, when contacts between different cultures have become so much more extensive, the Revolution's liberal ideals have renewed importance. Broadened to cover all of the world's citizens, they still appear to offer the best hope for a common set of principles on the basis of which the ancient Biblical promise of a world in which all nations can live together in harmony might be realized.

THE FRENCH REVOLUTION AS HISTORY

The experience of the French Revolution helped form the modern historical consciousness. Those who lived through it learned that a long-established society could be shattered and remade almost overnight. They also learned that events could overpower those who set them in motion and lead them into totally unexpected situations. Throughout Europe, the French Revolution was a tremendous stimulus to the study of history—not just the history of the French Revolution, but the study of the general mechanisms that shape historical events. The way in which historians interpret the French Revolution often serves as a model for the understanding of other great historical occurrences.

The first important histories of the French Revolution were strongly affected by the political currents of nineteenth-century French life. During the Restoration, when the official policy of the French government was to repress all memory of the Revolution, the liberal historian Adolphe Thiers's *History of the French Revolution* was a manifesto in favor of the ideals of 1789. Thiers celebrated the reformist leaders of the National Assembly and tried to exculpate them of any responsibility for the radicalism and violence of the Reign of Terror. Under the July Monarchy, Jules Michelet produced a populist narrative of the Revolution, insisting that the Revolution could not be understood without taking into account the role of the common people. His work, strongly colored by the romantic spirit of the times, can be seen as the first attempt to capture the experience of the Revolution "from the bottom up."

Historians writing after the failure of the Revolution of 1848 tended to be more critical of the 1789 movement. Alexis de Tocqueville's masterpiece, *The Old Regime and the Revolution*, published in 1856, was the first serious attempt to analyze and explain the revolutionary process, rather than simply to narrate its major events and judge its major actors. Without realizing it, Tocqueville maintained, the revolutionaries were continuing the work of the Bourbon monarchy, creating a centralized, bureaucratic government and destroying the organic connections between citizens. As a result, he concluded, they had undermined the preconditions for the liberty they thought they were establishing. Tocqueville's insistence on the connection between the Old Regime and the revolutionary era and his recognition that what the revolutionaries intended was quite different from what they achieved were fundamental contributions to the historical understanding of 1789. His essay remains essential reading for anyone trying to understand the Revolution.

THE JACOBIN HISTORICAL SYNTHESIS

Modern scientific scholarship on the French Revolution began with the appointment of Alphonse Aulard to the first academic chair of revolutionary history in the early 1880s. Aulard stressed the importance of detailed and thorough archival research, setting standards that still govern serious historical inquiry in the field today. He edited publications of primary source materials that are still of value and used his mastery of the archives to clarify many important episodes of revolutionary politics.

Aulard was also the founding figure in what has come to be called the classic or Jacobin interpretation of the Revolution. A firm supporter of the Third Republic, he argued that the history of the Revolution demonstrated that only the democratic republicans of the 1790s had really defended the national interest and ensured the victory of the ideals articulated by the liberal revolutionaries of 1789. Compared to Tocqueville, Aulard stressed the differences between the Old Regime and the Revolution rather than the continuities between them. He blamed the Terror and the Revolution's difficulties on the necessity of combatting counterrevolutionary forces at home and their foreign allies. In his view, Georges Danton, the energetic leader who had rallied the country in 1792 and 1793, personified the spirit of the democratic and republican revolution.

By the beginning of the twentieth century, the socialist doctrines of Karl Marx had come to have considerable influence in French politics and intellectual life. The great French socialist leader Jean Jaurès inspired the publication of a *Socialist History of the French Revolution* (1901–1904), which put new emphasis on the social and economic aspects of the movement. Earlier liberal and republican historians, including Aulard, had acknowledged the leading role of the bourgeois class in the Revolution. The socialist analysis explained this role in terms of the bourgeoisie's interest in creating the conditions for an expanding capitalist economy.

Between them, Aulard and Jaurès provided a basic framework that governed most scholarly analysis of the French Revolution until the 1960s, and which still has considerable influence today. Historians trained in this tradition see the Revolution as a sharp break with the Old Regime that preceded it and as a necessary and inevitable step toward modern secular democracy. They generally argue that "the Revolution is a bloc," in the words of the French republican politician Georges Clémenceau. By this, they mean that the liberal reforms enacted by the National Assembly in 1789 could only have been put into effect through the radical measures taken by the Jacobins after 1792. In this interpretation, the Terror is seen as a necessary aspect of the revolutionary process, essential to defeating the hostile forces at home and abroad that would otherwise have restored the Old Regime. Historians in this tradition generally accept the notion that the entire revolutionary process was led by self-conscious members of the bourgeoisie and assert that this class reaped the major benefits of the upheaval.

Many twentieth-century historians, sympathetic to the plight of the proletariat, claimed that the "bourgeois" revolution of 1789 provided a model for a future proletarian revolution that would finally ensure liberty and equality for all classes of the population. Many—but by no means all—historians of the French Revolution came to see the Bolshevik Revolution of 1917 in Russia as a confirmation of the Marxist interpretation of history. This in turn influenced their understanding of 1789, leading them to emphasize the theme of class struggle and to highlight those aspects of the French experience which anticipated what had happened in Russia.

The most prominent historians who contributed to this classical interpretation of the French Revolution after Aulard were the three French scholars Albert Mathiez, Georges Lefebvre, and Albert Soboul. Each in turn occupied the Sorbonne's chair of the history of the French Revolution, training numerous students and influencing research on the Revolution not only in France but in other countries as well. Each also broadened the scope of the classical interpretation in important ways. Albert Mathiez waged a bitter polemic against Aulard's hero, Danton, and in favor of Robespierre. Only Robespierre, Mathiez claimed, had understood the necessity of uniting the bourgeoisie and the common people and of using extreme measures to defend the Revolution's achievements. Mathiez also contributed to a better understanding of the way in which economic conditions affected the course of the Revolution. He demonstrated that there was a close correlation between high bread prices and lower-class unrest in Paris throughout the 1790s. Mathiez's work helped make sense of the radical Montagnard movement, which, he claimed, under pressure from the lower classes, had begun to propose measures that went beyond bourgeois democracy and foreshadowed the development of socialism.

Georges Lefebvre is remembered above all for elucidating the vital role of the peasants in the Revolution. His meticulous regional study of the department of the Nord showed that peasant communities were not an inarticulate mass, simply reacting to decrees from Paris. Peasants had concerns of their own, different from those of the bourgeois deputies in the Paris assemblies. Lefebvre's study of *The Great Fear of 1789* was a pioneering study of collective mentalities, and his clear and readable synthesis, *The Coming of the French Revolution*, published in 1939, introduced several generations of French and American students to revolutionary history. Lefebvre offered a sophisticated Marxist analysis that explained the course of the Revolution in terms of changing alliances between four basic social classes: the aristocracy, whose blind resistance to necessary reforms set the Revolution in motion, the bourgeoisie, which provided leadership and a revolutionary program, the peasantry, whose uprising in 1789 assured the Revolution's success, and the urban working class, whose pressure drove the bourgeois leadership to take the measures necessary to protect the Revolution after 1792.

Lefebvre's student Albert Soboul turned his attention to the sans-culottes, the urban militants who played such an important role in the Revolution's radical phase. He gave new precision to historians' picture of the sans-culottes, showing that they were not the poorest members of the Paris population but rather shopkeepers, skilled artisans, and small businessmen, generally literate and capable of forming their own political ideas, independent of bourgeois leaders. While Soboul continued the Jacobin historical tradition in France, several English-speaking historians trained by Lefebvre introduced the social-historical approach to the subject to the English-speaking world. George Rudé's *The Crowd in the French Revolution* showed that urban revolutionary violence was neither random nor purposeless. The crowd was made up of the better-off, more aware members of the urban lower classes, and its actions expressed a definite political agenda. Richard Cobb's *The People's Armies* added to historians' understanding of the role of the sans-culottes during the Terror. In many subsequent books and articles, Cobb broadened our understanding of ordinary people's experiences during the Revolution. Over time, however, he broke away from the Marxist emphasis on the importance of class conflicts, arguing that individual experience during the Revolution was too diverse to be understood in such categories.

THE REVISIONIST CRITIQUE

By the early 1960s, historians throughout the world seemed in agreement on the basic issues involved in understanding the French Revolution. Only a few scholars questioned the idea that 1789 had been above all an expression of social conflict, of the bourgeoisie's dissatisfaction with the Old Regime, and of the lower classes' resentment of their lot. To be sure, there were always some dissenters. In an essay entitled "The Myth of the French Revolution," an argumentative English historian, Alfred Cobban, charged that Marxist historians such as Lefebvre and Soboul had misread their own evidence. He denied that bourgeois merchants and manufacturers had fueled a revolt on behalf of a modern capitalist order. The bourgeois participants in 1789, Cobban maintained, were primarily owners of royal offices, irate because the Old Regime's incompetence was undermining their hard-won positions. An American historian, G. H. Taylor, challenged the notion of a conflict between a "feudal" aristocracy and a "capitalist" bourgeoisie by showing that both groups tended to invest their wealth in similar ways, above all by acquiring landed estates.

In the 1970s, these scattered calls for a revision of the standard approach to the French Revolution were brought together and given new polemical vigor by a French scholar, François Furet. In essays later gathered together in English under the title *Interpreting the French Revolution* (1981), Furet denounced what he called the "catechism" of historical orthodoxy that had come to dominate the field. Critical of Marxism, Furet questioned whether a model based on social classes corresponded to the reality of eighteenth-century life and pointed out that the revolutionary decade retarded the growth of capitalism, rather than promoting it. He also denied that pressure from counterrevolutionary forces explained the Revolution's path from liberal reforms to bloody dictatorship. In Furet's view, the politics of the Revolution was not a reflection of underlying class conflict. It was rather a violent competition of "discourses," as rival groups sought to capture control of strategic slogans. Furthermore, Furet questioned whether the Revolution had contributed to the development of liberal institutions. Like Tocqueville, whom he greatly admired, Furet seemed to suggest that the Revolution had been unable to break away from the authoritarian framework of the French past and that it did more to set back the cause of freedom than to advance it. Going beyond Furet, some French historians, particularly those who studied the Vendée rebellion, went so far as to label the Terror an instance of genocide.

POSTREVISIONIST STUDIES OF THE REVOLUTION

Furet's outspoken essay, the best summation of what has come to be known as the "revisionist" critique of the Jacobin historiographical tradition, galvanized new interest in the Revolution's history throughout the late 1970s and the 1980s. Caught up in the general crisis of the Marxist tradition, the defenders of what was now stigmatized as the "orthodox" view of the Revolution were thrown on the defensive. By 1980, a leading English historian, William Doyle, began his reconsideration of *The Origins of the French Revolution* by announcing that the traditional historical framework for the subject had "collapsed." As Doyle acknowledged, however, there was no consensus on how it should be replaced. Doyle himself was one of a number of historians who argued for a return to the primacy of political history. In the

Marxist tradition, political parties and movements had been seen as representatives of distinct social classes. If class struggle was no longer understood as the main force behind all political conflicts, the way was open for a renewed interest in the political events that led up to it and determined its outcome. Doyle's own *Oxford History of the French Revolution* (1988) offers a detailed narrative from this point of view.

Historians who questioned whether the French Revolution was best defined as a sudden shift from a feudal and aristocratic order to a capitalist and bourgeois epoch implicitly raised the question of how much of a break with the past the events of 1789 to 1815 actually represented. Most recent researchers have concluded that the Revolution did not mark a radical break in France's economic development. The fundamental transition to economic modernity that we label "the industrial revolution" did not arrive in France until the 1830s and 1840s. Although the Revolution abolished the political privileges of the nobility, French life remained dominated until the middle of the nineteenth century by an elite of "notables" whose wealth was still mainly in the form of landed estates. Among peasants and workers, old patterns of collective protest persisted until at least the 1830s, suggesting that the Revolution had not caused a fundamental change in mentalities. If there was a distinct period when France changed rapidly from a "traditional" society to a "modern" one, many recent historians have suggested that this happened not during the French Revolution but around the middle of the nineteenth century.

Most historians who specialize in the French Revolution have continued to argue that it did represent a fundamental crisis in France's history. They have reacted to the evidence that the Revolution did not bring about massive changes in economic or social structures by turning in new directions for inspiration, drawing on insights from anthropology and linguistics to demonstrate that 1789 created a new culture and new patterns of thought and behavior. Examples of what is nowadays often labeled "the new cultural history" include Mona Ozouf's study of *Festivals and the French Revolution* (1988), Lynn Hunt's *Politics, Culture, and Class in the French Revolution* (1984), and Timothy Tackett's *Religion, Revolution, and Regional Culture in Eighteenth-Century France* (1986). All three emphasize the importance of new rituals, new symbols, and new patterns of social behavior in defining the Revolution, as opposed to stressing the redistribution of property or the actions of political leaders. Keith Baker's *Inventing the French Revolution* (1990) takes an approach that is more linguistic and philosophical than anthropological. Baker dissects the different "languages" or "discourses" in which political issues were discussed in France before and during the Revolution. He argues that the words in which political debates are conducted limit and define their possible outcomes. Like Furet, and in contrast to the "new cultural historians," Baker sometimes seems to imply that the course of the Revolution was determined by the arsenal of political concepts inherited from the Old Regime, which militated against the creation of a genuinely liberal polity.

By deemphasizing the importance of socioeconomic class in the Revolution, the revisionist critics also opened the way for a new interest in the history of groups whose experience had previously been regarded as marginal. Historians of women have made the most of this opportunity, turning this into one of the liveliest areas of current revolutionary historiography. Joan Landes, in her *Women and the Public Sphere in the Age of the French Revolution* (1989), has argued that the revolutionary movement was fundamentally antifeminist. Other scholars, however, including Lynn Hunt, Dominque Godineau, and Darline Levy and Harriet Applewhite, see the Revolution as providing important opportunities for women's political participation, even though it culminated in a determined effort to confine women to their "proper" domestic concerns. Whereas recent historians who concentrate on peasants or workers have tended to see the social changes of the 1790s as less significant than those of the 1830s or 1840s, women's historians have suggested that the 1790s were indeed a defining decade in which new definitions of gender roles that persisted throughout the nineteenth century were established.

Research on other aspects of the social history of the revolutionary era has of course continued. The most recent social historians tend to be more cautious in defining social categories and generalizing about their experiences under the Revolution than their predecessors, however. An awareness of the importance of gender in shaping historical experience is one reason why it is now harder to make blanket statements about categories such as peasants. Today's historians are also acutely aware that different regions experienced the Revolution very differently. Variations in patterns of land tenure, religious loyalty, proximity to endangered frontiers, and prerevolutionary social and administrative structures have all been shown to have affected local reactions to the Revolution. No simple generalizations seem to describe the mosaic of experiences that has emerged from a proliferation of regional studies.

The celebration of the bicentennial of the French Revolution in 1989 took place at a moment when the revisionist and feminist critiques of the French Revolution had challenged long-established interpretations. In the second half of the 1990s, proponents of what can be called a neo-liberal or neo-democratic interpretation of the Revolution have reacted against these critiques and reaffirmed the movement's fundamental contribution to the causes of freedom and equality. Isser Woloch's *The New Regime* (1993) showed that, for all its excesses, the Revolution had in fact successfully implemented more of its democratic program than the revisionists had been willing to acknowledge. John Markoff's *The Abolition of Feudalism* (1996) and

Timothy Tackett's *Becoming a Revolutionary* (1996) both, in differing ways, reasserted the importance of economic interests and social class divisions in explaining revolutionary politics and countered the revisionists' tendency to portray the period's conflicts as purely ideological. In *Goodness beyond Virtue* (1998), Patrice Higonnet, a scholar often associated with the revisionist critique, offered a complex new interpretation of the Jacobin movement that saw it as being, despite its flaws, a forerunner of contemporary democracy. In 2000, Patrice Gueniffey, one of François Furet's most important disciples, published an important new study of the Terror that significantly modified Furet's assertions that 1789 had marked the decisive descent into revolutionary violence and that the Revolution's struggle with its enemies had nothing to do with the resort to extreme measures.

The understanding historians have of the French Revolution today is thus more nuanced and harder to sum up than it was a generation ago. Rather than a simple confrontation between past and future, feudalism and capitalism, or nobles and bourgeois, the events of the Revolution now seem to show us that the introduction of liberal and democratic principles was a complex and uneven process that undeniably exacted a regrettably high human cost. The revolutionaries made mistakes. They rejected compromises that might have reduced the antagonisms that wracked France after 1789, such as those caused by the attempt to reform the Church without taking devout Catholics' concerns into consideration. From a modern point of view, their treatment of women appears to be in flagrant contradiction with their own proclamations about universal human rights. Above all, the fact that the French Revolution not only turned to violent means to achieve its ends but that, for one brief but tragic period, it also made one-sided trials and public executions central to its policies, must always be deeply troubling to those who sympathize with its ideals. Even as we recognize the French Revolution's shortcomings and contradictions, however, it is impossible to exclude the movement that first proclaimed that "men are born and remain free and equal in rights," granted citizenship to religious minorities, voted to abolish slavery, and took so many initiatives to try to mitigate the effects of poverty and ignorance, from a central place in the development of modern notions of freedom.

NOTES

1. Alfred de Musset, *La confession d'un enfant du siècle* (Paris: Gallimard, 1973), 26.
2. Cited in Steven Kaplan, *Farewell, Revolution* (Ithaca, N.Y.: Cornell University Press, 1995), 137, 140.

SUGGESTIONS
FOR FURTHER READING

This short bibliography is meant to direct students to reference works that will help them find more specialized readings, to some of the more general books in the field, and to a selection of specialized monographs of particular interest. With a few exceptions, it is limited to titles available in English. References to works in French can be found in the bibliographies of most of the books listed here.

BIBLIOGRAPHIES, JOURNALS,
AND GENERAL REFERENCE WORKS

The *Bibliographie annuelle de l'histoire française* (1963—), published yearly, provides the most comprehensive bibliography of recent scholarly books and articles on French history, in both French and other languages. There are three scholarly journals in English devoted to French history that frequently publish articles on the revolutionary and Napoleonic periods: *French Historical Studies, French History*, and the *Proceedings of the Western Society for French History*. The French journal *Annales historiques de la Révolution française*, now accessible online via www. calenda.org, is devoted entirely to the subject. Many other historical journals also publish articles in this field.

Three indispensable reference works are Samuel Scott and Barry Rothaus, eds., *Historical Dictionary of the French Revolution*; Owen Connelly, ed., *Historical Dictionary of Napoleonic France*; and Colin Jones, *The Longman Companion to the French Revolution*. François Furet and Mona Ozouf, eds., *Critical Dictionary of the French Revolution* (1989) includes longer interpretive articles reflecting the revisionist perspective on the Revolution.

SPECIALIZED TITLES: SELECT BIBLIOGRAPHY

General Histories   There is a wide choice of recent general histories of the Revolution in English. Simon Schama's *Citizens* (1989) is a long and readable narrative history, somewhat one-sided in its stress on the Revolution's violence. William Doyle, *Oxford History of the French Revolution* (1988) is a detailed political account extending through 1802; Donald Sutherland, *France, 1789-1815* (1985) gives greater attention to social history and covers the entire Napoleonic period. Alan Forrest, *The French Revolution* (1995) is a concise overview organized on thematic, rather than chronological, lines; David Andress, *French Society in Revolution, 1789-1799* (1999) reemphasizes the movement's social dimension. Two older works that are still worth consulting are the synthesis by the leading French historian of this century, Georges Lefebvre, *The French Revolution*, 2 vols. (1962); and the exceptionally clear account of Norman Hampson, *Social History of the French Revolution* (1963). Useful collections of translated documents are Paul Beik, *The French Revolution* (1970), J. H. Stewart, *Documentary Survey of the French Revolution* (1951), and Laura Mason and Tracey Rizzo, *The French Revolution: A Document Collection* (1999). Lynn Hunt and Jack Censer, *Liberty, Equality, Fraternity* (2001) is a pioneering collection of documents and images from the period on CD-ROM. Gary Kates, ed., *The French Revolution: Recent Debates and New Controversies* (1998) is a collection of scholarly articles. Lynn Hunt, ed., *The French Revolution and Human Rights* (1996) gives the main speeches from revolutionary debates on this issue. Frank Kafker and James Laux, *The French Revolution: Conflicting Interpretations* (1990) provides excerpts from many older historical works.

The Old Regime and the Origins of the Revolution   A classic interpretation of the connection between the Old Regime and the Revolution, still valuable for its many brilliant insights, is Alexis de Tocqueville, *The Old Regime and the Revolution* (1955; orig. 1856). Two general overviews of Old Regime society and institutions are Roland Mousnier, *The Institutions of France under the Absolute Monarchy*, 1598–1789 2 vols. (1979, 1984), and Pierre Goubert, *The Ancien Regime* (1973). Daniel Mornet, *Les Origines intellectuelles de la Révolution française* (1933) is a fundamental work on the spread of Enlightenment ideas that has never been translated. Roger Chartier, *Cultural Origins of the French Revolution* (1991) and Robert Darnton, *The Forbidden Best-Sellers of Pre-Revolutionary France* (1995) broaden and update Mornet's approach. The development of an independent public opinion is a major theme in Thomas Crow, *Painters and Public Life in Eighteenth-Century France* (1985). Sarah Maza, *Private Lives and Public Affairs* (1993) studies how prerevolutionary scandals undermined the regime. Two recent interpretations of the sociology of the French Enlightenment are Dena Goodman, *The Republic of Letters* (1994) and Daniel Gordon, *Citizens without Sovereignty* (1994). David Bell, *Lawyers and Citizens* (1994) looks at the prerevolutionary role of an important professional group.

Interest in the contribution of prerevolutionary politics to the origins of the Revolution has revived strongly in recent years. Dale Van Kley has summarized his extensive research on the influence of Jansenism in *The Religious Origins of the French Revolution* (1996). Steven Kaplan's *Bread, Politics, and Political Economy in the Reign of Louis XV* (1976) deals with issues concerning economic modernization. The impact of the political crisis resulting from Louis XV's final attempt to silence the parlementary opposition is the subject of Durand Echeverria, *The Maupeou Revolution* (1985) and of many of the essays in Keith Baker, *Inventing the French Revolution* (1990). Douglas Dakin, *Turgot and the Ancient Regime* (1939) and Robert Harris, *Necker* (1981) deal with Louis XVI's two most controversial ministers, while Orville Murphy, *Charles Gravier, Comte de Vergennes* (1982) traces French foreign policy in the era of the American Revolution. Jean Egret, *The French Prerevolution* (1977) is the standard account of the political events of 1787 and 1788. Georges Lefebvre's *Coming of the French Revolution* (1947) is a classic synthesis by the century's greatest scholar of the subject. William Doyle's *Origins of the French Revolution*, 2nd ed. (1988) offers an updated analysis. In *Reform and Revolution in France* (1995), P. M. Jones argues for a continuity between the reform efforts of the Old Regime and the legislation of the Revolution's early years.

Revolutionary Politics Colin Lucas, ed., *The Political Culture of the French Revolution* (1989) contains contributions dealing with many aspects of revolutionary politics. Timothy Tackett, *Becoming a Revolutionary: The Deputies of the French National Assembly and the Emergence of a Revolutionary Culture* (1996) studies the politics of the Revolution's first assembly. Michael Kennedy, *The Jacobin Clubs in the French Revolution*, 3 vols. (1982, 1988, 2000) explains the workings of the club network; Alison Patrick, *The Men of the First French Republic* (1972) studies the deputies of the National Convention. Timothy Tackett, *Religion, Revolution, and Regional Culture in Eighteenth-Century France* (1986) and Suzanne Desan, *Reclaiming the Sacred* (1990) examine the social bases underlying the religious conflict, whose stages are recounted in John McManners, *French Revolution and the Church* (1970). Paul Hanson, *Provincial Politics in the French Revolution* (1989) looks at the contrast between Paris and the provinces. Isser Woloch, *The New Regime* (1993), provides a comprehensive look at the movement's impact on civic institutions.

Patrice Higonnet, *Goodness beyond Virtue* (1998) is a difficult but stimulating reappraisal of the Jacobin movement. Patrice Gueniffey, *La Politique de la Terreur* (2000) reevaluates the Revolution's most controversial phase. The multivocal approach of Norman Hampson, *Life and Opinions of Maximilien Robespierre* (1974) dramatizes the conflicting interpretations that have been offered of the most controversial revolutionary leader. R. R. Palmer, *Twelve Who Ruled* (1943) explains the Committee of Public Safety's policies. R. B. Rose, *Gracchus Babeuf* (1978) looks at one of the most extreme revolutionary thinkers, while Jacques Godechot, *The Counter-Revolution* (1964) covers both thought and action. Stanley Loomis's highly readable *The Fatal Friendship* (1972) is the best work on the royal family and its fate. David P. Jordan's *The King's Trial* (1979) vividly describes one of the Revolution's turning points; speeches from the trial are translated in Michael Walzer, ed., *Regicide and Revolution* (1992), and John Hardman, *Louis XVI* (1993) gives a portrait of the king. T. C. W. Blanning, *Origins of the French Revolutionary Wars* (1986) explains international aspects of the revolutionary conflict.

Revolutionary Culture François Furet's essay *Interpreting the French Revolution* (1981) opened a new era of historiography, focused on the Revolution's political culture. Lynn Hunt, *Politics, Culture and Class in the French Revolution* (1984) and Mona Ozouf, *Festivals and the French Revolution* (1988) offer stimulating explorations of this subject. Jeremy Popkin, *Revolutionary News* (1990) and Jack Censer, *Prelude to Power* (1976), deal with the newspaper press; *French Caricature and the French Revolution* (1988) deals with visual propaganda, while Daniel Roche and Robert Darnton, eds., *Revolution in Print* (1989) surveys all the major media of revolutionary propaganda, Carla Hesse, *Publishing and Cultural Politics in Revolutionary Paris, 1789-1810* (1990) examines the book trade, and Emmet Kennedy, *Cultural History of the French Revolution* (1989) covers the entire range of cultural activities. Laura Mason, *Singing the French Revolution* (1996) describes popular revolutionary music, while H.-J. Lüsebrink and Rolf Reichardt, *The Bastille: A History of a Symbol of Despotism and Freedom* (1997) looks at the development of the most potent symbol of the Revolution. R. R. Palmer, *The Improvement of Humanity: Education and the French Revolution* (1985) examines school-reform plans and their fate. Revolutionary ideology and its implications are treated in Patrice Higonnet, *Class, Ideology, and the Rights of Nobles during the French Revolution* (1980); George A. Kelly, *Victims, Authority, and Terror* (1982); and the psychologically oriented work of Lynn Hunt, *The Family Romance of the French Revolution* (1992).

Social and Women's History With the dissolution of the Marxist paradigm, there is no convincing synthesis of the complex social history of the revolutionary period. Peter Jones, *The Peasantry in the French Revolution* (1988) gives an overview of the revolution in the countryside, while Charles

Tilly, *The Vendée* (1967) uses the counterrevolutionary peasant revolt to build a general model explaining social protest. John Markoff, *The Abolition of Feudalism* (1996) is a major reexamination of the peasantry's role in the Revolution. The urban revolutionary movement is the subject of Albert Soboul, *The Sans-Culottes* (1964); George Rudé, *The Crowd in the French Revolution* (1959); and Richard Cobb, *The Police and the People* (1970). Much new work has recently appeared on women during the Revolution, including a documentary collection, Darline Gay Levy et al., *Women in Revolutionary Paris* (1979); the provocative interpretation offered by Joan Landes, *Women and the Public Sphere in the Age of the French Revolution* (1989); Sara Melzer and Leslie Rabine, eds., *Rebel Daughters: Women and the French Revolution* (1992); Olwyn Hufton, *Women and the Limits of Citizenship in the French Revolution* (1992); and Dominique Godineau, *The Women of Paris and their Revolution* (1998). Madelyn Gutwirth et al., eds., *Germaine de Staël* (1991) treats the epoch's most important female writer. Alan Forrest has examined two important groups in the revolutionary period in his *The French Revolution and the Poor* (1981) and *Soldiers of the French Revolution* (1990). Dora Weiner's *The Citizen-Patient in Revolutionary and Imperial Paris* (1993) looks at the impact on medicine. Michael Fitzsimmons, *The Parisian Order of Barristers and the French Revolution* (1987) provides a case study of how the Revolution affected a major professional group. On the revolution in Saint-Domingue, see the classic account in C. L. R. James, *The Black Jacobins* (1963) and the more recent but less comprehensive work of Carolyn Fick, *The Making of Haiti: The Saint Domingue Revolution from Below* (1990). George Tyson, *Toussaint L'Ouverture* (1973) provides selected documents about the great insurrectionary leader.

Directory Period After a flurry of interest in the 1960s and 1970s, the Directory has reverted to its traditional status as the Revolution's most neglected period. Bronislaw Baczko, *Ending the Terror* (1994) explains how the thermidorians tried to deal with the legacy of 1794. Martyn Lyons, *France under the Directory* (1975) is a good overview; Isser Woloch, *Jacobin Legacy* (1970) looks at the period's left-wing movement, while Harvey Mitchell, *The Underground War against Revolutionary France* (1965) examines royalist intrigues. Jeremy Popkin, *The Right-Wing Press in France, 1792–1800* (1980) is a study of domestic political opposition to the Republic. R. R. Palmer, *The World of the French Revolution* (1971) provides a brief account of the "sister republics."

Napoleonic Period Most of the literature on this period focuses on Napoleon, rather than on France. A major exception is Louis Bergeron's *France under Napoleon* (1981), which emphasizes the experience of the French people rather than Napoleon's life. Georges Lefebvre, *Napoleon* (1969) is a standard survey. Martyn Lyons, *Napoleon Bonaparte and the Legacy of the*

French Revolution (1994) and Geoffrey Ellis, *Napoleon* (1997) incorporate more recent scholarship. Felix Markham, *Napoleon* (1963) is a reliable biography. J. C. Herold, *The Mind of Napoleon* (1955) gives selections from his letters and memoirs. Robert Holtman, *Napoleonic Propaganda* (1950), and Irene Collins, *Napoleon and his Parliaments* (1979) discuss domestic political aspects of the reign. Gunther Rothenberg, *The Art of Warfare in the Age of Napoleon* (1979) and Owen Connelly, *Blundering to Glory* (1987) cover various aspects of its military history. Geoffrey Ellis, *Napoleon's Continental Blockade* (1981) studies the effects of Napoleon's economic warfare. Peter Geyl, *Napoleon: For and Against* (1949) and Frank Kafker and James Laux, eds., *Napoleon and his Times* (1989) document historians' changing views of Napoleon over time; the latter title has a good bibliography.

The Memory of the Revolution   The bicentennial of the French Revolution inspired new interest in the event's long-term impact and its place in French memory.   François Furet, *Revolutionary France 1770–1880* (1992) describes the gradual consolidation of democratic republicanism in nineteenth-century France.   Steven Kaplan, *Farewell, Revolution* (1995) is a fascinating account of how France marked the 200th anniversary of the Revolution in 1989.

CHRONOLOGY
OF PRINCIPAL EVENTS
DURING THE FRENCH REVOLUTION

PREREVOLUTIONARY CRISIS
(JANUARY 1, 1787–MAY 5, 1789)

February 22, 1787: Assembly of Notables opens.

November 19, 1787: Compromise plan to solve fiscal crisis falls apart when Paris Parlement protests king's arbitrary order to accept it.

May 8, 1788: Royal ministers announce plan to abolish parlements and create new judicial system, setting off widespread protests.

July 5, 1788: Government announces convocation of Estates-General and suspends censorship.

July 13, 1788: Hailstorm damages crops in much of northern France, causing fears of famine.

August 26, 1788: Jacques Necker appointed as finance minister.

December 27, 1788: Royal Council announces "doubling of Third Estate," allowing commoners twice as many deputies as other Estates in Estates-General.

January-April 1789: Convocation of electoral assemblies for Estates-General.

April 28, 1789: Reveillon riot in Paris shows extent of social tensions in capital.

May 5, 1789: Opening session of Estates-General.

THE LIBERAL REVOLUTION
(MAY 5, 1789–AUGUST 10, 1792)

June 17, 1789: Deputies of Third Estate declare themselves the National Assembly.

June 20, 1789: National Assembly deputies swear Oath of the Tennis Court.

June 23, 1789: National Assembly defies Louis XVI's order for estates to meet separately.

June 27, 1789: Louis XVI orders deputies of clergy and nobility to join National Assembly.

July 11, 1789: Dismissal of Necker announced.

July 14, 1789: Paris crowd and soldiers storm the Bastille.

July 20–early August 1789: Wave of rural violence ("Great Fear") sweeps most of the country.

August 4-5, 1789: National Assembly decrees the abolition of seigneurial dues and special privileges.

August 26, 1789: National Assembly passes the "Declaration of the Rights of Man and Citizen."

September 11, 1789: National Assembly votes to give king suspensive rather than absolute veto.

October 5-6, 1789: Crowd of women and National Guards marches on Versailles and forces king and National Assembly to move to Paris.

November 2, 1789: National Assembly votes to expropriate Church lands.

July 12, 1790: Enactment of church-reform plan, the Civil Constitution of the Clergy.

July 14, 1790: Festival of the Federation commemorates first anniversary of storming of Bastille.

May 15, 1791: Assembly votes to give political rights to some mulattoes and free blacks in colonies.

June 14, 1791: Le Chapelier law, abolishing guilds and prohibiting formation of trade unions.

June 20, 1791: Louis XVI and his family flee Paris. They are stopped at Varennes on June 22.

July 16, 1791: Paris Jacobin club splits; supporters of the king form a new club, the Feuillants.

July 17, 1791: Paris National Guard kills sixty demonstrators in "massacre of Champ-de-Mars."

August 22, 1791: Beginning of slave insurrection in Saint-Domingue.

August 27, 1791: Austrian and Prussian rulers issue Pillnitz declaration, demanding restoration of Louis XVI's rights.

September 27, 1791: National Assembly votes to make all French Jews full citizens.

October 1, 1791: First session of the Legislative Assembly.

April 20, 1792: France declares war on Austria.

August 10, 1792: Sans-culotte militants attack royal palace, force Legislative Assembly to suspend king and call for election of National Convention.

The Radical Revolution
(August 10, 1792–July 27, 1794)

September 2-5, 1792: "September massacres": Revolutionary activists kill suspected counterrevolutionaries in Paris prisons.

September 20, 1792: French victory at Valmy halts advance of the Austrian-Prussian army.

September 20, 1792: National Convention meets. On September 22, the Convention declares France a republic.

January 21, 1793: Execution of Louis XVI.

March 11, 1793: Vendée counterrevolutionary revolt breaks out.

May 31-June 2, 1793: Revolutionary activists force Convention to decree arrest of Girondins.

June 6, 1793: Start of federalist revolts against Convention.

July 13, 1793: Charlotte Corday assassinates Marat.

July 27, 1793: Robespierre elected to Committee of Public Safety.

August 23, 1793: Convention decrees the "levée en masse."

September 5, 1793: Convention decrees that "terror is the order of the day"; general maximum on prices and wages.

September 17, 1793: Passage of Law of Suspects.

October 5, 1793: Convention establishes revolutionary calendar, prelude to radical phase of de-Christianization campaign in November 1793.

October 16, 1793: Execution of Marie-Antoinette.

October 31, 1793: Execution of twenty-one Girondin deputies.

December 4, 1793 (14 frimaire II): Convention puts all local officials under the authority of the Committee of Public Safety.

January 17, 1794: "Infernal columns" begin the bloodiest phase of the repression in the Vendée.

February 26, 1794 (8 ventôse II): Convention votes for distribution of confiscated emigré property to poor patriots.

March 24, 1794 (4 germinal II): Revolutionary Tribunal condemns Hébert, the *Père Duchesne.*

April 6, 1794 (16 germinal II): Execution of "Indulgents" (Danton, Camille Desmoulins, and supporters).

June 8, 1794 (20 prairial II): Robespierre presides over Festival of the Supreme Being.

June 10, 1794 (22 prairial II): Law accelerating Revolutionary Tribunal's procedures marks start of "Great Terror."

June 26, 1794 (8 messidor II): French victory at Fleurus drives enemy armies out of France.

July 27, 1794 (9 thermidor II): Convention votes the arrest of Robespierre and his supporters.

THE THERMIDORIAN AND DIRECTORY PERIODS
(JULY 27, 1794–NOVEMBER 9, 1799)

April 1, 1795 (12 germinal II): Hunger crisis provokes sans-culottes to invade the Convention.

May 20-3, 1795 (1-4 prairial III): Final sans-culotte uprising; one Convention deputy is killed.

October 5, 1795 (13 vendémiaire IV): Defeat of counterrevolutionary uprising in Paris clears way for installation of new Directory regime.

May 10, 1796 (21 floréal IV): Arrest of Gracchus Babeuf and members of the "Conspiracy of the Equals."

September 4, 1797 (18 fructidor V): Coup d'état ousts counterrevolutionaries from Directory and legislature; start of "Second Directory."

October 17, 1797 (26 vendémiaire VI): Napoleon's treaty with Austria at Campo-Formio.

May 11, 1798 (22 floréal VI): Coup d'état prevents election of neo-Jacobin deputies.

June 18, 1799 (30 prairial VII): Coup d'état ousts four members from Executive Directory.

November 9, 1799 (18 brumaire VIII): Directory overthrown by Sieyès and Napoleon.

THE NAPOLEONIC PERIOD
(NOVEMBER 9, 1799–JUNE 18, 1815)

December 13, 1799: Napoleon Bonaparte made First Consul.

June 14, 1800: Napoleon's victory at Marengo consolidates his power in France.

February 9, 1801: Treaty of Lunéville between Austria and France.

July 16, 1801: Signature of Concordat between France and the Papacy, officially published on April 8, 1802.

March 25, 1802: Peace of Amiens between France and England.

May 19, 1802: Establishment of Legion of Honor.

August 4, 1802: Napoleon becomes First Consul for Life.

March 28, 1803: War resumed between France and England.

March 20, 1804: Execution of duc d'Enghien.

March 21, 1804: Proclamation of the Civil Code (Code Napoleon).

December 2, 1804: Napoleon crowns himself as Emperor, with Pope in attendance.

December 2, 1805: Battle of Austerlitz.

October 14, 1806: Battles of Jena and Auerstädt shatter Prussian army.

November 21, 1806: Napoleon declares Continental Blockade against trade with Britain.

July 7, 1807: Treaty of Tilsit with Russia.

March 1, 1808: Napoleon announces creation of new system of nobility.

May 1808: Anti-French uprising in Madrid leads to reprisals that fan Spanish resistance.

June 11, 1809: Pope Pius VII excommunicates Napoleon.

July 5-6, 1809: Battle of Wagram.

April 2, 1810: After divorcing Josephine, Napoleon marries the Austrian princess Marie-Louise.

June 1812: Napoleon starts invasion of Russia. Forced into disastrous retreat in late October, he loses most of his army.

October 16-19 1813: "Battle of the Nations" at Leipzig.

April 6, 1814: Napoleon abdicates as Emperor.

March 20, 1815: After landing in southern France on March 1, Napoleon arrives in Paris and inaugurates the "Hundred Days."

June 18, 1815: Allied forces under the command of Wellington defeat the French at Waterloo.

INDEX

Aboukir, battle of, 107
Absolutism, definition of, 3
Academies, 4-5
"Additional Act" (1815), 138
Aelders, Etta Palm d' (feminist), 89 (doc.)
Alembert, Jean d' (philosophe), 17
Alexander I, Tsar, 127, 135, 136
Alsace, 10, 62, 120, 128
Amalgame, 92
American Independence, War of, 4, 21
Ami du Peuple (newspaper), 54, 59 (illus.)
Amiens, Peace of, 118, 120, 125
Anglas, F.A. Boissy d' (revolutionary politician), 102 (doc.)
Applewhite, Harriet (historian), 149
Arch of Triumph, 132
Aristocratic reaction, 22
Armoire de fer, 76
Army, 65, 125, 133, 134, 135, 136
    in Directory period, 102, 106, 109
    National Assembly and, 65
    prerevolutionary 4, 10
    victories during Terror, 92–93
    See also Grand Army; Imperial Guard; *levée en masse*; Ségur edict; war
Army of Italy, 106, 114
Artisans 13, 65. *See also* sans-culottes; workers
Artois, Count of (brother of Louis XVI), 37. *See also* Charles X
Assembly of Notables, 22, 23-4 (doc.)
Assignats, 50, 77, 99, 104
Auerstädt, battle of, 127
August 4, 1789, decrees of, 38, 42, 43, 87
August 10, 1792, *journée* of, 67-9 (doc.), 76
Aulard, Alphonse (historian), 144
Austerlitz, battle of, 127
Austria, 4, 62-3, 76, 93, 106, 109, 114, 118, 126-7, 135, 136, 138
Avignon, annexation of, 62

Babeuf, Gracchus (radical leader), 107
Bailly, Sylvain (mayor of Paris), 33, 34, 57, 82
Baker, Keith (historian), 37, 148
Bank of France, 117
Barnave, Antoine (revolutionary politician), 57, 82
Barras, Paul (revolutionary politician), 103, 108, 114
Basel, Peace of, 105
Bastille, 1, 32 (illustration), 33 (doc.), 37
Batavian Revolution, 105
"Battlefield of Eylau" (painting), 132
Beauharnais, Josephine (wife of Napoleon Bonaparte), 114, 115, 124, 135
Becoming a Revolutionary (by Timothy Tackett), 149
Belgium, 76, 93, 105, 106, 118, 128, 138
    annexation of, 106
Belley, J.B. (black deputy to Convention), 90
Berlin, 127
Bernadotte, General, 136
Berthier, Alexander (Napoleonic minister), 117
Bicentennial of French Revolution, 149
Bill of Rights (U.S.), 41, 42
Billaud-Varennes (revolutionary politician), 82
Birth control, 20
Blacks, 47, 62, 89-90. *See also* colonies; slavery
Bonald, Louis de (social theorist), 122-3
Bonaparte, Joseph (brother of Napoleon), 126, 128

Bonaparte, Lucien (brother of Napoleon), 110
Bonaparte, Napoleon, 93, 102-3, 106, 110, 111-29, 132-38
    abdication of (1814), 137
    becomes First Consul, 111, 113 (illustration), 115-6
    and Catholic Church, 119, 121, 129, 135
    childhood and youth, 114
    coronation of as Emperor, 124, 126
    and coup d'état of 18 brumaire, 110
    defeat at Waterloo, 138
    and Directory, 106-7, 114
    Egyptian expedition, 106-7, 115
    establishes Empire, 124
    exile to Saint Helena, 138
    foreign policy of, 118–19, 125-7, 135-6
    and "Hundred Days," 137-8
    ideas of (doc.), 125
    invades Russia, 136
    leads invasion of Italy, 106, 110, 114
    military campaign during Consulate, 118
    opposition to, 121-3
    and vendémiaire uprising, 102-3
    victory at Toulon, 93, 114
    See also Buonaparte, Napoleone; Consulate; Empire
Bordeaux, 11, 61, 63, 80
Borodino, battle of, 136
Bourbon dynasty, 3, 5, 126, 137, 139
Bourbon Restoration. *See* Restoration
"Bourgeois republic," 97
"Bourgeois revolution," 12–13, 44, 145
Bourgeoisie, 11–13
Bread price, impact of, 25, 43, 78, 145
Brienne, Loménie de (royal minister), 24, 25
Brissot, Jacques-Pierre (journalist and politician), 63. See also Girondins
Britain, 4, 6, 16, 25, 76, 101, 106, 109, 118, 124, 125-7, 134, 135-8
    free trade treaty with (1786), 13, 25
    See also England
Brittany, 8, 97, 101
    in pre-Revolution, 25, 26
18 brumaire Year VIII, coup d'état of, 110, 112, 113 (illus.), 115
    See also Bonaparte, Napoleon; Sieyès, Emmanuel
Brunswick, Duke of (general), 67
Brunswick Manifesto, 67
Buonaparte, Napoleone, 93. *See also* Bonaparte, Napoleon
Burke, Edmund (political theorist), 16, 58, 91

Caen, 80
Cahiers de doléance, 27–29
Calas, Jean (Protestant), 17
Calendar, revolutionary. *See* Revolutionary calendar
Calonne, Charles Alexandre de (royal minister), 21–22, 23–24
    reform proposals of, 21–22, 23 (doc.), 24
Campo-Formio, treaty of, 106, 109, 118
Candide (novel), 16
Carnot, Lazare (revolutionary politician), 82, 92
Carrier, Jean-Baptiste (revolutionary politician), 90, 97
Catholic Church
    and dechristianization campaign, 86
    under Directory, 97, 104-5, 107, 108
    and Enlightenment, 13, 16, 19
    National Assembly's reform of, 48–52

Catholic Church, *continued*
    Napoleon and, 114, 119, 129, 135
    prerevolutionary, 4, 8–9, 19
    revival of support for, 121-2
    See also Civil Constitution of the Clergy; clergy;
        Concordat; dechristianization; Jansenism; Pius
        VII; Pope; refractory priests
Cercle social (club), 55
Chaptal, Jean-Antoine (Napoleonic minister), 117
Charles X (king of France, 1824–1830), 139 *See also*
    Artois, Count of
Chateaubriand, François-René de (author), 121-2
Chaumette, Anaxagoras (revolutionary politician), 88
China, 142
Chouans, 101
Church. *See* Catholic Church; clergy
Church lands, expropriation of, 48–50, 87, 119
Civil Code, 120-1, 140
Civil Constitution of the Clergy, 50-2 (illus.), 56, 71, 119,
    121
    opposition to, 51-2, 56, 60, 77, 88
Classic interpretation of French Revolution. *See* Jacobin
    interpretation of French Revolution
Clémenceau, Georges (French politician), 145
Clergy, 8-9, 50-2, 119, 121
    Civil Constitution of the, 50-2
    in Estates-General, 26–27, 30
    prerevolutionary, 8–9
    See also Catholic Church; Civil Constitution of the
        Clergy; refractory priests
Club Massiac (club), 55
Clubs, 54-5
    women's, 55
    See also Cercle social; Club Massiac; Cordeliers
        club; Feuillant club; Jacobins
Cobb, Richard (historian), 146
Cobban, Alfred (historian), 146
Code civil. See Civil Code
Code Napoléon. See Civil Code
Collot d'Herbois (revolutionary politician), 82
Colonies, 29, 47, 61, 89-90, 106, 118–19
    prerevolutionary, 4
    See also blacks; mulattoes; Saint-Domingue; slavery
Coming of the French Revolution, The (by Lefebvre), 145
Commissioners of the executive power, 104, 116
Committee of General Security, 83
Committee of Public Instruction, 47
Committee of Public Safety, 82, 83-4, 90–92, 94. See also
    Robespierre
Committee on the Needy, 47
Commune of Paris, 70, 88
Compte rendu (by Necker), 23
Concordat, 119, 121, 129
    See also Catholic Church; Pius VII
Concorde, Place de la, 76
Condorcet, marquis de (revolutionary politician), 78
Conseil d'état, 116–17
Conservatism. *See* Bonald, Louis de; Burke, Edmund;
    counterrevolution
Constant, Benjamin (author), 122, 138
Constituent Assembly. See National Assembly
Constitution, American, 40-1
Constitution of 1791, 38, 62, 64, 68, 71-2, 74
    See also August 4, 1789, decrees of; Declaration of
        the Rights of Man; National Assembly
Constitution of 1793, 80, 99, 100
Constitution of 1795 (Year III), 97, 101, 102 (doc.), 108,
    110, 112
Constitution of 1800 (Year VIII), 115
Constitutional monarchy, theory of, 16, 71-2
Consulate, 111, 115–17, 120
    Life Consulate, 120

Continental System, 127-8, 131, 135–36
Convention. *See* National Convention
Corday, Charlotte (assassin), 81
Cordeliers Club, 55, 56, 60, 67, 70
Corneille, Pierre (playwright), 123
Corsica, 114
Council of Elders, 101
Council of 500, 101, 110, 115
Council of State. *See* Conseil d'état
Counterrevolution, 58, 60, 64 (doc.), 71, 100-1, 107–8,
    121–3, 126 *See also* Burke, Edmund; Club Massiac;
    emigrés; Verona, declaration of
Crowd in the French Revolution, The (by Rudé), 146

Danton, Georges (revolutionary politician), 55, 70, 74,
    82, 91, 144, 145
Dantonists, 91, 94
Dauphiné, 25, 26
David, Jacques-Louis (artist), 87, 91, 132
Décade philosophique (journal), 132
Décadi, 108. *See also* revolutionary calendar
December 4, 1793, law of, 83
Dechristianization, 86, 121
Declaration of Human Rights (1948), 42, 142
Declaration of the Rights of Man and Citizen, 38-43, (doc.),
    44, 61, 62, 78, 112, 140, 142
"Declaration of the Rights of Women," 88
Departments, 47–48, 49 (map), 141
Desmoulins, Camille (journalist), 54, 55, 91
Diamond Necklace affair, 19. *See also* Marie-Antoinette
Diderot, Denis (author), 17
Directory, Executive, 96–97, 101, 103-110, 111, 114
    and foreign affairs, 105-7
    overthrow of, 110
Discourse on the Origins of Inequality (by Rousseau), 17
Divorce legislation, 60, 88, 120
"Doubling of the Third [Estate]," 27
Doyle, William (historian), 147
Dubarry, Madame (royal mistress), 19
Dumouriez, Charles-François (general), 64, 76

Ecole normale, 104
Ecole polytechnique, 104, 121
Economic conditions
    during Directory, 103-4
    historians' analysis of, 145
    in Napoleonic Empire, 133–34
    prerevolutionary, 14–15
Education, 14, 47, 104, 119, 121, 129, 141-2
Egyptian expedition, 106-7, 115, 119, 132
Elba, 137
Elections
    in 1791, 58
    in 1797, 107
    in 1800, 115–16
    in 1802, 120
Emigrés, 56, 62, 63, 64 (doc.), 76, 101, 117, 126, 137. *See
    also* Counterrevolution
Emile (by Rousseau), 17
Empire, Napoleonic, 120, 124, 128-35 (map), 130 (doc.)
    131
"Empire" style (in art), 132
Encyclopédie. See Encyclopedia
Encyclopedia (by d'Alembert and Diderot), 17-18
Enghien, Duke of, 126
England, 4, 6, 16, 25, 62, 133. *See also* Britain
Enlightenment, 16–18, 105, 122
Enragés, 78, 79 (doc.), 81, 88, 90
Equality (in Declaration of Rights of Man), 38, 42
Estates, prerevolutionary, 8. *See also* Clergy; nobility;
    Third Estate

Estates-General, 6, 22, 24, 25, 26-30
  elections to, 27
  meeting of, 29–30
  summoning of (1788), 25
État civil, 60
Execution of king, 75, 76 (illus.)
Exposition of the System of the World (by Laplace), 105
Eylau, battle of, 127, 132

Faubourg Saint-Antoine, 32, 99
Federalist movement, 80-81
Federation, festival of, 53, 55
Fédérés, 67 (1792), 138 (1815)
Fesch, Cardinal, 129
Festival of the Supreme Being, 87, 91, 93 (illus.)
Festivals, public, 53, 56, 87, 91, 93 (illus.). *See also* Federation, festival of; Festival of the Supreme Being
Festivals and the French Revolution (by Ozouf), 148
Feuillant club, 57, 60, 63
Flanders, 14
Flesselles (royal official), 33
Fleurus, battle of, 93
22 floréal Year VI, coup of, 108
"Foreign plot," 90
Fouché, Joseph (revolutionary politician and Napoleonic minister), 97, 117, 137, 138
Fouquier-Tinville (revolutionary politician), 97
Frederic the Great (king of Prussia), 4
Frederic William II (king of Prussia), 63
Freemasons, 12, 18
Friedland, battle of, 127
18 fructidor Year V, coup of, 108
Furet, François (historian), 91, 147, 148, 150

Gabelle, 8
Gaudin, Charles (Napoleonic minister), 117
General will, theory of, 17, 41
Genoa, siege of, 118
Genius of Christianity (by Chateaubriand), 121-2
Germany, 106, 118, 121, 127, 128, 135, 140. *See also* Prussia
"Germinal franc," 117
12–13 germinal Year III, *journée* of, 99
Gironde, department of, 63
"Girondin" constitutional plan, 78
Girondins, 63, 74, 76, 78-80, 82
  defeat of (May 1793), 80
  execution of (October 1793) 82
Godineau, Dominique (historian), 149
Goethe, J. W. (author), 70
Gouges, Olympe de (revolutionary activist), 88
Grand Army, 127, 136, 138
"Great Fear," 34
Great Fear of 1789, The (by Lefebvre), 146
"Great Terror," 91
Grégoire, abbé Henri (revolutionary politician), 47, 61
Grenoble, 25
Gros, Antoine-Jean (artist), 132
Guadeloupe, 61
Guéniffey, Patrice (historian), 150
Guerre des Dieux, La (by Parny), 108
Guilds, 8, 10, 13
  abolition of (1776), 7, 13
  abolition of (1791), 41, 47
Guillotin, Dr. (revolutionary legislator), 70
Guillotine, 70, 98 (illus.)
Guizot, François (French politician), 131 (doc.)

Haiti, 118-9. *See also*: Saint-Domingue
Hébert, Jacques (journalist and politician), 81, 90-1. *See also Père Duchesne*

Helvetic Republic, 106
History of the French Revolution (by Thiers), 143
Hoche, Lazare (general), 101
Hostages, law of, 110
Hôtel-de-Ville (Paris), 43, 69 (map), 94
Hondschoote, battle of, 93
Hugo, Victor (author), 129
"Hundred Days," 138
Hunt, Lynn (historian), 148, 149

Idéologie, 105. *See also* Idéologues
Idéologues, 105, 107, 121, 122, 132-3
Imperial Catechism, 129
Imperial Guard, 135, 138
Imperial University, 129
"Incorruptible, The." *See* Robespierre, Maximilien
India, French possessions in, 4
"Industrial revolution," 148
Ingres, J.-A.-D. (artist), 132
Institut de France, 104, 121
Intendants, 5, 116
Interpreting the French Revolution (by Furet), 147
Inventing the French Revolution (by Baker), 148
Italy, 118, 128
  French invasion of, 106, 114

Jacobin interpretation of French Revolution, 144–46
Jacobins, 54-5, 57, 60, 63, 67, 70, 72, 74, 99, 107
  closing of club, 99
  and declaration of war (1792), 63
  during Legislative Assembly, 60, 67
  under Napoleon, 116
  during National Convention, 74
  revival of under Directory, 107, 108–10. See also Girondins, Montagnards
Jansenism, 18–19
Jaurès, Jean (French politician and historian), 144
Jena, battle of, 127
"Jeunesse dorée," 99, 101
Jews, 10-1, 47, 119–20, 141
  political rights granted to, 47
Josephine, Empress. *See* Beauharnais, Josephine
Journal de l'Empire, 133
Journal des Débats, 123, 133
Journalists, 54, 59 (illus.). *See also* newspapers
Journals, 18
July 17, 1791, massacre of, 57
"July Monarchy," 139, 143
July Revolution. *See* Revolution of 1830
June 20, 1792, *journée* of, 67

Lacombe, Claire (political activist), 78
Lafayette, Marquis de (revolutionary politician), 33-4, 43, 45, 57
Lamennais, Félicité de (priest), 129
Landes, Joan (historian), 149
Language reform (during Reign of Terror), 86-7
Laplace, Pierre-Simon (astronomer), 105
Larochefoucauld-Liancourt, Duke of, 1
Last Judgment of Kings (play), 86
Launay, de (military commander), 33
Le Chapelier law, 47
Lefebvre, Georges (historian), 22, 71, 145-6
Legion of Honor, 120
Legislative Assembly, 58, 60–64, 67–70
Legislative Body, 117, 129
Leipzig, battle of, 136
Leopold II (Emperor of Austria), 63
Levée en masse, 81, 82, 92
Levy, Darline (historian), 149

Libelles, 19
"Liberal revolution," 44
Liberty (in Declaration of Rights of Man), 41-3, 44
"Liberty trees," 55
Lille, massacre in, 65
Lindet, Robert (revolutionary politician), 82
Livrets, 129
Local government (in Revolution), 48
Loménie de Brienne. *See* Brienne, Loménie de
Louis XIV (king of France, 1643–1715), 4, 5, 10, 16, 19
Louis XV (king of France, 1715–1774), 3, 7, 15, 19
Louis XVI (king of France, 1774–1793), 1, 3, 4, 19, 21–22, 34, 45, 56-7, 68
   coronation of (illus.), 2
   demonstration against (June 20, 1792), 67
   dismisses Calonne, 24
   dismisses Necker, 31
   execution of, 75-6 (illus.)
   flight to Varennes, 56-7
   grants rights to Protestants, 10
   and October Days, 43
   and prevolutionary crisis, 24, 27, 29–30
   supports declaration of war, 63-4
   suspended from office, 68
   trial of, 74–76
   vetoes law against emigrés, 62
Louis XVIII (king of France, 1814/5–1824) 100, 137, 138, 139
   manifesto of, 64 (doc.)
Louisiana Purchase, 118
L'Ouverture, Toussaint, 61
Lunéville, Treaty of, 118
Luxembourg, 118
Lycées, 129
Lyon, 14, 80-81, 99
   siege of, 80-1

Machault d'Arnouville (royal minister), 7
Mahomet (play), 16
Mainz, 105 *See also* Rhineland
Makandal conspiracy, 61
Malesherbes, Lamoignon de (king's lawyer), 75
Malta, 125
Mandats, 104
Marat, Jean-Paul (journalist), 54, 55, 59 (illus.), 74, 79, 99
   assassination of, 81, 87
Maréchal, Sylvain (playwright), 87
Marengo, battle of, 118
Marie-Antoinette (queen of France, 1770–1793), 19, 45, 82.
   See also Diamond Necklace affair; Varennes, flight to
Marie-Louise (empress), 135
"Marseillaise, La," 67
Marseille, 11, 63, 67, 80-1, 99
Martinique, 61
"Martyrs of prairial," 100
Marx, Karl, 12, 144
Masonic movement. *See* Freemasons
Mathiez, Albert (historian), 145
Maupeou, René (royal minister), 7, 24
Maury, abbé (counterrevolutionary spokesman), 45, 50
Maximum, 78, 82, 99
May 31, 1793, *journée* of, 80
Medical schools, 104
Ménétra, Jacques-Louis (artisan), 13
Mercure de France (journal), 132
Metric system, 86
Michelet, Jules (historian), 143
Milan, 114
Mirabeau, Honoré Gabriel Riqueti, Count of (revolutionary politician), 31, 45, 46, 83
Mitterrand, François (French politician), 142

Monarchiens, 46
Monasteries, abolition of, 50
Montagnards, 74, 76, 78-82, 87–88, 99, 145. *See also* Jacobins; Louis XVI, trial of; Robespierre, Maximilien; Saint-Just, Louis-Antoine
Montesquieu, Charles de (author), 16, 17, 18, 19
Moreau, Jean Victor (general), 118
Moscow, 136
Motherhood, attitudes toward, 17. *See also* women
Mounier, Joseph (revolutionary politician), 26, 46
Mulattoes, 47, 61. *See also* colonies; Saint-Domingue
"Municipal Revolution," 34
Museum of Natural History, 104
Musset, Alfred de (author), 139
"Myth of the French Revolution, The," (by Cobban), 146

Nancy, army mutiny in, 65
Nantes, 11, 26, 77, 90
Nantes, Edict of, 10
Naples, Kingdom of, 106
Napoleon. *See* Bonaparte, Napoleon
Napoleon II (son of Napoleon Bonaparte) 135
"Napoleonic legend," 112
"Napoleonic settlement," 117, 137
National Assembly, 30–31, 32, 34, 37–38, 43–51, 53-4, 55-8, 62, 65
   and army reform, 65
   and Church, 48–52
   conclusion of, 57–58
   and Declaration of Rights, 37–43
   and flight to Varennes, 56-7
   and foreign affairs, 62
   formation of, 30
   and "Great Fear," 34
National Convention, 67-70, 73–84, 86-92, 94, 96-7
   composition of, 73
   divisions in, 76, 78-80
   establishes Committee of Public Safety, 82
   overthrows Robespierre, 94
   purge of (1793), 80
   and rights of women, 88–89
   suspends 1793 constitution, 80
   after 9 thermidor Year II, 96-7, 99-102, 114
National Guard, 33, 43, 45, 55, 57, 65, 67, 76, 80, 99
   establishment of, 33
   and massacre of July 17, 1791, 57
Necker, Jacques (royal minister), 7, 23, 25, 27, 29–30, 34
   dismissal of, 31
   reappointment of, 34
Nelson, Horatio (admiral), 106-7, 125
Netherlands, 4, 105, 118, 128
"New cultural history," 148
New Héloïse, The (by Rousseau), 17
New Regime, The (by Woloch), 149
Newspapers, 29, 37-8, 54, 59 (illus.), 141
   and coup d'état of 18 fructidor Year V, 108
   Girondin, 80
Nîmes, 50
Nobility, 8-12, 20
   in Estates-General, 26–27
   Napoleonic, 133
   prerevolutionary privileges of, 9–11
   and Restoration, 139-40
   See also Seigneurialism
Notables, Assembly of. *See* Assembly of Notables
Notre-Dame cathedral, 86, 122

October Days (1789), 43–44. *See also* violence
Old Regime and the Revolution,The (by Tocqueville), 143-4
On Germany (by Madame de Staël), 132

Orders. *See* Estates, prerevolutionary
Origins of the French Revolution (by Doyle), 147
Oxford History of the French Revolution (by Doyle), 147
Ozouf, Mona (historian), 148

Paine, Thomas (revolutionary writer), 76
Palais-Royal, 31
Papal States, 128
Paris, 1, 3, 18, 31, 34, 43–44, 54, 55, 65-7, 69 (map), 79-80,
    94, 99-100, 121, 132
    Girondins and, 79–80
    Napoleonic plans for, 132
Parlements, 5, 6, 12, 22
    and Jansenist movement, 19
    in Montesquieu's writings, 16
    and pre-Revolution, 24-26
Parny, Evariste (poet), 108
Parthenopean Republic, 106
Patriots (in 1789), 29, 33-34
Paul I (tsar), 109
Peasants, 8, 10, 14–15, 20, 29
    after Revolution, 140–42
    and August 4 decrees, 38
    gains during Terror period, 87
    Georges Lefebvre's studies of, 145-6
    in Napoleonic period, 133
    prerevolutionary, 14–15, 20
    and "revolutionary army," 82
    and Vendée uprising, 77
People's Armies, The (by Cobb), 146
Père Duchesne (newspaper), 81, 90. *See also* Hébert,
    Jacques
Persian Letters (by Montesquieu), 16
Pétion, Jérôme (mayor of Paris), 68 (doc.)
Petty bourgeoisie, 13
Peuple, 13–14. *See also* artisans; petty bourgeoisie; sans-
    culottes
Philosophes, 16–18
Physiocrats, 7
Piedmont, 114
Pillnitz Declaration, 63
Pius VII (pope), 119, 126, 135
Poland, 63, 105, 127
Political culture (in French Revolution), 53–55, 86-7
Politics, Culture, and Class in the French Revolution (by
    Hunt), 148
Pope, 51, 129.
    Pius VI 56
    Pius VII 119, 126, 135. *See also* Concordat; Pius VII
Portugal, 134
Poverty, National Assembly's concern with, 47
22 prairial Year II, law of, 91
1–4 prairial Year III, journée of, 99-100
30 prairial Year VII, coup of, 109-10
Prefects, 115
Pre-Revolution, 22–27
Press. *See* newspapers
Press, freedom of, 47, 141
Privilege (definition of), 8–9
Privileged orders. *See* clergy; nobility
Property (in Declaration of Rights), 41
Protestants, 10, 17, 47, 119, 141
    civil rights granted to, 10
    political rights granted to, 47
Provence, Count of. *See* Louis XVIII
Provinces, 8, 49 (map)
    abolition of, 48
    revolution in (map), 66
Prud'hommes, conseils de, 131
Prussia, 4, 67, 105, 127, 136, 138
Public opinion, prerevolutionary, 18-20

Pyramids, battle of, 106

Quebec, 4
Quiberon landing, 101

Rabaut Saint-Etienne (revolutionary politician), 27, 28
    (doc.)
Racine, Jean (playwright), 123
Reading rooms, prerevolutionary, 18
Reform efforts, prerevolutionary, 6–8, 10, 21–24
    Refractory priests, 60, 62, 70, 108. *See also* Catholic
    Church; Civil Constitution of the Clergy; clergy
Reign of Terror. *See* terror, policy of
*Religion, Revolution, and Regional Culture in Eighteenth-
    Century France* (by Tackett), 148
René (by Chateaubriand), 122
Rennes, 26
Republic, proclamation of, 74. *See also* National Con-
    vention; republicanism
Republicanism, 56, 74
Restoration, 137-8, 139, 143
    Second Restoration, 138
Reveillon riot, 31
Revisionist historians of French Revolution, 146–50
Revolution, definition of, 36–37
Revolution of 1830, 134, 139
Revolution of 1848, 139, 143
Revolutionary army, 82
Revolutionary calendar, 86, 97
Revolutionary government, 69, 82, 84, 85 (doc.)
Revolutionary Tribunal, 70, 82, 90-91, 97
Révolutions de France et de Brabant, 54
Révolutions de Paris, 33 (doc.), 36
Rhineland, 76, 105, 106
    annexation of, 118
    See also Germany
Robespierre, Augustin (revolutionary politician), 114
Robespierre, Maximilien (revolutionary politician), 45,
    46, 60, 63, 70, 74, 82, 91-2, 93 (illus.), 94, 96, 97, 98
    (illus.), 145
    execution of, 94
    joins Committee of Public Safety, 82
    in National Convention, 74
    opposes dechristianization, 86
    role in Reign of Terror, 91-2, 98 (illus.)
    speech on revolutionary government (doc.), 85
    urges execution of Danton, 91
Rohan, Cardinal de, 19. *See also* Diamond Necklace
    affair
Roland, Madame, 63, 84-5 (doc.)
Romanticism, 122, 132
Rome, 106
Rousseau, Jean-Jacques (author), 17–18, 19, 41, 83
Roussillon, 93
Roux, Jacques (enragé leader), 78, 79 (doc.)
Rudé, George (historian), 146
Russia, 63, 105, 109, 118, 126-7, 135, 136, 138
    Napoleon's invasion of, 136
Russian Revolution, 142, 145

Saint-Domingue, 47, 61, 89-90, 118-9
    slave revolt in, 47, 61, 89-90
    See also colonies; slavery
Saint Helena, 138
Saint-Just, Louis-Antoine (revolutionary politician), 76,
    82, 84, 87, 91, 94
Salons, 18
Sanhedrin, 119–20
Sans-culottes, 65, 67, 70, 72, 73, 74, 77-8, 80, 82

Albert Soboul's study of, 146
leaders arrested, 90
political program of, 78
social composition of, 77-8
and 9 thermidor Year II, 94
and thermidorian Convention, 99–100
See also artisans; journée of May 31, 1793; journée of
Sept. 5, 1793; revolutionary army; sections
Say, Jean-Baptiste (economist), 122
"Second Directory," 108
Second Empire, 139
Second Republic, 139
"Second Revolution" (1792), 71
Sections (in Paris), 67, 69 (map), 70, 78, 80, 91, 101. See
also sans-culottes
Secularization, 20
Ségur edict (1781), 10
Seigneurialism, 10
Self-denying ordinance, 58, 73
Senate, Napoleonic, 115, 117, 129, 137
September 5, 1793, journée of, 82
September massacres, 70, 78
Seven Years' War, 4
Sieyès, abbé Emmanuel (revolutionary politician), 26-7,
30, 45, 101, 110, 112, 115
"Sister republics," 105, 108, 114, 127
Slavery, 7, 29, 47, 61, 89-90, 119
National Convention's abolition of, 89-90
Smith, Adam (economist), 122
Soboul, Albert (historian), 145, 146
Social Contract, The (by Rousseau), 17, 41
Socialist History of the French Revolution (by Jaurès), 144
Société des amis des noirs, 29
Society of Friends of the Constitution. See Jacobins
Society of Revolutionary Republican Women, 78, 81, 88
Sonthonax, L.-F. (revolutionary politician), 90
South America, 142
Sovereignty (in Declaration of Rights of Man), 41
Spain, 62, 76, 93, 106, 128, 134-5, 136
Spirit of the Laws, The (by Montesquieu), 16
Staël, Madame de (author), 122, 132
Subsistence, right of, 80
Suspects, Law of, 82, 97
Sweden, 136
Switzerland, 106

Tackett, Timothy (historian), 52, 148
Taille, 9, 10
Talleyrand, Charles-Maurice (Napoleonic minister),
117, 126, 137
Tax farmers, 6
Tax system, 6–7, 103
Taylor, G. H. (historian), 147
Tennis Court, Oath of, 30
Terray, abbé (royal minister), 7
Terror, policy of, 82, 85 (doc.), 90–92, 97, 101, 121
historians' views of, 142, 143, 144, 145, 150
Theater, revolutionary, 87
9 thermidor Year II, 94, 96
"Thermidorian reaction,"96-99, 100, 101
Thermidorians, 94, 96
Thiers, Adolphe (historian), 143
Third Estate, 11, 26-7, 28 (doc.), 30, 32 (illustration)
in Estates-General, 30-1
Third Republic, 140, 144
Tilsit, Peace of, 127
Tocqueville, Alexis de (historian), 8, 143–44, 147
Toulon, 81, 93, 114
Towns, prerevolutionary privileges of, 10
Trafalgar, Battle of, 125
Treatise of Political Economy (by Say), 122

Treilhard, Jean-Baptiste (revolutionary politician), 50
Tribunate, 117, 129
Turgot, Jacques (royal minister), 7, 13, 14
Two-thirds decree, 101-2
Tyrol uprising, 135

Ulm, battle of, 127
Unigenitus, Papal bull of, 19
United Nations, 42, 142
United States, 25, 118
Universal Declaration of Human Rights, 42, 142

Valmy, battle of, 70, 74
Varennes, flight to, 56-7, 63
Venality of offices, 5
Vendée uprising, 77, 80, 87, 89, 101, 147
13 vendémiaire Year IV, journée of, 101-3, 107, 114
Venice, 106
Ventôse decrees, 87-8
Verdun, 70
Vergennes, Count of (royal minister), 4
Vergniaud, Pierre (revolutionary politician), 90
Verona, Declaration of, 100
Versailles, Palace of, 1, 5
Veto, royal, 46
Vichy government, 141
Vienna, 106
Vieux Cordelier (by Camille Desmoulins), 91
Violence, in French Revolution, 31–34, 38, 43–44, 61, 67-
70, 142. See also September massacres; October days;
Terror, policy of
Voltaire (author), 16, 17, 18, 19, 123
Voting rights, 46, 101

Wagram, battle of, 135
War
Austro-Prussian defeat in (1792), 70-1
during Consulate, 118
declaration of (1792), 62–4
during Directory, 105-7
during Empire, 125–7, 134-7
French defeats (1793), 76
impact on politics of, 65
during Terror, 92–93
Waterloo campaign, 138
Washington, George (American president), 125
Waterloo, battle of, 138
Wattignies, battle of, 93
Wellington, Duke of (general), 134, 136, 138
What is the Third Estate? (by Sièyes), 26-7
Woloch, Isser (historian), 149
Women, 14, 55, 88–89, 134
in October Days, 43–44
limits on rights of, 88–89, 120, 140
political activities of, 43–44, 67, 78, 88-9 (doc.)
political clubs for, 55
Rousseau's attitude toward, 17
social condition of, 14, 120, 134
violence and, 43-44
Women and the Public Sphere in the Age of the French Rev-
olution (by Landes), 149
Workers, 47, 129, 131. See also artisans; sans-culottes

Young, Arthur (author), 14

Zadig (by Voltaire), 16